Road Maps to Prosperity

Development and Inequality in the Market Economy

The purpose of this series is to encourage and foster analytic and policy-oriented work on market-based reform in developing and post-socialist countries. Special attention will be devoted in the series to exploring the effects of free market policies on social inequality and sustainable growth and development.

Editor:
Andrés Solimano

Titles in the Series:

Andrés Solimano, Editor. *Road Maps to Prosperity: Essays on Growth and Development*

Road Maps to Prosperity

Essays on Growth and Development

Edited by Andrés Solimano

Ann Arbor
THE UNIVERSITY OF MICHIGAN PRESS

Published in the United States of America by
The University of Michigan Press
Manufactured in the United States of America
♾ Printed on acid-free paper

1999 1998 1997 1996 4 3 2 1

A CIP catalog record for this book is available from the British Library.

Library of Congress Cataloging-in-Publication Data

Road maps to prosperity : essays on growth and development / edited by
Andrés Solimano.
p. cm. — (Development and inequality in the market economy)
Originally presented at a conference in El Escorial, Spain, July
11–13, 1994.
Includes bibliographical references and index.
ISBN 0-472-10729-1 (hardcover : alk. paper)
1. Economic development—Congresses. 2. Economic development—
Case studies—Congresses. I. Solimano, Andrés. II. Series.
HD75.R6 1996
338.9—dc20 96-24890
CIP

Contents

Contributors

Alice H. Amsden
Massachusetts Institute of Technology
Cambridge, MA, USA

Javier Andrés
University of Valencia
Valencia, Spain

Pranab Bardhan
University of California at Berkeley
Berkeley, CA, USA

José E. Boscá
University of Valencia
Valencia, Spain

Vittorio Corbo
Pontífica Universidad Católica de Chile
Santiago, Chile

Rafael Doménech
University of Valencia
Valencia, Spain

José De Gregorio
Ministry of Finance
Santiago, Chile

Pablo E. Guidotti
Central Bank
Buenos Aires, Argentina

Klaus Schmidt-Hebbel
Central Bank
Santiago, Chile

Luis Servén
World Bank
Washington, D.C., USA

Andrés Solimano
Inter-American Development Bank
Washington, D.C., USA

Lance Taylor
New School for Social Research
New York, N.Y., USA

Preface

The creation of material wealth is central to improving living standards and promoting prosperity and social progress. But what initiates a period of rapid economic growth? How can growth and prosperity be sustained over time? How can countries avoid growth crises and stagnation? What would an analytically sound and policy-relevant development approach look like in the late twentieth century? What can be learned from the growth and development experiences of Latin America, East Asia, and the OECD countries? These are the key questions that this book, written by leading scholars in the field, tries to address.

The chapters in the first part of the book critically review and expand on recent work in the following specific subject areas. The new growth economics is assessed in proper analytical and historical perspective by looking at the main contributions made during the last two centuries. The complex links between savings, investment, and growth are examined through a careful review of the existing analytical and empirical literature. Development theory is subject to scrutiny by highlighting new directions for research and policy analysis using recent contributions to growth and trade theory, institutional economics, and the study of social processes. The elements of a "strategic growth approach" that build on the successes and failures of both state-led and market-driven growth experiences are discussed.

The second part of the volume is devoted to the analysis of the rich experience with economic growth and development in Latin America, East Asia, and the OECD in the last three decades. Themes studied include the causes of "golden age" versus growth crisis in different periods and regions, the growth response to policy reform in Latin America and East Asia, growth convergence in the OECD, and the role of finance in development.

An initial version of the chapters included in this volume were presented in a conference in El Escorial, Spain, on July 11–13, 1994, as part of a series on themes of economic reform, development, and social inequality. The kind permission of *World Development* to publish chapter 9, "Financial Development and Economic Growth," by J. De Gregorio and P. Guidotti, is appreciated. The conference series has been organized with the Universidad Complutense of Madrid and the journal *Pensamiento Iberoamericano,* with the collaboration of Professors Carlos Abad and Osvaldo Sunkel. The initiative has also had the support of the World Bank, the International Monetary Fund, the Inter-American Development Bank, the UN Economic Commission on Latin America, and the UN Conference on Trade and Development. I acknowledge the support provided by all these institutions.

I would also like to kindly acknowledge the logistical support of Pilar Brown of the Inter-American Development Bank in the preparation of this book, the outstanding editorial job of Melissa Vaughn, and the general collaboration of the staff of the University of Michigan Press.

CHAPTER 1

Introduction

Andrés Solimano

The creation of material wealth as a way to improve living standards and promote social progress and human fulfillment is the key objective of economics and public policy. After two decades of large global shocks, with a simultaneous deterioration in macroeconomic conditions and slowdown in growth in several industrialized and developing nations, the 1990s are witnessing a revitalization of analytical work and policy interest on themes of economic growth, savings generation, capital formation, and long-run development.

The chapters of this volume focus on the following basic questions:

What are the key ingredients that foster economic growth and material progress? What is the role of savings, investment, productivity growth, and demand factors in the growth process?

What are the factors that start a period of economic growth and prosperity? What causes growth to be halted, and how can it be reignited after large recessionary shocks?

What are the main analytical frameworks that explain the growth process, and how does the "new growth theory" build on earlier contributions to the subject?

What would be the main elements that a consensus on sustainable "progrowth" policies in developing countries must contain?

What would be the main elements of a "reconstructed agenda" of development theory encompassing macroeconomic, microeconomic, and institutional dimensions after the exhaustion of state-led development and the rise of free-market economics?

What are the main principles of modern development policies that, along with a growth orientation, would include an active concern about poverty reduction, equity, institutional design, and the quality of life?

What is the impact of alternative development strategies (state dirigisme, market-oriented policies, hybrid models) on the record of economic growth in Latin America and East Asia? What explains growth convergence and growth disparities within highly integrated economic regions like Western Europe?

What is the role of credit and finance in fostering growth and development?

Understanding Growth: New Theories and Empirics

A useful way to organize thinking on growth issues is to look at the "mechanics of growth." This methodology focuses on the growth rate of the labor force and the rate of (physical and human) capital accumulation and productivity growth as the sources of output expansion. Although this (supply-side) methodology does not establish causal relationships among the main variables that affect growth and does not spell out the fundamentals behind factor accumulation and productivity growth, its simplicity makes it appealing as a starting point from which to organize the analysis of growth issues.

At a more abstract level, growth theories differ in several respects: the role of supply versus demand factors in the determination of growth rates, the level of aggregation, the role of savings versus investment in "leading" growth, the treatment of time (logical versus historical, in the Hicks-Robinson parlance), the role attached to institutions and markets in growth, and the interactions between income distribution and the rate of economic growth.

More recently a revitalization of growth analysis (largely dormant since the late 1960s) has been associated with the emergence of the so-called new growth theory emphasizing increasing returns and endogenous technical change.

In this line, the discussion has centered around the endogeneity or exogeneity of long-run growth in aggregative models. As the "new" growth theory was started by a generation of neoclassical economists, the benchmark of comparison has been the Solow model, whose main result is that, in steady state, output growth is fully determined by the *exogenous* rates of technical progress and population growth.

The new vintage of growth models developed since the mid-1980s has relaxed the assumption of constant returns to scale and allowed for the *endogeneity* of technical progress, making it dependent on the rate of physical investment and/or human capital accumulation.

The endogeneity of technical progress in growth models, however, is not really a novel result of the new growth theory. Kaldor, Arrow, Uzawa, and others in the 1950s and 1960s set up growth theories in which technical progress is endogenous. In those models, endogenous technical progress was modeled as a "technical progress function" (Kaldor) or as a process of "learning by doing" (Arrow).

In any case, a beneficial by-product of the new vintage of growth models is the renewed interest in understanding the process of generating productivity growth, in terms of both its microeconomic and industrial organization underpinnings as well and its spillover effects at the macro level.

From a policy perspective, the Solow model implies a sort of fundamental policy ineffectiveness in growth matters. As the long-run rate of output growth is determined only by exogenous rates of productivity and population growth, no room is left for economic policies to affect steady-state growth. In contrast, the new growth theory recreates an important role for policy in affecting long-term growth rates through its impact on investment, education, and technological change.

This provides a renewed impetus for enhancing the policy relevance of growth theory. In fact, policy makers and academicians have always felt uneasy with the notion, associated with the neoclassical growth model, that "policies do not matter" in affecting the long-run growth performance of an economy.

In spite of these positive features, there are several shortcomings associated with the endogenous growth theory and its empirics. At an analytical level, the models are still very aggregative, making them incapable thus far of explaining patterns of structural transformation across productive sectors that take place in actual development processes. Moreover, very aggregative models hardly capture well-known sectoral disparities in the rates of technical change, a variable that plays a central role in the new theory.

Another limitation of the new theory is its excessive emphasis on steady-state growth paths, or "golden ages." The interplay between business cycles (booms and recessions) and trend or potential growth is often absent in the new analysis. Admittedly, these interactions are complex, but simplicity is bought at a high price in terms of leaving unexplained an important part of the growth story in the real world.

In addition, the new growth approaches are basically supply-driven models in which aggregate demand plays almost no role in output determination. Harrodian, Robinsonian, and Kaleckian models all show that aggregate demand, through the investment function, can play a significant role in the determination of long-run growth (see chapter 2). In this vein, the growth impact of fluctuations in savings and investment, central to Keynes and later generations of Keynesian economics, is also largely absent in the new growth tradition.

Other important pending issues leading to a more realistic and policy-relevant growth theory concern: *(a)* the need of an explicit treatment of distributive issues in a growing economy, *(b)* the explicit consideration of institutional and political economy constraints that shape any experience of long-run growth, *(c)* the recognition and identification of the economic actors that lead the growth process being either a Schumpeterian class of entrepreneurs devoted to activity creation and innovation (rather than rent seeking) and/or government strategic planners that devise and implement growth strategies in some partnership with the private sector.

At the empirical level, there are problems too. Reverse causality, omitted variables, and measurement problems cast serious doubts on the accuracy of the testing and verification of the new growth theory.

In this area, a clear overuse has been made of panel data for a large number of developing and developed economies without a more detailed scrutiny of the quality and comparability—both over time and across countries—of the data. Time-series analysis for individual countries, combining econometric methods with historical and institutional analysis to produce rich country detail and evidence, is rarely seen in the empirics of the new growth theory. The quest for "generality" in testing the new theory has left aside the richness of analyzing concrete historical growth experiences.

Regarding measurement, a main concern up to now has been to use national account data valued at internationally comparable prices. Relatively little attention has been devoted, however, to the examination of potential biases in the measurement of quantities across countries and over time. Moreover, explanatory variables in the standard growth regressions such as investment ratios, educational levels of the population, initial income, political variables, and others are particularly prone to face comparability problems as well as being subject to limited country coverage.

Blueprints for Prosperity: Growth Policies

What can be done to create and maintain an environment conducive to growth, economic dynamism, vitality, and progress?

There are several ways to approach this central policy question. One way is to look at the theory and its insights on the ingredients for growth. Another way, complementary to the first, is to look at successful experiences and extract useful lessons.

Clear success stories in the developing world are the economies of East Asia that managed to grow, in a sustained way, at annual rates of around 7–8 percent (or more) in the last three decades. More recently, in South America, Chile stands as a country that since the second half of the 1980s and throughout the 1990s has been growing at annual rates around 7 percent in a context of macroeconomic and social stability and external integration.

The stylized facts of these sustained growth experiences can be summarized as follows: *(a)* over the medium run, growth has come along with high investment rates, *(b)* capital formation has been financed to a large extent by high national savings, *(c)* productivity growth has been an important source of aggregate output growth; *(d)* underlying macroeconomic conditions have included moderately low inflation, an absence of significant fiscal imbalances, and consolidated balance of payments positions; *(e)* the trade regime has favored export expansion; moreover, external orientation has been a powerful device for enforcing domestic competition; *(f)* the private sector has been an "engine of growth." In East Asia this strong growth has taken place in close partnership with the state.

Are those progrowth principles transferable? In general, yes. Of course, their adoption will be shaped by a host of country-specific factors such as initial resource endowments and education levels, social and political constraints, and other historical, geographical, and cultural characteristics.

Besides learning from success stories, we must also consider the experiences of countries that managed to grow and prosper for several decades but in which growth ultimately slowed or ceased entirely once their entire economic policy regimes entered into crisis. Mexico and Brazil, two large Latin American economies, are cases in point. Brazil grew at an average annual rate close to 7 percent between 1940 and 1980. Moreover, it did so in a policy regime of state dirigisme and import substitution. However, over time the system brought forth macroeconomic imbalances and microeconomic inefficiencies that eventually sent the Brazilian economy into a period of escalating inflation, sluggish growth, and financial instability during most of the 1980s and early 1990s. Mexico grew at an average annual rate of about 6.5 percent from the early 1950s until the early 1980s under a policy regime similar to that of Brazil. Nevertheless, that dynamism collapsed in the early 1980s, as a serious foreign debt crisis developed. Despite very intensive economic reform—albeit punctuated by external shocks and domestic policy mistakes—Mexico has had considerable problems restoring its high growth rates of the 1950s, 1960s, and 1970s. The Mexican experience shows that the resumption of long-run growth after a systemic change from state dirigisme and import substitution to a market-based economy is complex and can take longer than expected.

Brazil's experience also teaches an important transitional lesson: once high growth is derailed in a context of unresolved macroeconomic crises, the gathering of social consensus needed to restore basic macro stability—a prerequisite for sound growth—might come only after extreme instability (hyperinflation) takes place. A similar lesson could be drawn from the Argentinean experience of the 1980s and early 1990s. Another case of high growth that ran out of steam is the former Soviet Union, which managed to grow at a rapid rate between the 1930s and the early 1970s.

To sum up, the lessons from East Asia and Chile are more related to the role of national savings, capital formation, productivity growth, and supportive policies in a steady growth path. Other dirigiste Latin American and socialist growth experiences are important in highlighting the exhaustion of growth dynamism in the final phases of their old policy regimes and transitional difficulties of restoring growth after economic reform. The dynamics of growth crisis and growth recovery and their links to changes in policy regimes is then a subject of great importance.

Development Theory: Evolving Views

The peak years of development theory were the 1940s and 1950s, with some follow-up in the 1960s. In contrast, as discussed before, the 1970s and 1980s were mainly concerned with short-term problems of macroeconomic stabilization and adjustment. Moreover, that period witnessed a resurgence of free-market economics that openly challenged some basic postulates of traditional development theory.

Traditional development theory stressed market failures, increasing returns, coordination problems in the investment process, and the externalities of technical progress. In addition, traditional development analysis featured an overly optimistic belief on the ability of the state to carry out tasks underperformed by decentralized markets and the private sector.

These views also reflected historical experiences at that time. The great crisis of the early 1930s showed, rather dramatically, how laissez-faire capitalism could fail to overcome massive unemployment, output slump, and financial fragility. Moreover, the Soviet Union since the 1930s and the emerging socialist camp in Eastern Europe in the 1950s were in a sort of "golden age" of industrialization and rapid growth helped by the extensive use of planning and state ownership. These experiences certainly contributed, in the 1940s and 1950s, to shaping an intellectual climate more favorable to state-led development and planning than to free-market economics as the blueprint for development.

In the late 1960s and 1970s things started to change. The breakdown of the Bretton Woods system, the two oil shocks of the 1970s and the ensuing appearance of "stagflation" in the North, and the debt crisis of the 1980s in the South combined to challenge the postwar consensus on macroeconomics and development.

As a consequence, a central element of that consensus—that because market failures were particularly pervasive in the developing world, the state needed to step in and *lead* the development process—was contested.

The new neoclassical critique no longer viewed the state as a benevolent and effective entity, routinely able to correct market failures and match market and social values. On the contrary, the state apparatus also faced shortcomings: its informational, organizational, and administrative structures were limited and could be overwhelmed when attempting to cope with increasingly complex economic and social problems. In addition, in practice the state departed significantly from the naive view of it as a direct representative of the average citizen implementing a mandate to maximize a well-defined social welfare function. In contrast, the state became more an accommodative body under pressure by rent seekers, coalitions, and private interest groups. The message was clear: divest the state of many of its allocative, distributional, and entrepreneurial roles that it was increasingly unable to perform well, and allow the market and the private sector to unleash their productive and innovative capacities to generate rapid growth and development.

As the 1990s go by, a more balanced consensus that combines insights from both the old development theory and the new neoclassical critique seems to be emerging. The old themes of the early development economists—increasing returns, market imperfections, indivisibilities, and spillover effects from technical progress—are now part of the mainstream of economics, as the new growth theory eloquently shows. There is also a growing recognition of the failures of the state alongside the failures of the market. Informational and coordination problems and incentive incompatibilities point up common failures of both market-based and government-based institutions, rendering the old dichotomy of markets versus the state not very illuminating. The real challenge lies in the design of social institutions that deliver outcomes that are economically efficient, socially equitable, and politically feasible.

Development Policy

Nowadays it is difficult to separate growth from development policies and, in fact, any sustainable development strategy must include economic growth as a key component. Development, however, goes beyond growth: it includes broad issues of living standards and the quality of life. This in turn encompasses aspects of income distribution and social equity, the physical environment, institution building, social participation in public decision making, democracy, and freedom.

In contrast to the development paradigm of the 1950s and 1960s, the emerging new consensus on development gives a prominent role to the market as a key mechanism of economic coordination. On the role of the state, two basic views can be identified: one is a "laissez-faire" position that gives the state a role only as a provider of: *(a)* macroeconomic stability, *(b)* the legal framework that governs private activity, and *(c)* the provision of public goods. The other view is more dirigiste and redistributivist than the former and sees the state as also playing a part in correcting social inequalities and defining and implementing industrial policy. The attitude toward the state's role in the maintenance of macroeconomic stability and the regulatory framework would be, in general, similar in both views.

Development policy faces new challenges beyond the "market versus state" debate, including issues of institutional design and how to fill the vacuum left by the conjunction of both state and market failures. The management by local organizations of common resources like water and the delivery of social services such as education, health, and housing highlights the potential role for intermediate organizations (e.g., nongovernmental organizations) in performing activities traditionally managed by the state or simply underperformed. In fact, "civil society," nongovernmental or communitarian organizations, could be a bridge between the individual (or household) and the state, enriching the menu of coordinating mechanisms in society.

The topic of inequality and social policy is not new of course and has always been at the core of development economics. The new consensus reinforces the idea that growth is a basic and necessary condition for poverty alleviation; moreover, any sustainable strategy of redistribution must be "growth conforming." Recent analytical work in this area stresses a channel of causality running from initial inequality to subsequent growth; the chief finding of this new literature is that inequality hampers growth. The previous discussion on institutions is also linked to social policy in the sense that the poor and other vulnerable groups need some organizations both to voice their demands for benefits as well as to coordinate, perhaps, the delivery of social services at the local level.

Broader issues of democracy and human freedom are also important in the design of broad and politically feasible development policies. In this area, intellectual and policy interactions with other disciplines and political institutions are critical and must be explored actively through a dialogue between economists, political scientists, philosophers, and politicians.

This volume is organized in two parts. The first part, chapters 2–5, presents overviews and new perspectives on growth and development issues. The second part, chapters 6–9, comprises country and regional studies of actual growth and development experiences along with an empirical study on the role of finance in the growth and development process.

Let us take a brief look at the content of each chapter. Chapter 2, by Lance Taylor, examines a broad set of growth theories that precede and inspire the new growth theory in terms of their substantive themes, logical structure, and empirical relevance. These theories have been developed during a couple of centuries or so of economic history and include work by Smith, Marshall, Ricardo, Marx, Ramsey, Keynes, Preobrazhenski, Schumpeter, Solow, Hirschman, Lucas, and others.

Chapter 3, by Pranab Bardhan, highlights new directions in development theory that elaborate on both the traditional development theory of the 1940s and 1950s and the ensuing neoclassical critique of the 1970s and 1980s. The chapter discusses the new growth theory from a development perspective: it addresses the issue of how to start growth and avoid poverty traps, identifies compatibilities between growth-promoting and equity-enhancing policies, and defines the scope for state and market failures, highlighting the need for sound institutional design.

Chapter 4, by Klaus Schmidt-Hebbel, Luis Servén, and Andrés Solimano, explores the determinants of savings and capital formation and the links with output growth, covering causality issues, compositional problems of savings and investment, the role of productivity growth in output expansion, and interactions with investment. The chapter also conducts an in-depth analysis of savings determinants and identifies new themes in savings and investment analysis.

Chapter 5, by Alice H. Amsden, explores the rationale of "strategic" government intervention in fostering industrialization and development. Late industrialization and growth is examined in the context of resource-poor economies that rely on technological adaptation and effective state promotion of investment, exports, and innovation as the engines for economic development; special attention is devoted in this chapter to the transferability of these experiences to other developing economies.

Chapter 6, by Vittorio Corbo, contrasts the actual growth experiences of Latin America and East Asia in the last two or three decades. The determinants of growth in both regions are assessed, using panel data regressions, in terms of the empirical specifications of the new and old growth theory for a period covering the 1960s, 1970s, and 1980s.

Chapter 7, by Andrés Solimano, analyzes the growth record and potential of two alternative development strategies: state-led import-substitution development and market-based development. The first regime was implemented in Latin America from the 1940s to the 1980s; the second strategy has been adopted more recently in Chile, Mexico, and several other Latin American countries. The analysis devotes attention to two main issues: *(a)* the transition from adjustment to sustainable growth in the aftermath of reform; and *(b)* the relative contribution of factor accumulation and total factor productivity growth to overall output expansion in state-led and market-based development strategies.

Chapter 8, by Javier Andrés, José Boscá, and Rafael Doménech, examines the postwar growth experience of OECD economies in light of recent contributions of new growth theory regarding factor accumulation, the process of generating technical progress, and the role of a highly educated and well-trained work force in fostering growth. The authors pay particular attention to growth and the debate on convergence in a highly integrated economic region.

Chapter 9, by José De Gregorio and Pablo E. Guidotti, analyzes the role of finance in long-run growth, examining the "active credit" school that focuses on credit availability as a binding constraint to finance investment and growth, and the "passive credit" school that poses, in Schumpeterian fashion, that innovation and investment are the driving forces behind output expansion, with finance and credit playing a passive or accommodative role. At an empirical level, the focus is on transmission mechanisms such as the level of investment and its productivity, through which credit affects output growth and the rate of increase in factor productivity.

Part I
Overviews and Perspectives

CHAPTER 2

Growth, the State, and Development Theory

Lance Taylor

The sun rarely shines on new ideas in economics; the days are even fewer when economists' novel thoughts are of great intrinsic worth. These truisms reflect the nature of the discipline. To expand upon Robert Heilbroner's (1991) classic description, worldly philosophers are philosophers still, doomed to mull over a collection of concepts that does not expand at a rapid pace.

Contrary to current academic practice, this observation means that economics should be conscious of its own history—all the neat models were not created during the last ten years. Real philosophers still ponder Plato and Aristotle with benefit, just because they happened to get to most of the good ideas first. Economists proposing "new" theories of growth, trade, or development could gain from their more unworldly colleagues' example. In the context of usable theory, the moral is that good minds have grappled for two centuries with problems of development and causes of growth. In the long run, their insights are likely to prove more useful than the models that fit this decade's fashions best.

Such thoughts are especially relevant when one recognizes that there are many distinct theories of growth, only a small selection of which are reflected in the new mainstream literature. Somewhat arbitrarily, six theoretical traditions are categorized in summary fashion in sections A–F of figure 2.1, with additional effects cataloged in section G. "Filiation" (a phrase coined by Schumpeter [1954]) runs roughly horizontally in the different sections, with cross-category linkages pointed out by solid lines. Dashed lines show oppositional reactions of importance.

The diagram provides background for the three main themes of this chapter. The first is that past thinking about growth and development does encompass diverse lines of thought; many are relevant to the current policy debate. "New" growth theories draw upon just a few of these ideas, and are correspondingly deficient. Second, "new" or "market-friendly" development strategies that became popular in the 1980s suffer

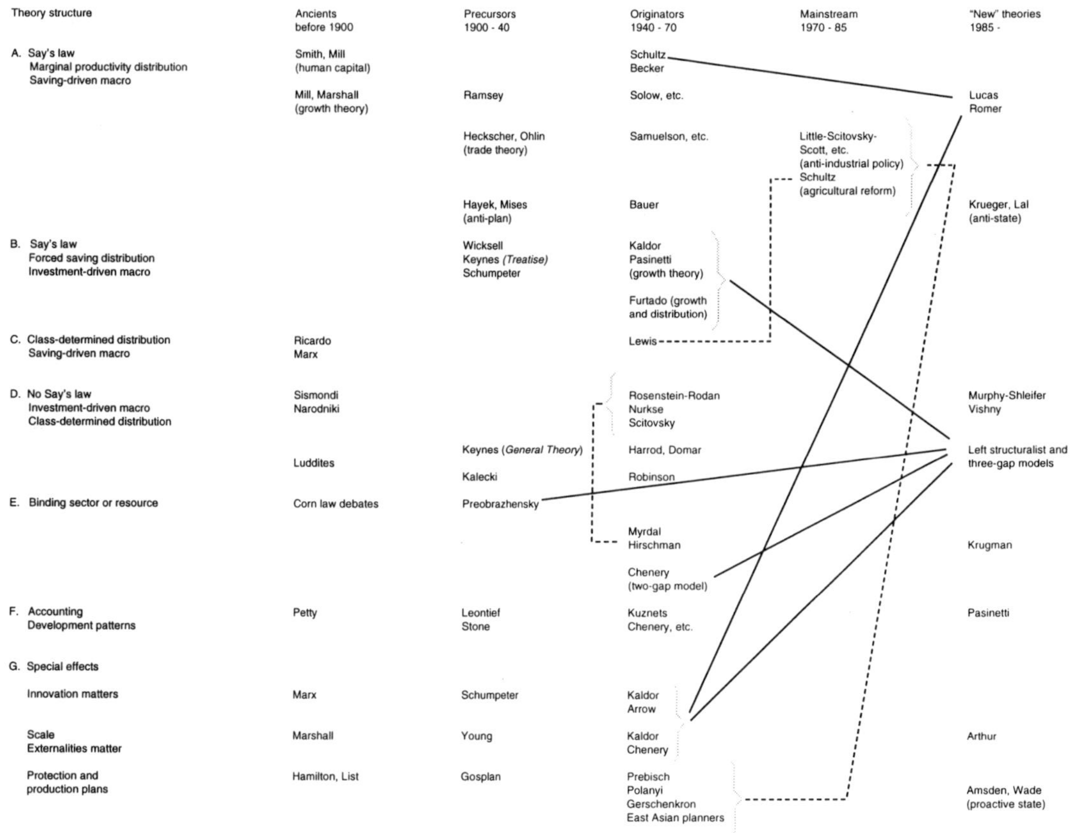

Figure 2.1 Filiations and oppositions in growth and development theory
Note: Solid lines denote filiations, and dashed lines oppositions.

from the same problem. Their orthodox advocates have an extremely limited pespective. How both mainstream discourses might be widened is the final topic. It can be clarified in part by considering specific issues with regard to generation and absorption of technical progress. These are mentioned at various points, with semiformal models banished to three appendixes.

New Growth Models and Say's Law

Section A is the Tory Row of figure 2.1—mainstream growth theorists dwell almost exclusively there. They postulate Say's law that all scarce production inputs are fully utilized and claim that flexible prices in markets dominated by optimizing "agents" vary to permit the economy to arrive at such a state. In macroeconomic terms, the supply of saving is determined by forces of productivity and thrift, and capital formation adjusts correspondingly (perhaps aided by a variable interest rate in the market for "loanable funds" with laws codified by John Stuart Mill). From Mill through Marshall to Solow and beyond, this vision of the economic system has animated orthodox thought. It supports an engine of considerable analytical power; the trouble is that all its energy is easily dissipated on manipulating models with weak connections to the institution- and ignorance-ridden economies in which we live.

The concerns of new growth theory underline these points. Its basic motivations appear to be twofold. The first is to break away from Solow's (1956) regime in which output and employment (plus exogenous productivity) growth rates are forced to be equal in steady state. Mathematical tricks have been employed to widen the spectrum of possible growth rates.

The second goal is to "endogenize" productivity growth by tying it to other variables in the system, ideally through the use of rational actor "microfoundations." One approach has been to relate the level of productivity to a stock variable such as physical capital or the human capital built into the (fully employed) labor force. Some sort of externality is often postulated to this end. A question that might seem natural to enthusiasts of market processes is why an externality that increases a variable as important as macroeconomic productivity is not internalized by perceptive economic actors. This question, however, is never posed by new growth theorists.

The other way to endogenize productivity has been to tie its observed increases to realized economies of scale. To carry out this task, tractable formal models of imperfect competition are required; most are borrowed from the new industrial organization literature, with their verisimilitude subject to doubt.

Saving drives capital formation in all new growth theory, as it must in models incorporating Say's law and marginal productivity distribution rules. Most efforts presume that saving is determined "optimally" by some immortal, representative, utility-maximizing "agent" with perfect foresight (up to a random error, perhaps). Aside from demonstrating that a model's creator has studied control theory, this approach at best adds ornamentation to an exogenously postulated saving rate and at worst is downright misleading (as shown presently). It is not pursued here.

Let X stand for output and K the capital stock; *pace* Cambridge controversies we treat both as being made from the "same" (malleable) commodity. The output-capital ratio $u = X/K$ becomes a measure of input substitution (not capacity utilization as in the demand-driven models discussed in appendixes A and B). If there is full employment of labor L at all times, then the labor-capital ratio $\lambda = L/K$ follows from dynamic equations for L and K respectively. Let ξ be the output-labor ratio, or average labor productivity, and s the economywide saving rate.

Old neoclassical growth models are based on the accounting conventions that

$$\frac{\text{Saving}}{\text{Output}}\frac{\text{Output}}{\text{Capital}} = \frac{\text{Investment}}{\text{Capital}} = \frac{\text{Increase in capital}}{\text{Capital}} = \frac{\text{Increase in output}}{\text{Output}}$$

$$= \frac{\text{Increase in Employment}}{\text{Employment}} + \frac{\text{Increase in (Output/Employment)}}{\text{(Output/Employment)}}$$

or

$$su = I/K = \hat{K} = \hat{X} = n + \rho, \tag{2.1}$$

where a "hat" denotes a growth rate $[\hat{K} = (dK/dt)/K]$ and depreciation is ignored for simplicity. With exogenous growth rates of employment and labor productivity after the last equals sign (with values $n = \hat{L}$ and $\rho = \hat{\xi}$ respectively) and savings-determined investment, then either the saving-output ratio s or output-capital ratio u has to adjust to allow all the equalities to hold in a steady state.

Solow's road to a such an equilibrium is based on the assumptions that the saving rate s is fixed while the output-capital ratio u is an increasing function $f(\xi\lambda)$ of the "effective" labor-capital ratio $\xi\lambda = \xi L/K$

via which the labor input of employed workers is scaled by their average productivity ξ. A well-behaved neoclassical production function is usually invoked to explain the dependence of u on $\xi\lambda$.

Using (2.1), the growth rate of $\xi\lambda$ becomes

$$\hat{\xi} + \hat{\lambda} = \rho + n - \hat{K} = \rho + n - su = \rho + n - sf(\xi\lambda). \qquad (2.2)$$

For easy comparison with the models set up in appendixes A and B, (2.2) describes the growth process in terms of changes in the labor-capital ratio λ as opposed to its more commonly used inverse (the capital-labor ratio).

Although some new growth models presume otherwise, the usual hypothesis is that the function $f(\xi\lambda)$ is increasing; that is, for a given capital stock, output rises when there is a bigger labor input. One implication is that subject to proper boundary conditions (the "Inada conditions"), there will be a stable steady-state growth path with $\hat{\lambda} = 0$ and $n + \rho = sf(\xi\lambda) = \hat{K}$. The effective labor-capital ratio $\xi\lambda = \xi L/K$ is constant at steady state, meaning that $\hat{X} = \hat{K}$.

One of the new theory's advertised advances is to get away from boring steady growth at an exogenous rate $n + \rho$ by relaxing the Inada conditions (a possibility already recognized by Solow). For example, u can simply be made constant as in Rebelo's (1991) "AK" model. The implication is that $\hat{X} = \hat{K} = su$ automatically, in a restatement of the "Harrod-Domar equation" used to crank out growth rates in numerous development planning exercises since the 1950s (the quotation marks signal the fact that the equation does not reflect the stability questions raised by both Harrod and Domar).

To satisfy (2.1), the productivity growth rate ρ becomes an endogenous variable in an AK world, adjusting as a true "residual" (in the traditional sense of that word) to satisfy the growth accounting balances. The fact that Solow's introduction of capital-labor substitution was originally billed as an improvement over Harrod and Domar's formulations is usually not mentioned in descriptions of AK models. Affinities between AK machines with several capital goods and von Neumann's (1938) and Sraffa's (1960) formulations are not pointed out either.

Other new growth models can be described in the Solow framework, if one writes a simplified version of (2) as

$$d\lambda/dt = \lambda[n - sf(\lambda)]. \qquad (2.3)$$

In this equation, ξ no longer plays its labor-augmenting role. Also, $f(\lambda)$ is no longer assumed to be monotonically increasing.

Suppose that the economy begins its growth process without much capital, or a high labor-capital ratio λ. As the capital stock rises relative to population and λ falls, the output-capital ratio $u = f(\lambda)$ may not decline very much or even go up if accumulation generates externalities. In other words, the right-hand side of (2.3) may remain negative, with capital deepening going on forever. Output per worker X/L will keep on rising in response to the increase in $\lambda^{-1} = K/L$. Unfortunately for ordinary workers (as opposed to "representative agents" getting income from both labor and capital sources), the wage share in output will also tend toward zero.

Once again, ρ could be introduced as a residual in (2.1) to reflect per capita income growth, although movement along a production function rather than "technical progress" is being observed. In any case, growth becomes "endogenous" along the lines suggested by Jones and Manuelli (1990), who in terms of the present discussion would postulate a function $f(\lambda)$ with a range strictly bounded from below. A constant elasticity of substitution (CES) production function will do the trick so long as the elasticity exceeds one. Econometric estimates of CES functions usually reject this hypothesis.

A variant story involves changes in the saving rate s. If $m(\lambda)$ is the marginal product of capital (again, a function of the labor-capital ratio), then a saving function might be written as $s = \sigma[m(\lambda)/i]$, where i is a reference rate of interest (e.g., the social discount rate in an optimal growth context). If m rises due to externalities as λ falls, then it could induce enough extra saving to keep $d\lambda/dt < 0$ for a long time (or maybe forever) in (2.3).

Contrary to the old, standard view, su might even be a monotonic *inverse* function of λ, leading to an unstable growth process in which a decrease in λ induces s and/or u to rise strongly enough to ensure that $d\lambda/dt < 0$. If λ is initially "too high" (capital is "too scarce" relative to population), then both s and u may be low, making the right-hand side of (2.3) positive so that λ will rise further. In other words, there can be a knife edge between limitless capital deepening and a poverty trap.

Three comments are in order about this possibility. The first is that it reflects the usual outcomes of optimizing endogenous growth models with strong externalities (Easterly 1994). In such models' solutions, accumulation is determined by saving that responds to changes in m. The formal rule takes a form such as

$$d\lambda/dt = h[i - m(\lambda)], \tag{2.4}$$

where $h(\ )$ is an increasing function. If $dm/d\lambda < 0$ and λ is slightly below the value at which $m(\lambda) = i$, then it will diverge toward zero and the capital-labor ratio will grow without a bound.

In the simple accounting of (2.3), however, such a growth path seems unlikely on empirical grounds. Output-capital ratios do not vary over a wide range in practice; that is, $df/d\lambda$ is not likely to be large in absolute terms even if it is negative for some values of λ. More important, in practice national savings rates do not appear to be responsive to rates of return, so that if even m goes up, it will bring forth at most a modest savings increase. By overstressing the sensitivity of saving to price signals, optimal growth formulations such as (2.4) signal the presence of knife edges that in all likelihood do not exist.

Second, knife edges have long been postulated in growth theory from the side of investment demand, which cannot figure in neoclassical models based on Say's law. Investment has been said to be highly sensitive either to the profit rate (see appendix A on Kaldor's growth model) or to the level of capacity use (the source of potential instability in Harrod's pioneering model of 1939). From a Keynesian perspective, knife edges are more likely to be sharpened by investment rather than saving behavior, but none have been empirically observed to date.

Finally, unstable growth dynamics can arise from many other sources. About forty years ago, Leibenstein (1954) and Nelson (1956) pointed out that high labor-capital ratios accompanied by Malthusian population dynamics and an absence of externalities can lead to poverty traps. Following many Latin American authors, Taylor and Bacha (1976) argued in an investment-driven model that the growth rate may rest on a knife edge determined by distributional conflicts and tastes for different sorts of commodities by different social classes—a poverty trap or unequalizing growth led by luxurious consumption can result. These ancient development models foreshadowed the knife edges formalized in the new growth theory when most of the formalizers were unborn or in grammar school.

As noted in the preceding, two sorts of microeconomic behavioral rationales have been suggested for endogenous productivity growth. One is externalities, via which a productivity level like ξ can be tied to a stock or state variable in a growth model. Such specifications have a long history. As discussed in appendix A, Kaldor's (1957) "technical progress function" makes ξ rise along with K/L, or capital deepening. In a macroeconomic restatement of the learning curves familiar to industrial planners, Arrow (1962) tied ξ to "learning by doing," as proxied by accumulated output over the years. To fit such phenomena into optimal growth models, however, a dilemma that plagued Marshall has to be resolved.

One horn is the desire of neoclassical economists to retain marginal productivity distribution theory under conditions of perfect competition. To carry out that project, they have to assume that economic agents behave as if there are nonincreasing (preferably constant) returns to the scale for all production inputs. Otherwise, second-order conditions for dynamic optimization cannot be satisfied and marginal productivity distribution rules make no sense.

The other horn is that positive externalities give rise to increasing returns. For example, in his well-known new growth model, Lucas (1988) postulates an aggregate production function of the form

$$X = K^{\beta}[(1 - \tau)H]^{1-\beta}(H^*)^{\gamma}, \tag{2.5}$$

where H is the total stock of human capital and τ is the share of their time that agents devote to acquiring new H (ambitious beings, they are fully employed in commodity production the rest of the time). "Normal" production takes place according to constant returns of scale for work effort $(1 - \tau)H$ and physical capital K, but via the externality factor $(H^*)^{\gamma}$, more human capital raises the overall productivity level. The asterisk in the H^* term is a reminder that human capital is subject to personal decisions but also boosts overall productivity.

The agents make their saving and time allocations by maximizing the discounted utility of consumption subject to (2.5) and accumulation equations over infinite time. Leaving aside this exercise's ontological absurdity, agents *cannot* recognize the externality due to H^*, else their calculations fall apart for the reasons noted above.

Solving infinite horizon optimal growth problems with unrecognized externalities has been billed as a mathematical step forward, a claim that would make a real applied mathematician smile. More disconcerting should be the smiles that externalities even as transcendent as human capital provoke from severe neoclassical economists, including members of the "Austrian" school. If extra learning generates more output, Austrians argue that sooner or later somebody should start making money from that fact (say, by providing education more cheaply than the state). Were such internalization of the benefits of a higher H^* to occur, Lucas's rationale for the importance of human capital accumulation ceases to make sense.

At least one ambitious piece of data analysis points to an absence of externalities. In a multidecade project, Jorgenson (1990) has tried to grade components of the U. S. labor and capital stocks in detail by their "quality" in a sources-of-growth accounting framework; the owners of these inputs have full claim to their returns. For the United States at least, his results consistently show a minor contribution of the residual (or "technical progress") to growth. In other words, the mathematical contortions required to fit the externality in (2.5) into an optimal growth framework may not be worth the effort—on strictly neoclassical empirical grounds.

An alternative approach to explaining productivity growth is to drop perfect competition to bring in decreasing average production costs. For example, Romer (1987) assumes that production depends on a number of intermediate inputs, with each one supplied subject to constant marginal cost plus a fixed capital cost that can be "spread" over a greater production volume. Subject to strong behavioral assumptions, Romer shows that this form of decreasing costs translates into an aggregate production function for final goods in which the capital tied up in intermediates shows up as an externality like H^* in (2.5).

Romer's empirical spirit is willing, but the analytical flesh is weak. Realistic analyses of decreasing costs under imperfect competition point to two strong conclusions. First, authors such as Sraffa (1926), Young (1928), and Kaldor (1972) emphasized that scale economies can underlie "cumulative processes" that upset the balanced, mutual, and self-adjusting equilibria characteristic of Walrasian theory. Firms that initially exploit decreasing costs can gain a commanding position, or else unstable price and investment cycles can arise (as noted, Japanese and Korean planners in their push for scale economies in production avoided such problems by hands-on market interventions to preclude what they called "excessive competition"). Under such circumstances, there is no reason for exit and entry of firms to drive "pure" profits to zero.

Second, as development economists such as Hirschman (1958) emphasized and Chenery (1959) formalized, relative product prices can shift over wide ranges depending on which production processes with increasing returns are present or absent in the economy (think of the decision about whether to import, produce for the domestic market, or produce for export some tradable good, or the impact of decreasing costs on the price of a usually nontraded good such as electricity). Cost-based prices arising from one configuration involving the presence or absence of members of a set of possible decreasing cost production processes are not an adequate guide for investment project decisions to create another configuration with a markedly different price vector.

Like many recent modelers of imperfect competition, Romer relies on a specification devised by Dixit and Stiglitz (1977) that cleverly sweeps these problems under the rug. In his version, final goods producers choose "varieties" of intermediates that substitute for one another subject to a CES function. The more varieties put into operation, the greater is supposed to be the level of final output (just why a farmer using several brands of gasoline instead of just one in his tractor will produce more crops is not carefully explained). Firms with identical cost structures enter symmetrically into production of intermediates until pure profits are driven to zero. The trade-off between a decreasing marginal product of greater input diversity and decreasing supply cost limits the size of each firm—there is no possibility for cumulative processes to get going!

Aghion and Howitt (1992) extend the model to take into account the search for cheaper technologies to produce intermediates, with "innovations" arriving according to a stochastic process. Their model is tractable just because of the convexifying properties of the Dixit-Stiglitz specification. Without it, potential innovators would face an insoluble computational problem in infinite horizon stochasic dynamic programming because of the potentially wide range of relative price configurations discussed above. The inspiration that true entrepreneurs possess to cut through this computational knot was what Schumpeter (1934) celebrated. Aghion and Howitt don't get the point.

The Romer and Aghion-Howitt models serve a useful function in emphasizing the importance of intermediate inputs in production processes. Although in practice intermediates enter technologically with highly asymmetric input-output coefficients, their share in the gross value of output does rise with income, going from about one-third to one-half in poor and rich countries respectively. Moreover, a big proportion of the macroeconomic residual is "explained" by shifts in the sectoral composition of output from low- to high-productivity sectors in an input-output framework.

The problem is that the new growth models leave out the dynamic, cumulative effects of decreasing costs coupled with the backward and forward production linkages that underlie these changes, which were fully recognized by Hirschman, Chenery, and a host of other early development economists. *The Strategy of Economic Development* is a far better guide to these connections than exercises in optimal growth with the behavioral irrealism that they impose—just to smooth out the imbalances that Hirschman thought were at the heart of the development matter.

Say's Law without Marginal Conditions

Other growth theories can be situated in opposition to the mainstream—not because they are less relevant to serious questions, but because orthodoxy provides a well-known standard of reference. Schumpeter

(1934) in section B of figure 2.1, for example, did not adhere to marginal productivity theory when he described an economy "developing" from one configuration of steady-state growth or "circular flow" to another. Rather, he took over much of Marx's supply-side vision and combined it with a provocative analysis of technical innovation to forge a spirited defense of capitalism. A sketch of his *Theory of Economic Development* goes as follows:

As just hinted, the starting point is rather like Mill-Marshall-Solow steady growth from figure 2.1's section A—this is Schumpeter's own interpretation of "circular flow." An economy in circular flow may be growing, but it is not "developing" in his terminology. Development occurs only when an entrepreneur unveils an innovation—a new technique, product, or way of organizing things—and shifts production coefficients or the rules of the game. He or she gains a monopoly profit until other people catch on and imitate, and the economy moves to a new path of steady growth.

A key analytical question about this process refers to both the financial and real sides of the economy: how does the entrepreneur obtain resources to innovate? An endogenous money supply and redistribution of real income flows are required to support the new mode of economic operation.

To get the project going, the entrepreneur must invest—an extra demand imposed on an economy already using its resources fully in circular flow. To finance investment, he or she obtains loans from the banks; new credit and thereby money are created in the process. The bank loans are used to purchase goods in momentarily fixed supply. Their prices are driven up, so that real incomes of other economic actors decline. The most common examples are workers receiving temporarily fixed nominal wages or the cash flows of non-innovating firms. There is "forced saving" as workers' lower real incomes force them to consume less; groups that receive windfall income gains are assumed to have higher saving propensities, so that demand apart from the entrepreneur's declines. Meanwhile, routine investment projects may be cut back.

In summary, the transition between states of circular flow is demand driven from the investment side (though of course the innovation may involve production of new goods or increases in productivity), and short-run macro adjustment takes place through income redistribution via forced saving with an endogenously varying money supply. This story illuminates the section B typology in several ways.

First, the forced saving adjustment story is not just Schumpeter's;

he shared it with Wicksell, the Keynes of the *Treatise on Money,* and a whole host of other "post-Wicksellian" macroeconomists (Amadeo 1989). In the guise of the widow's cruse, forced saving survived World War II into Kaldor-Pasinetti growth theory. Together with related mechanisms such as the inflation tax (faster inflation erodes wealth in the form of real money balances and induces people to save more), forced saving is virtually the only means that can bring an independent investment function together with supply-constrained output. If investment or some other demand injection goes up, consumption must be crowded out by changing (typically rising) prices; the marginal productivity distribution rules that underpin new growth theory go by the boards.

Just what determines output from the supply side is another question. Institutions as in Pasinetti's (1981) accounting-based descriptive model or else a shortage of a critical input such as foreign exchange are two possibilities discussed later.

Kaldor's (1957) theories in section B complement Schumpeter's through their emphasis on technical progress stemming from economies of scale and new investment. As has been noted, his "technical progress function" and "Verdoorn law" relating the rate of productivity growth respectively to the rate of growth of capital per worker and the rate of growth of manufacturing output fit directly into new growth theory models (typically without citation, since mainstream authors seem to find it necessary to refer only to themselves!). Although they may be subject to instability problems in the short run, Kaldor's models form a nice synthesis of forced saving macroeconomic adjustment and endogenous technical change. They tie together his "stylized facts" of a stable capital-output ratio and profit rate in the long run, together with a falling labor-output ratio and a rising capital-labor ratio over time. For the record, a brief formal presentation is given in appendix A.

Finally, the Schumpeter-Kaldor causal scheme can be extended to several sectors, as by Latin American structuralists like Furtado (1972). If industrialization beyond production of simple goods like food and textiles is to occur, they said, then under present social conditions greater income concentration is necessary to sustain demand for more sophisticated commodities, because their production is likely to be subject to minimum cost-effective size requirements due to economies of scale. The Taylor-Bacha (1976) knife edge mentioned above comes from increasing income concentration through a variant of forced saving. It provides macroeconomic adjustment in response to (and feeds back into) rising investment in a luxury goods sector catering to rich people's demands.

Distribution and Growth

Section C of figure 2.1 refers to a line of growth theories that takes income distribution as determined by institutional factors prior to the economic system. This idea of course traces back to the classics, and found vibrant form at the hands of Marx.

To summarize Marx's views on growth (or anything else, for that matter) in a way acceptable to all his readers is impossible. All we can do here is set out a number of points that he raised, which can be inserted into simple, formal models that fall well short of capturing the complexity and internal contradictions of his perceptions of growth under capitalism and other modes of production:

1. Indeed, the first thing to note is that Marx emphasized that economies change in irreversible historical time in an overall institutional framework such as "capitalism," "feudalism," or "oriental despotism." Any such mode of production can be characterized by specific social devices for appropriation of surplus product over necessary consumption. This classical insistence on the primacy of processes determining the income distribution is adopted by many non-mainstream authors.
2. Marx concentrated on the capitalist mode, in which growth results from both accumulation and endogenous technical change. Producers adopt new methods to edge out competitors or because rising labor power can wipe out surplus value, thereby wiping out laggard capitalists as well. Schumpeter gave a specific form to such processes when he wrote about innovation-induced "creative destruction" of obsolete technologies and firms.
3. Competition among capitalists tends to equalize profit rates across sectors. Sectoral demand and supply levels may not mesh, however, giving rise to a "disproportionality crisis." Similarly, aggregate demand may not equal supply. Money provides a vehicle for hoarding purchasing power, which can lead to a "realization crisis" or slump.
4. Both kinds of crises interact in a cyclical theory of growth, well described by Sylos-Labini (1984). At the bottom of a cycle, the real wage is held down by a large "reserve army" of unemployed workers, and capitalists can accumulate freely. As output expands, however, the reserve army is depleted and the real wage may rise. Capitalists search for new labor-saving technologies and also invest to build up the stock of capital and reduce employment via input substitution. Excessive funds tied

up in machinery, sectoral imbalances, and lack of purchasing power on the part of capitalists to sustain investment (or of workers to absorb the output that new investment produces) can all underlie a cyclical collapse.

5. Although he cited Ricardo and ignored Marx, Lewis (1954) translated this story of cyclical upswing into a long-run theory of economic growth, with "surplus labor" replacing the reserve army. This view from section C of the diagram provoked a strong reaction from the neoclassical line A, as discussed later. More recent, explicitly Marxist authors stress the fall in investment that may occur in response to a profit squeeze as labor gains in bargaining power over a sequence of cycles. This view shows up in the demand-driven growth models discussed in section D. They provide an interesting alternative to mainstream stories.
6. Finally, accumulation and growth may occur as these processes unfold, perhaps accompanied by a falling rate of profit, increased immiserization of the working class, or both. Marx and some recent authors see cyclical profit squeezes culminating in a steadily declining rate of profit over time.

Models without Say's Law

In their macroeconomics, both Marx and Lewis largely stick with saving-determined capital formation; in this regard they differ little from neoclassicists. But why, after Kalecki and the Keynes of the *General Theory,* should we believe that growth dynamics are determined by saving from the supply side? In the short run, output can vary to bring saving in line with investment, with prices and the income distribution relatively fixed. Over time, distribution can evolve according to conflicting income claims; if the process is dynamically stable (a counterexample is discussed in a moment), the economy will tend toward a "long-run" steady state with constant relative shares.

"Stagnationist" or "left structuralist" growth models built on these ideas show up in section D. They underlie much discussion of the economic development process, as by Lustig (1980) and Chakravarty (1987). Analysis of rich countries, Kalecki (1971) and Robinson (1962) are among the original exponents of this tradition (with forerunners tracing back to Malthus and beyond). Robinson, for example, determines short-run equilibrium at the intersection of saving and investment functions that depend positively on the rate of profit (the first functional relationship can reflect forced saving). A Marx-inspired dynamic evolu-

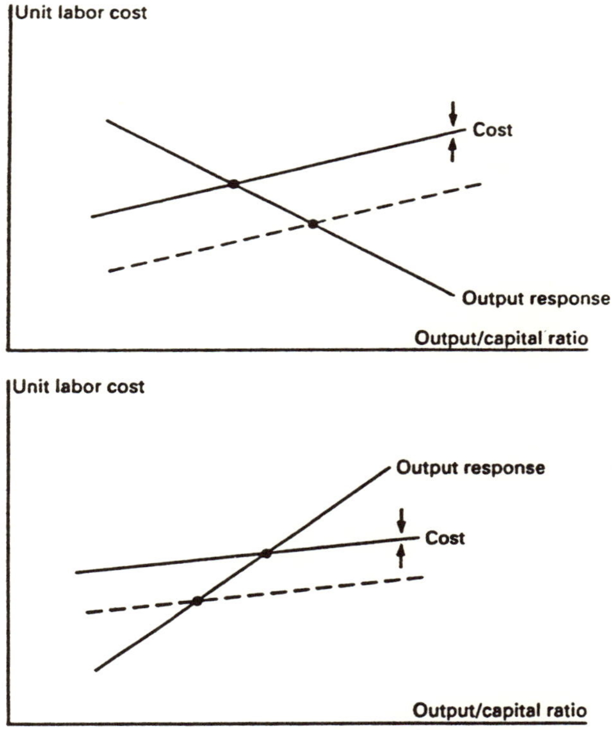

Figure 2.2 Effects of faster labor productivity growth in profit-led (top) and wage-led (bottom) economies

tion of factors influencing the profit share can drive such a model over time, as discussed by Marglin (1984).

Figure 2.2 is a natural extension of the Robinson diagram—discussed by Gordon (1995), Taylor (1991), and others—which puts a distributional variable (the profit rate or real wage) on the vertical axis and output or capacity utilization on the horizontal. An output response or IS schedule plots points along which investment equals saving (at some endogenous output level) for a given distribution. A supply-rated curve then shows how distribution responds (either in the short run or steady state) to changing output. Figure 2.2 has a rising "Cost" schedule in the capacity utilization versus real wage plane, as the latter variable responds positively to increases in the former.

Within this structuralist framework, the slope of the IS curve becomes an interesting parameter, as pointed out by Rowthorn (1982) and

Dutt (1984). For instance, its sign determines whether or not the economy can easily absorb labor productivity growth, which in the first instance wipes out jobs and workers' spending power. Capitalism's classic compensatory mechanism for falling labor-output ratios has been growth of real wages to support aggregate demand. Almost two centuries ago, members of the Luddite movement reflected by economists such as Malthus and Ricardo recognized that this process can break down when full employment is not presupposed (as by Kaldor, Schumpeter, and the economists who operate in section A of fig. 2.1).

Luddite arguments can be valid if an economy with less than full employment is "wage led" in the sense that a higher real wage or wage share stimulates aggregate demand. In an economy closed to foreign trade, an increase in the wage share has two immediate effects on effective demand: (*a*) If the propensity to consume from wage income exceeds the propensity from nonwage income (an econometric truism), then consumer demand will increase, possibly stimulating investment through the accelerator as well; (*b*) contrariwise, the corresponding reduction in the nonwage share may cut back on investment via reduced profitability. If the first effect dominates, then demand will increase with the wage share. By an obvious contrast, the economy becomes "profit led" if the second effect is more important.

If the economy is open to trade, further complications arise. One follows from the fact that the wage share, or the product of the real wage and the overall labor-output ratio, is a good approximation to labor costs per unit output. An increase in the share therefore may provoke higher export costs and a reduction in effective demand via falling sales abroad, that is, an economy in which exports are cost-responsive is more likely to be profit led.

The econometric evidence (such as it is) suggests that developing economies are typically wage led. A positive wage-output linkage can complicate adjustment to increases in labor productivity; this is how Luddite arguments come in. If unemployed labor is present, a productivity gain (or a fall in the labor-output ratio) is not likely to be accompanied immediately by a higher real wage. At the initial level of output, total wage payments will decline as the cost schedule shifts downward (to the dashed line) in the lower diagram of figure 2.2. The output-capital ratio decreases along the output response curve as unit labor costs fall toward their new steady-state level where the schedules cross. There is reduced consumption demand and possibly lower investment and potential output growth via the accelerator, as shown in more detail in appendix B.

Wage-led economies are also subject to distributional instability, which occurs when the cost schedule is steeper than the output response. A wage increase then raises aggregate demand, which in turn bids up wages further as labor markets tighten. This positive feedback can upset macroeconomic stabilization efforts, as it did for example after "heterodox shock" anti-inflation programs in Latin America in the mid-1980s. By freezing prices, these packages offset forced saving and the inflation tax, leading to an initial jump in output due to consumption demand. The resulting wage pressures contributed to making the freezes rapidly melt.

If exports are sensitive to local production costs, they may jump up enough to raise total output in the profit-led adjustment shown in the upper diagram. The price elasticity of "our" exports becomes a crucial parameter, key to absorbing productivity growth. In practice, market mechanisms alone are not likely to make export demand responsiveness rise. A government agency or publicly backed large enterprise such as a South Korean *chaebol* or a transnational corporation may be needed to search out buyers and pressure local producers into making goods and services that sell.

Finally, profit-led economies also may not be easy to guide, especially if the cost curve in the upper diagram is nonlinear, with a steep slope at high levels of capacity utilization (Gordon 1995). Attempts to raise output by shifting the output response curve outward will then mostly be diverted into real wage increases in a full employment profit squeeze. Investment demand may well decline, if it is more sensitive to profitability than output through the accelerator. In a profit-led world, attempted expansionary policy can lead to slower potential output growth, just as faster productivity advance can have the same effect when effective demand is led by wages.

Another set of models in section D can be developed on a multisectoral basis, with steady states defined by stable income distributions and all sectors expanding at the same rate. Such a framework for redistribution lies behind reform proposals that have appeared over the years. The French-Swiss reformer Sismondi (1815) recommended progressive redistribution in the wake of the Napoleonic Wars to stimulate French industrialization—more prosperous workers would demand clothing and textiles and propel investment in those sectors. Similar themes appeared in the writings of last century's *Narodniki* or Populists in Russia, and are debated in India today.

As with Furtado's work, the key idea here is that demand and distributional changes can stimulate cumulative processes à la Myrdal (1957) and Kaldor (1972) to alter the nature of supply. Many authors have pointed out that redistribution and public investment projects may raise demand enough to make profitable production processes with fixed overheads that have constant marginal but decreasing average costs. Activating economies of scale in this fashion can have profound economywide effects of the sort invoked by Young (1928) and his student Rosenstein-Rodan (1961) with his "Big Push."

New growth theorists such as Murphy, Shleifer, and Vishny (1989) came late in picking up such possibilities, which were commonly accepted by the post–World War II generation of development economists. Unhindered by Say's law, they shared a set of ideas that fit well with the growth theories of sections B through E, and included the following:

1. Schumpeter's views about the disequilibrium nature of the development process are valid, and provide an underlying framework that can be applied widely.
2. One can postulate conditions under which development will be increasingly rapid, capital-intensive, and reliant on a greater role of the state. In nineteenth-century Europe, for example, greater relative "backwardness" called forth more dramatic transitions (Gerschenkron 1962).
3. Economies of scale are important. As already noted, coordinated investment across many sectors in a Big Push may be required to give balanced output and demand expansion to take advantage of decreasing average costs economywide (Rosenstein-Rodan 1943; Nurkse 1953). Building on Schumpeter's metaphor, the idea was to get the economy from a "vicious" to a "virtuous" circle of growth.
4. The investment must be planned, because pervasive market failures such as decreasing costs and imperfect tradeability mean that price-driven, decentralized investment decisions will not be socially optimal (Scitovsky 1954).
5. Modern analytical tools such as input-output models and social cost-benefit analysis make public investment planning possible (Chenery 1959).
6. On the other hand, planning tools are at best approximations, so that one should be on the lookout for inflationary, balance of payments, and other bottlenecks, and figure out how to break them in a process of perpetually unbalanced expansion (Hirschman 1958).

The distinction between Hirschman's dialectical worldview and Rosenstein-Rodan's "balanced growth" ideas was sharp. But to anticipate later discussion, neither Hirschman nor Rodan disappeared from the mainstream's view because his work was insufficiently formalized, contrary to what Krugman (1993) asserts. Indeed, the mathematics of Chenery's (1959) and contemporaries' planning models with economies of scale was more sophisticated than the apparatus Krugman habitually works with. The difference is that Chenery and friends used integer or dynamic programming methods to solve centralized or firm-level planning problems while Krugman (with the new growth theorists) uses devices such as the Dixit-Stiglitz (1977) formulation outlined above to convexify a putative general equilibrium in which firms have fixed costs. Once again, the interesting questions of multiple equilibria posed by nonconvexities are simply ignored.

Contrary to Krugman's arguments, the old development literature lost impact because it had two ideological drawbacks. One was that although it was rich with diagnoses of development problems, it provided little concrete policy advice. Circular flow, cumulative processes, relative backwardness, balanced and unbalanced growth, etc., were intriguing metaphors but didn't help much with practical decisions. Planning models and cost-benefit analysis proved to be more of academic interest than managerial worth. Later neoclassical approaches claimed (falsely) to be more practical.

The second problem is that the early development economists placed limitless faith in the capacity of the state to intervene in the economic system. Its inability to carry out its assigned development role(s) became apparent almost equally fast. This defect had already been emphasized by first Mises (1935) and then Hayek (1935) in the "calculation debate" about socialist planning. Their teachings were reanimated by Bauer (1972) in the developing country context; the neoliberal resurgence of the 1980s brought them to prominence later on.

Realistically or not, neoclassical economics at most requires that the state should be a "night watchman." The early development economists needed the state to be proactive and effective, but provided no reasons why it could or should fulfill its tasks. This omission was soon seized upon by neoclassical economists who forged a new "market-friendly" consensus about how to further development and growth, a topic to be addressed in the following section.

Models with Binding Resource or Sectoral Supply Constraints

In models that don't postulate Say's law, specific supply limits can still provoke distributional changes like those underlying forced saving.

Examples include shortages of crucial inputs like foreign exchange, or else interactions between sectors adjusting to excess demand respectively via changes in output and a flexible price. Growth models along these lines have been elaborated by economists in section E of figure 2.1.

The ever-present danger of "external strangulation" in developing economies is an old theme in structuralist thought, dating at least to the work of the Economic Commission for Latin America in Santiago in the 1950s. The notion was formalized by Chenery and Bruno (1962) in their two-gap model incorporating separate foreign exchange and saving restrictions on growth.

The saving constraint follows naturally from Harrod-Domar or "AK" algebra: investment has to be financed by either national saving or capital inflows from abroad. But the inflows also cover the trade deficit. Industrialization via import substitution (the only way to build up local production capacity that has been discovered so far) means that the economy becomes dependent on imports of intermediate goods—without them, local factories cannot work. At the same time, import substitution rarely extends to capital goods, so that up to half of investment spending takes the form of purchases from abroad. There is a sharp trade-off between current production and capital formation, which only additional foreign exchange can relieve. If domestic output is limited by scarcity of convertible dollars or yen, inflationary forced saving macroeconomic adjustment often occurs. As a consequence, during the 1980s real wages fell on the order of 50 percent in many economies externally strangled by the debt crisis.

The saving and foreign gaps have been extended in recent work (Bacha 1990; Taylor 1991) to take into account two important fiscal effects. First, after the debt crisis, many governments nationalized foreign obligations—the state was liable for external payments on debt. Second, econometric work in the 1980s typically showed that there is a strong "crowding in" effect of public on private capital formation (contrary to the crowding out of private by public spending through rising interest rates in financial markets that is frequently presumed). The consequence is a "fiscal gap" limiting growth because public (and therefore total) capital formation is cut back. Attempts to relieve fiscal burdens by relying on forced saving or the inflation tax became ever more frequent in the 1980s. The multiple, interacting problems posed by saving, foreign exchange, fiscal, and inflation gaps are a source of much current policy concern. They are not adequately addressed by growth models in the mainstream tradition, which typically assume that sufficient relative price flexibility will make such woes go away.

Turning to section E models with two broad commodities domestically supplied, a frequently used specification is based on one sector where supply is limited by available capacity and the price adjusts to clear the market, plus a second sector in which production meets demand. This two-sector specification blends forced saving, Engel demand effects, and output adjustment in an illuminating fashion. It can be applied in various contexts (e.g., to analyze the agricultural terms of trade, to discuss "Dutch disease" problems when a traded goods sector has its price fixed from the world market and a nontraded sector has an adjusting price, and to do global macroeconomics between a "North" exporting industrial goods and a "South" selling primary products). The nature of the model can be illustrated with the first interpretation here.

Models focusing on the relative price of food (or agriculture's terms of trade) date at least from the controversy between Ricardo and Malthus about whether England's Corn Laws limiting grain imports should be repealed. To address this question, we assume that "industry" has prices fixed by a mark-up over prime costs and its output is determined by demand, while "agriculture" has fixed supply and a market-clearing price in the short run.

To see how the model works, we can ask how the two markets interact. Suppose that the terms of trade shift toward agriculture, say, due to a reduction of food imports. Industrial output can either rise or fall. It will be pushed up by increased demand from higher agricultural income, but also held down by reduced real nonagricultural spending power (real wages drop due to forced saving from dearer food). The latter effect will be stronger insofar as Engel's law makes food demand income inelastic, so that the loss in workers' spending power primarily forces down their demand for industrial goods. Under such circumstances, letting more imports into the economy will doubly benefit the industrial sector—food prices fall and output expands. Although he used a different model to argue his case, this outcome is consistent with Ricardo's advocacy of repeal of the Corn Laws.

The alternative view was espoused by Malthus in his *Principles of Political Economy,* where the argument can be interpreted in terms of distributional effects on aggregate demand. Agriculture is responsible for a big proportion of income and consumer spending. Farmers (or landlords for Malthus) hit by adverse terms of trade will cut their purchases, reducing economic activity overall. Whether a Ricardian or Malthusian distributional configuration applies in developing countries today is highly relevant for policy—the answer according to applied computable general equilibrium models seems to go either way.

Besides import policy, other state interventions can affect the terms of trade. Fiscal expansion or increased investment, for example, will bid up the flexible price to generate forced saving to help meet the increased injection of demand. Ellman (1975) argues that food price-induced forced saving supported the Soviet industrialization push of the 1930s, in contrast to Preobrazhenski's (1965) suggestion that the terms of trade be shifted *against* agriculture by a monopsonistic state to extract an investable surplus.

Fix-price/flex-price models (a terminology due to Hicks [1965], one of the many co-inventers of such specifications) can also be used to describe growth. Determination of the growth rate depends crucially on how causality in the macroeconomic system runs. If saving-investment balance in the North, for example, regulates expansion of the world economy, then the primary export terms of trade and capital formation in the South will tag along as adjusting variables. Contrariwise, slow growth in a dominant fixed-supply sector can determine behavior of the whole system. How the agrarian question may (or may not) be resolved is an obvious application not taken up by recent mainstream theories.

A final observation about section E is that ideas like Myrdal's cumulative processes and Hirschman's succession of bottlenecks fit well into a category of models based on binding sectoral performances and constraints. Whether they can be formalized tractably is another question. The fact that the answer is often in the negative does not detract from the usefulness of disequilibrium or dialectical approaches to thinking about the world.

Accounting for Growth

Section F appears in figure 2.1 to emphasize that accounting schemes and contemplation of how the entries within them change over time can provide insight into the development process. The discovery that it makes sense to peruse the numbers was made centuries before running endless regressions of GDP growth rates on a host of right-hand side variables (re)appeared as a recent fad. It dates back 300 years to the "political arithmetick" of William Petty and contemporaries, who for example recognized that the GDP share of agriculture declines as per capita income goes up—a consequence of now predictable technological trends and Engle's law. Kuznets and Chenery were able uncoverers of similar regularities, whose findings are well summarized by Syrquin (1988).

The other theme that should be mentioned in connection with section F is that manipulation of accounting schemes themselves can provide useful insights. In a recent example, Pasinetti (1981) closes the input-output accounts by assuming that operating surpluses of firms at the sectoral level just finance their investment demands. This hypothesis (a disaggregated version of the widow's cruse) is not a bad approximation to the nature of investment finance under industrial capitalism, and points to several interesting conclusions (details of the model appear in appendix C):

1. A labor theory of value broadly applies, with mark-up rates on labor costs varying across sectors according to their capital intensity and capacity growth rates;
2. If one aggregates gross outputs over sectors using direct and indirect labor inputs, taking into account investment requirements as weights, a material balance of the form $\Sigma h_i c_i = 1$ emerges, where the h_i are "hyperintegrated" labor inputs (in Pasinetti's usage) and the c_i stand for public and private sectoral consumption levels per worker (ignoring net exports).
3. In this accounting scheme, Pasinetti first observes that the h_i coefficients decrease when there is labor productivity growth, which historically runs between zero and a few percent per year under modern capitalism. Second, although per capita demand for a given commodity or service may rise for a time, ultimately it tends to slow or even decline. For example, in the United States in the 1920s and Europe after World War II, surging consumption of automobiles and associated products supported employment growth, even though productivity was going up. But by now, cars are no longer income-elastic items and their c_i coefficient is stable or going down while their h_i also continues to fall.

Both trends can stifle employment expansion—in Marx's hoary language, the material balance condition can fail to be satisfied due to either a realization or a disproportionality problem. Even if enough work is available in principle, disproportional demand and productivity trends across sectors may require substantial labor force reallocations if full employment is to be maintained. Such movements are never socially simple; most countries rely on public action to make them as painless as possible.

Similarly, if the employment realization—or stagnation—problem is severe, it can be offset in several ways, but all entail their own complications. One familiar mechanism is capitalism's continual introduction of new goods that people feel impelled to buy—few households had cell phones and compact disk players even a few years ago. Whether entrepreneurs can continue to deluge us with novel temptations with rapidly growing c_i coefficients is always an open question. Second, real wages can rise to offset lower h_i

coefficients. We have seen how Luddite barriers can impede this process when the economy is wage-led. Finally, policymakers can attempt demand stimulation; in a profit-led economy such an effort can easily break down. Contrary to the facile optimism underlying the models of figure 2.1's section A, there is no automatic mechanism that makes the $h_i c_i$ terms for currently functioning sectors add up to one.

4. Finally, Pasinetti uses his labor theory of value to rediscover and generalize the theory of the terms of trade proposed by Lewis (1969). The gist is that there is a common set of traded goods for which poor countries have relatively low productivity (levels or growth) in comparison to rich countries. Poor countries have somewhat higher productivities in their exclusive traded goods (tropical food crops, raw materials) than in the common ones, while the reverse is true for rich countries. The result is to swing the terms of trade and real income relative to the common traded goods against poor countries. The moral is that real income growth in developing economies depends crucially on their attaining rapid rates of productivity increase for the common set of traded goods.

A variant trade story concentrates not so much on primary exports as on manufactures. Following Japanese and South Korean practice, how successful have developing economies been in shifting demand composition toward export commodities with high income elasticities in trading partners and rapid productivity growth (perhaps due to decreasing per unit costs)? A material balance with the c_i terms decomposed into domestic demands and exports (and imports treated as leakages) would be a natural means to address this question.

Other Perspectives

Concern about the forces supporting East Asia's economic success carries over to section G, along with restatements of the scale economy and technical innovation mechanisms already discussed. These feed indirectly into endogenous growth theory, and with more force appear in Arthur's (1989) observations about the likely irreversibility of sensibly modeled processes of technological advance (especially when there are production nonconvexities). Harking back to the balanced/unbalanced growth debate, his results suggest that the unbalanced team was closer to getting the story right.

A related and distinctly nonmainstream view about the importance of "productive forces" traces back to exponents of protectionism as a basis for industrial development such as Hamilton and List. Along parallel lines, Polanyi (1944) argued that the state played an essential role in building up the institutions that supported nineteenth-century growth.

From the orthodox point of view, such notions sound heretical, but they certainly encouraged people like Prebisch (1959) in their advocacy of import-substituting industrialization, or ISI. List on *The National System of Political Economy* was more widely read than Anglo-Saxon economists in Japan in the 1930s, and his ideas strongly undergird the East Asian "model" that emerged at that time. Studies of South Korea and Taiwan by Amsden (1989) and Wade (1990) respectively describe the model's features. Because East Asia raises issues that any realistic growth or development theory should address, it is worthwhile to summarize the basic points:

1. A theme continually developed in South Korea's official documents was that "the market mechanism cannot be entirely trusted to increase competitive advantage by industries," so that branches likely to enjoy high productivity growth and income-elastic demand were to be promoted as "promising strategic industries" (Chang 1993). They were given custom-designed financial, technical, and administrative support. Picking winners turned out to be an operational concept in an economy like South Korea's (and, earlier, Japan's), which was not operating on world technological frontiers. As Dore (1986) emphasizes in the Japanese case, in "catching up" situations, it is fairly easy to pick out which sectors to favor and what kinds of support they need for success.

   Corrective feedback to the selection process was provided by ongoing, broad reporting of activities of "priority" firms to the government. The economic bureaucracy thus had access to detailed business information, which proved essential for effective industrial policy. "Creative destruction" was assured by the government's use of its business information to weed out inefficient production operations in successive waves of rationalizations, mergers, and liquidations. Individual *chaebols* were clearly subject to discipline, even though as a group they had privileged access to state resources. Noise and static in dealings between the state and producers were reduced by the fact that apex organizations were engaged on both sides of the dialog.

2. In line with this strategy, intense effort was devoted to acquiring technology (the huge public investment in education was economically mobilized exactly in this fashion). For this reason, direct foreign investment was strictly regulated while foreign technologies

were banned in sectors in which domestic counterparts were available. Firms were encouraged to practice reverse engineering, along with licensing and purchase of technologies not available at home—all under bureaucratic guidance.

3. There was a consistent emphasis on attaining economies of scale. This goal was reflected in many mergers of small firms initiated or subsidized by the government (e.g., in the chemical, automobile, fertilizer, and other sectors). There was an ongoing campaign to restrict entry and control capacity expansion in various sectors to curtail "excessive competition" in the form of big swings and destabilizing cumulative processes in investment and price wars in industries with decreasing costs.

4. Within the generally expansionary macroeconomic environment, credit allocation was aggressively practiced. The banking system was nationalized early in the Korean industrial drive, giving the state effective control over all important financial flows (aided by tight foreign exchange restrictions). "Policy loans" with subsidized interest rates and priority rationing accounted for over half of bank credits in the 1960s and 1970s.

These features of East Asian industrial planning suggest several conclusions relevant to other developing economies. One is that there can be a bargaining solution among peak organizations to restrain "rent-seeking" à la Krueger (1974), with rapid output growth and the state's power to punish recalcitrants in the background. Rents (or better, Marshallian quasi-rents or Marxian/Schumpeterian profits) were certainly created for the *chaebols* by their privileged position, yet they became production powerhouses and not leeches thriving on public largesse. Moreover, they were effectively guided by the bureaucracy, because channels were created for it to get access to business information.

The economic bureaucracy itself was an essential player. In the terminology of economic sociology of the sort pioneered by Polanyi (Evans 1992), it was "embedded" in the society in the sense that it could act autonomously for the public good as it saw fit, without completely being taken over by patronage and rent seeking.

Dialog among the bureaucracy and enterprises permitted the East Asian nations to practice economic planning effectively in a capitalist environment. Short-term allocative efficiency ("getting prices right") was often sacrificed to long-term productive efficiency or rapid productivity growth. Conscious rent creation on the part of the state was the key to constant industrial upgrading and realization of economies of scale. In the long run, huge steel mills and shipyards made sense.

Finally, following Japan, the institutional basis for other East Asian miracles was put in place over a relatively short time. *Chaebols,* trading companies, planning bureaucracies, and the macroeconomic policy mix all emerged in the early 1960s in a creative burst. Obviously, such institutions cannot be transferred without modification to other national contexts, but partial functional equivalents may well prove relevant elsewhere in the world. Exploring such possibilities would be a proper domain for realistic theories of economic growth.

The Mainstream Policy Response

The theories of sections B–F of figure 2.1 might conceivably be up to such an exploration, but the same cannot be said for the orthodox views summarized in section A. In fact, they emerged as part of a strong reaction against public guidance of the economy, which got under way in its most recent form in the 1960s. Of course, Mises, Hayek, and predecessor liberals had raised the same ideas long before, while the Polanyis of their times fired back.

The first wave of recent critics concentrated on the "inefficiency" of state intervention as it had evolved, particularly in the emphasis that development economists of the Rosenstein-Rodan vintage placed on ISI. Trade theorists, who are imbued with the evils of protectionism at an early age, took the lead. Using then novel analytical tools such as effective rates of protection and domestic resource costs, authors such as Little, Scitovsky, and Scott (1970), Krueger (1984), and many others showed that the incentive structures created by import substitution were highly unequal for different economic actors. They further sought to correlate "distorted" policy regimes with poor economic performance. Their modest success in this endeavor is a continual embarrassment for the school (Fanelli, Frenkel, and Taylor [1993] criticize the latest attempts in the World Bank's 1991 *World Development Report*).

One of the empirical problems is worth flagging now. The "welfare losses" due to distortions emerging from solutions of computable general equilibrium models—the highest-tech analytical tools—are usually meager: 100 percent price wedges might reduce GDP by one-half percent. Implicitly, then, the initial neoclassical critique reduced to an assertion that eliminating distortions will lead the economy to jump to a noticeably more rapidly growing configuration of circular flow. But just how is such a transition supposed to occur? The dynamics of miracles instigated by the invisible hand are not easy to describe, perhaps because they seldom happen.

Regardless of this difficulty, when the critics showed that many industries in developing countries had "negative value-added" at world prices, they took the profession by storm. But they also transmitted a more powerful message. Read between the lines, these economists advocated laissez-faire as the only viable alternative to an incentive mare's nest. The rapid growth rates of Taiwan and South Korea—at the time unrealistically postulated to have noninterventionist governments—were cited in support of the free market. Although they are not easy to substantiate, the notions that observed distortions inhibit growth and that rapid growers are noninterventionist now permeate the rhetoric and advice of mainstream development scholars and lending institutions; they are built solidly into the policy recommendations offered by the World Bank and International Monetary Fund.

Similar developments took place on the agricultural front, where Lewis- and Preobrazhenski-style concerns about the dual economy were swept aside by authors emerging from an anti-interventionist American Middle Western agricultural economics tradition such as Schultz (1964). Their diagnosis was that farmgate prices had been held down in developing countries, in comparison to world market prices (however distorted by rich country interventions) as a point of reference. Accumulation processes as well as income distribution within the sector and politicoeconomic difficulties in altering the way it works were alien to the new price mechanists' ways of thought. Although food production in some countries was aided by subsidies to big farmers to utilize the new technologies offered by the Green Revolution, price reform alone has not been capable of stimulating agriculture over much of the developing world. Africa is only the saddest case.

In the 1980s, the debate on economic policy took another turn. Echoing Bauer (1972), who had questioned the efficacy of state intervention early on, more recent authors postulate that "bureaucratic failure" is worse than "market failure." Figure 2.3 is a schematic representation of the latest neoclassical critiques. The point that it tries to depict is that the critics are not fully relevant because their models push them into extreme positions with regard to the nature of both the market (highly distorted or fully competitive) and the state (pluralistic and reacting passively to pressures or monolithic and proactive). On the other hand, the obstacles to intervention that they emphasize do help understanding of blocked attempts at economic reform.

For example, Olson (1982) argues that because of bargaining costs and the presence of free riders, coalitions within the society form

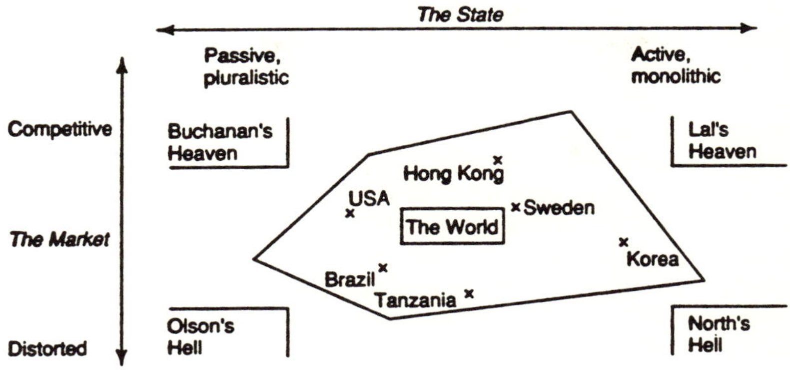

Figure 2.3 Neoliberal views of state/market interactions

to protect their own interests. They seek to redistribute income toward themselves, instead of increasing efficiency in the national interest. A weak state cannot intervene, so the system tends toward a highly distorted market structure with the coalitions distributing the spoils: "Olson's Hell" in the diagram. Developing countries that have helped coalitions form themselves around ISI or other strategic interventions may drift toward infernal situations as the subsidized groups take over decision making: Argentina comes to mind for this pathology (along with numerous others).

The public choice school led by Buchanan (1980) follows Krueger (1974) in elevating "rent seeking" induced by government interventions—lobbying for state favors, paying a bribe to get an import quota or Pentagon contract, fixing a ticket for a traffic violation—to a deadly social ill. If real resources are devoted to pursuing rents or "directly unproductive profit-seeking" (DUP) activities in the jargon, the outcome can be a form of suboptimality resembling Olson's for the society as a whole.

Inventing DUP was a technical advance because deep wells of postulated corruption allowed numerical models to give satisfyingly large estimates of welfare losses from distortion. Moreover, the saving social grace becomes a thoroughly night-watchmanly state supervising a competitive market—the latter condition to be guaranteed by international free trade. Under these conditions, DUP activity supposedly becomes unrewarding, and the invisible hand will guide society toward "Buchanan's Heaven." Unpleasant externalities such as transnational corporations taking advantage of a country's fully unregulated trade and external capital markets are banished from the scene.

A second form of bliss takes a more authoritarian cast. For Buchanan, the ideal state mimics the Cheshire Cat by vanishing to avoid being taken over by the interests. Alternatively, the state can force the interests to vanish or in Lal's (1983) words, "A courageous, ruthless, and perhaps undemocratic government is required to ride roughshod over these newly created special interest groups"—before Chiapas, the current Mexican leadership may have shared such dreams. In the diagram, we ascend to another Heaven, although it is not clear why Lal's ruthless generals and bureaucrats will abstain from taking over the market also. The record of Third World authoritarian states in avoiding corruption and distortions is not encouraging in this regard.

Indeed, a market distorted by the state for its own ends is a final extreme possibility in the diagram, which can be associated with North's (1981) theories of economic history—not to mention Kennedy's (1987) good read about how their military-industrial complexes force great powers into economic decline. In a typical North example, a state may choose to raise revenue by creating monopolies and then marshall political arguments in their support. The fate of Leninist centrally planned systems suggests that economic damnation may well lie at the end of such a path.

The message of the diagram is that the state and market in principle can arrive at extreme configurations that are easy to characterize. However, the Buchanan combination of a purely night watchman state and a completely undistorted market has never been observed in practice (certainly not in eighteenth-century Britain and contemporary Hong Kong—the two most widely cited putative examples). If it were ever created, a Lal equilibrium would probably not be stable, and recent events suggest that even North's Hell is not forever (the same is true for Olson's form of anarchy).

Indeed, as the central section of the picture illustrates, existing societies combine mixtures of state activism with market distortions—the national placements are arbitrary but are meant to illustrate stylized facts. Moreover, if it were possible to attach numerical coordinates to nations' points in the diagram, statistical analysis would almost certainly detect scant association between their positions or movements and indicators of economic performance such as GDP growth rates, except for the likelihood of poor growth in countries with Hellishly distorted markets.

Beyond this hypothetical regression, a much more fundamental point is that the new neoclassical theory of the state is ahistorical and timeless—although it may shed light on tendencies, it elides the messy dynamics of transitions. As with the new growth theory, a typical model would please Dr. Pangloss: all of its "agents" successfully optimize over all possible choices so that the system inevitably arrives at the best (and only, presuming uniqueness) possible world. Not much hope for "development," in Schumpeter's sense of jumping from one pattern of circular flow to another, in such specifications.

Where Theory Might Sensibly Go

We are left to ponder how formal growth theory might incorporate some of the foregoing ideas, to become practically useful for policy formation. No instant answers are at hand, but a few thoughts are worth noting:

1. Mechanisms supporting growth and factors restraining it clearly vary from place to place and time to time. The different ways in which the broadly similar accounting schemes that underlie all growth models can be "closed" by behavioral assumptions along the lines laid out in figure 2.1 do matter, as pointed out by Sen (1963) and elaborated by Marglin (1984), Taylor (1991), and many others.

   Formalizations of the ideas in all the sections of figure 2.1 can be fit to any single economy's data and will give different answers about its likely evolution and sensitivity to policy moves. Statistical techniques like Granger causality (or lead-lag) tests are of little use in sorting out the closure question, because of absent data and multiple causal patterns. When they are applied, however, they rarely support the macroeconomic vision underlying section A of figure 2.1 (Gordon 1995). Serious political economy or institutional discussion provides a better means to consider the causal patterns at hand.

2. Even so, the ideas of Mises and Hayek as propagandized by Thatcher and Reagan continue to dominate the current policy scene. In growth and development theory, the corollaries are an emphasis on price-induced supply responses and the wonders of the invisible hand. The big role played by human capital accumulation in new growth models is a case in point.

   The idea that more education can have productive payoffs was raised by Smith and Mill and popularized by Schultz (1963) and Becker (1964) quite some time ago. Dissidents like Amsden (1989) likewise stress the role that a skilled labor force played in East Asia's economic success. The question is whether education is more a necessary or concomitant condition for economic development instead of sufficient for it to occur. A few examples shed light on possible answers.

South Korea's numerous engineers may well have been unemployed or unemployable had the Economic Planning Board not practiced its Hamiltonian (as in Alexander, not William Rowan) strategies for growth. A country with a poor education performance like Brazil grew rapidly until it hit a foreign resource bottleneck in the 1980s; countries with ample human capital like Sri Lanka only began to grow fast when external donors turned on the hard currency tap at about the same time. These stories suggest that economic growth is a multifactoral process, and that all available inputs will not automatically be used à la Say. However impressive their manipulations of nineteenth-century mathematics, models ignoring these mundane observations fail the credibility test.

3. As many authors noted in figure 2.1 pointed out, growth can be strongly influenced by distributional processes unfolding within social, political, and economic structures. Old Ricardo and Marx were not wrong in setting up models based on socioeconomic classes; the not-so-old *General Theory* was built on an institutional vision of capitalism that is still valid to a great extent. Structuralist modelers are inspired by these examples, which strike them as far richer than the world of Walras.

Indeed, structure as reflected in low-order dissipative differential equation systems may be more tractable to deal with than the not necessarily well-behaved Hamiltonian (à la William Rowan, this time) dynamics utilized by neoclassicists. In phase spaces of $2n$ dimensions where n exceeds one, chaos can easily arise to confute the saddlepaths beloved of optimal growth adepts (Lorenz 1989). On a less formal level, it makes sense to heed the justes limites to Walras's program raised by Poincaré himself: ". . . you regard men as infinitely selfish and infinitely farsighted. The first hypothesis may perhaps be admitted in a first approximation, the second may call for some reservations" (letter of 1 October 1901, cited by Ingrao and Israel 1990).

4. In the "really existing" world, even the first approximation is not very good—the planet is evidently populated by impurely "economic" men and women, who certainly have neither unlimited computational capabilities nor perfect foresight. In such a place, development is a transformation that deep minds besides Mises's and Hayek's have tried to understand, without clear-cut success. Nonetheless, one can learn from the theories of capitalism proposed by Marx, Weber, Polanyi, and others. As already observed, Marx stressed the importance of the institutions supporting accumulation

and technical advance. Despite Bretton Woods tutelage over the past dozen years, they show no signs of emerging in much of the developing world under allegedly "market-friendly" reform programs.

The mature Weber (1968) pointed to a complex causal pattern underlying capitalism's origins: "All in all, the specific roots of Occidental culture must be sought in the tension and peculiar balance, on the one hand, between office charisma and monasticism, and on the other between the contractual character of the feudal state and the autonomous bureaucratic hierarchy." All were essential in setting up capitalism as a system of institutionalized strife among shifting but well-defined social groups (Collins 1980). At a more practical level, all successful or semisuccessful reform programs in semi-industrialized countries in recent decades—Spain, Chile, Korea, Taiwan—have involved complex causal patterns and contingent historical events.

Polanyi's great insight has also been noted, that the institutions supporting the market system arose historically with state guidance from within society, which also defended itself against their worst excesses—child labor laws were passed early in the nineteenth century and the collapse of real wages in Eastern Europe was arrested at 30–40 percent late in the twentieth. "Double movements" of this sort will continue to occur as other countries develop, peacefully only if the tensions of change do not become unbearable.

As society's superordinate actor, the state will also have to play a central role in forcing both sides of the double movement—markets will be neither created nor regulated without public action. Developing country experience surely shows that states can fail in several dimensions (Evans 1992). They operate under fundamental uncertainty, and may or may not respond to the uneven advances of different sectors, disproportionalities, and balance of payments and inflationary pressures that will inevitably arise (Hirschman 1958). They can try to do too much, thereby achieving little. They can become purely predatory, as in countless petty dictatorships around the world. Nonetheless, as theoreticians of backwardness from Gerschenkron to Amsden have pointed out, when backward economies do catch up the process is mediated by the state, in particular by an autonomous bureaucracy accepted by (and embedded in) the society overall.

Somehow, new growth theory manages to ignore all these considerations, while authors operating in sections B through F of figure 2.1 have kept them foremost in their minds.

APPENDIX A: KALDOR'S GROWTH MODEL

Let π be the share of profits in output and b the labor-output ratio. Then, using the notation developed in the discussion of new growth models, the breakdown of the value of output (ignoring intermediate inputs, indirect taxes, etc.) takes the form $PX = wbX + \pi PX$, or

$$P = wb/(1 - \pi), \tag{A.1}$$

where w is the money wage. The factor $1/(1 - \pi)$ can be interpreted as a mark-up on labor costs, a point developed further in appendix B. The real wage ω is $\omega = w/P$, and we can define the profit rate $r = \pi PX/PK = \pi u$, where the output-capital ratio u now measures the level of economic activity as opposed to the results of factor substitution as in neoclassical growth models. Since $\omega b = 1 - \pi$, any one of the three distributional variables r, π, and ω determines the other two.

Assume that the aggregate saving function, reflecting class distinctions, is

$$g^s = \text{Savings}/PK = [s_\pi \pi + s_w(1 - \pi)]u, \tag{A.2}$$

in which s_π is the saving rate from profit income, s_w is the rate from wage income, and $s_\pi > s_w$.

Investment can be assumed to respond to capacity utilization as in Kaldor (1940) and Steindl (1952), as well as to the profit rate r:

$$g^i = I/K = g_0 + \alpha r + \beta u = (\alpha\pi + \beta)u, \tag{A.3}$$

where we ignore depreciation.

Macroeconomic equilibrium is determined by the condition $g^i - g^s = 0$. With u predetermined, we can solve for π as

$$\pi = \frac{g_0 + (\beta - s_w)u}{[s_\pi - (s_w + \alpha)]u}. \tag{A.4}$$

The macroeconomic stability condition with π as the adjusting variable in the short run is $\partial(g^i - g^s)/\partial\pi < 0$. Mindless differentiation shows that this inequality is equivalent to

$$\sigma = s_\pi - (s_w + \alpha) > 0. \tag{A.5}$$

For the private nonresidential U.S. economy with variables scaled by potential output, rough values for long-run investment and saving parameters are on the order of $\alpha = 0.25$, $\beta = 0.1$, $s_\pi = 0.5$, $s_w = 0.3$ (Gordon 1995). Subject to the vagaries of econometrics and the difficulties of blowing up these parameters to take into account tax and import leakages, other forms of investment, etc., stability of the Kaldorian adjustment process (were the economy really at full employment with forced saving as the main adjustment mechanism) would be precarious in the United States. As will be seen in appendix B where u is the adjusting variable with π fixed in the short run, Kaldorian instability translates into the statement that the economy is profit-led. In the present context, the message of instability is that an increase in π releases demand pressures that make it increase further still.

Be that as it may, when the stability condition (A.5) is satisfied equation (A.4) shows that the profit share rises with all three parameters of the investment function for given u; this is forced saving. The standard widow's cruse result shows up as $\partial\pi/\partial s_\pi < 0$.

When output is the macro adjusting variable in the short run, the usual Keynesian stability condition of $\partial(g^i - g^s)/\partial u < 0$ says that saving should respond more strongly than investment to a change in u, or

$$\Delta = s_\pi \pi + s_w(1 - \pi) - (\alpha\pi + \beta) > 0, \tag{A.6}$$

which is satisfied for the parameters above with a "reasonable" value of π (say between 0.1 and 0.2).

If this inequality is valid, then the sign of $\partial\pi/\partial u = -\sigma/\Delta\ u$ will be negative when (A.5) is satisfied. In a moment, we will want to assume that the derivative of the capital stock growth rate $g = (dK/dt)/K$ with respect to u is positive. From the investment function (A.3), this requirement will be fulfilled for a small positive σ.

Kaldor's technical progress function can be written as $\xi = f(K/L)$, or in log-linearized differential form as

$$\hat{\xi} = \phi_0 + \phi_1(g - \hat{L}), \tag{A.7}$$

where a "hat" denotes a growth rate: $\hat{\xi} = (d\xi/dt)/\xi$. Assume that $\hat{L}$ is exogenous. Since $u = \xi\lambda = \xi(L/K)$, we can write

$$\hat{u} = (1 - \phi_1)(\hat{L} - g) + \phi_0. \tag{A.8}$$

Away from the "trivial" solution where $u = 0$, we find that the differential equation for du/dt is stable around an equilibrium where $g = \hat{L} + \phi_0/$

$(1 - \phi_1)$ so long as $dg/du > 0$ and $\phi_1 < 1$. Along such a steady-state growth path, π and u are constant and the rest of Kaldor's stylized facts mentioned in the text hold true. Because $\pi = 1 - \omega b = 1 - \omega/\xi$ and is constant, we have $\hat{\omega} = \hat{\xi}$, or the real wage increases at the rate of productivity growth.

APPENDIX B: A LEFT STRUCTURALIST GROWTH MODEL

If we drop the hypothesis of full employment, then it is natural to treat u as the adjusting variable in the short run, with the income distribution evolving over time according to the dynamics of labor-management bargaining, conflicting claims to output, or class conflict (depending on which perspective one prefers). With π constant in the short run, equation (A.1) above becomes a mark-up price theory along Kaleckian lines.

An immediate question that arises is how output responds to changes in distribution. For the model set out in appendix A but closed by constant π and variable u, the answer is that the economy is "wage-led" with $\partial u/\partial \omega > 0$ when the inequality in (A.5) is satisfied and the stability condition (A.6) is valid. In words, wage-led adjustment happens when there is a big difference in saving parameters from profit and wage incomes, and the response of investment to the profit rate is weak. (As noted in the text, one should also take into account export demand as well as the fact that imported intermediate inputs into the production process represent a saving leakage not tied to wage income. Both factors push developing economies in the direction of being wage led—their exports are not price responsive and they become highly dependent on intermediate imports via ISI. In simple models, an output increase in response to a higher wage occurs when there is an output decrease in response to real devaluation. Devaluation is often, but not always, contractionary in the Third World.)

To explore how productivity growth influences long-run macro developments, we have to bring in distributional dynamics explicitly. Let $\theta = \omega b = 1 - \pi$ stand for the labor share (or, equivalently, labor cost per unit output in a simple model). Conventional wisdom after the famous Dunlop and Tarshis papers of the late 1930s suggests that the real wage ω increases with the level of economic activity; more recent "full employment profit squeeze" Marxists would argue the same for the labor share. If the social processes underlying wage determination are self-stabilizing ("the world is stable"), then wage dynamics might take the form

$$\hat{\omega} = h(\theta, u), \tag{A.9}$$

with negative and positive first partial derivatives for θ and u respectively. Higher capacity utilization puts upward pressure on the wage, and a bigger labor share dampens it down.

If there is ongoing labor productivity growth, a technical progress function could take the form

$$\hat{b} = -\phi(\theta, u) < 0, \tag{A.10}$$

replacing (A.7). Typically, one would suppose that $\partial\phi/\partial\theta > 0$, as more expensive labor spurs the search for productivity gains. Higher capacity utilization leading to greater investment from (A.3) should aid productivity growth as in Kaldor's formulation.

With productivity rising, unit labor costs become the natural object of distributional conflict. The relevant dynamic equation is

$$\hat{\theta} = \hat{\omega} + \hat{b} = h(\theta, u) - \gamma\phi(\theta, u) = h(\theta, u) + \gamma\hat{b}. \tag{A.11}$$

In these expressions, γ is the share of productivity growth that is passed through to lower unit cost in the short run (another tricky social question). We assume that $h_\theta - \gamma\phi_\theta < 0$ and $h_u - \gamma\phi_u > 0$ (i.e., induced changes in productivity do not outweigh the distributional effects on real wage changes mentioned in the preceding). Alternatively, (A.11) can be written as

$$\hat{\omega} = h(\theta, u) + (1 - \gamma)\phi(\theta, u),$$

so that a share $1 - \gamma$ of higher productivity feeds into real wages. In Korean experience, for example, γ takes a value around one-half.

A steady state for (A.11) is defined by $\hat{\theta} = 0$, so that $\hat{\omega} = -\hat{b}$ and there is a constant profit share. Changing levels of u and θ allow the steady state to be obtained via the adjustment process illustrated in figure 2.2. A wage-led scenario appears in the lower diagram in which $du/d\theta > 0$ along the "output response" curve. The diagram shows a stable equilibrium in which the "cost" schedule along which $\hat{\theta} = 0$ is less steep than the output response curve.

A burst of technical advance can be represented by an upward shift of the ϕ function, making real unit labor cost decline faster in (A.11). To bring $\hat{\theta}$ back up to zero, θ itself would have to fall. The cost schedule shifts downward, and at the new steady state both unit costs and capacity use are lower. If investment demand is relatively more sensitive to capacity utilization than the profit rate (the exact condition is $\beta(s_\pi - s_w) > \alpha s_w$), then the steady state capital stock growth rate would also decline.

The upper diagram in figure 2.2 is based on the hypothesis that the economy is profit led, for example because exports are highly responsive to falling unit labor costs. As a consequence, aggregate demand is an inverse function of θ. Faster productivity growth leads to a new steady state where u is higher and the capital stock growth rate speeds up. Such a virtuous shift in circular flow can occur in a nation at any income level, and has been typical in East Asia. How to find the export strategy that converts local rent seekers into aggressive entrepreneurs is the corresponding industrial policy task.

APPENDIX C: PASINETTI'S ACCOUNTING

Following Taylor (1994), Pasinetti's (1981) model is restated here in input-output notation, illustrated with a social accounting matrix (or SAM) for two sectors in table 2.1. The first two columns give breakdowns of sectoral costs P_iX_i into intermediate input costs $P_ia_{ij}X_j$) (where the a_{ij} are the usual input-output coefficients), labor costs wd_iX_i (where the d_i coefficients stand for "direct" labor inputs per unit of gross outputs X_i), and profits or operating surpluses $\pi_iP_iX_i$. The first two rows show that values of sectoral outputs are exhausted by intermediate, consumption, and investment demands. The c_i coefficients give consumption of sector i's product(s) per employed worker (total employment is L). The b_{ij} coefficients transform investment levels "by destination" I_i into commodity demands by sectors "of origin." They obey the columnwise restrictions $b_{1j} + b_{2j} = 1$, and represent a version of Leontief's "B" matrix. They also underlie price indexes for investment goods of the form $P_I^j = P_1b_{1j} + P_2b_{2j}$ $(j = 1, 2)$.

The third row defines labor income Y_w, and the third column shows

TABLE 2.1 Input-Output Accounts for Two Sectors with Investment Demands

$P_1a_{11}X_1$	$P_1a_{12}X_2$	P_1c_1L			$P_1b_{11}I_1$	$P_1b_{12}I_2$	P_1X_1	
	$P_2a_{21}X_1$	$P_2a_{22}X_2$	P_2c_2L			$P_2b_{21}I_1$	$P_2b_{22}I_2$	P_2X_2
	wd_1X_1	wd_2X_2						Y_w
	$\pi_1P_1X_1$							Y_π^1
		$\pi_2P_2X_2$						Y_π^2
				S_π^1				$P_I^1I_1$
					S_π^2			$P_I^2I_2$
Totals	P_1X_1	P_2X_2	Y_w	Y_π^1	Y_π^2	$P_I^1I_1$	$P_I^2I_2$	

Note: $P_I^i = P_1b_{1i} + P_2b_{2i}$.

that it is exhausted by consumption demand, so that workers are assumed not to save.

The remaining rows and columns summarize Pasinetti's key assumptions that (*a*) sector *i*'s investment is exactly financed by its operating surplus, and (*b*) each sector operates at full capacity use. Ignoring depreciation, in each sector we then have $I_i = k_i g_i X_i$, where g_i is the growth rate of capacity and k_i is an investment/incremental capacity ratio.

The savings assumption can be stated as $\pi_i P_i X_i = P_I^i I_i = P_I^i k_i g_i X_i$. The implication is that the operating surplus share π_i is given by the formula $\pi_i P_i = P_I^i k_i g_i$. The usual expression for the profit rate r_i would be $r_i = \pi_i P_i / P_I^i k_i = g_i$, so that fast-growing sectors are assumed to be more profitable. Such an observation is often made in practice; Pasinetti's saving-investment hypothesis is also consistent with the fact that sectors with high mark-up rates tend to be capital-intensive. Finally, an increase in a sector's capacity growth rate has to be met by a higher profit share, in a disaggregated version of forced saving.

Pasinetti undertakes two main tasks with this set-up: mapping labor costs into prices (or solving a "transformation problem"), and finding an expression relating labor/output and consumption/labor coefficients. Implications of both are discussed in the text.

It is simplest to do the transformation problem in matrix notation. Let A be the square matrix of the a_{ij}, B the matrix of the b_{ij}, and $\gamma_i = k_i g_i$ a "growth factor" for sector *i*. The square matrix γ^* has the growth factors along its main diagonal with zeroes elsewhere and the row vector of operating surplus shares can be written as $(\pi P)' = (\pi_1 P_1, \pi_2 P_2, \ldots)$. The price-cost breakdown in the first two columns of the SAM can be written as $P' = P'A + wD' + (\pi P)'$ where D' is the row vector of direct labor input coefficients.

The saving-investment assumptions imply that $(\pi P)' = P_I{}'\gamma^* = P'B\gamma^*$ where $P_I{}' = (P_I^1, P_I^2, \ldots)$ is the vector of investment goods price indexes. The price vector P' solves out as

$$P' = wD'(I - A - B\gamma^*)^{-1} = wH', \qquad \text{(A.12)}$$

where H' is a vector of "vertically hyperintegrated labor" coefficients in Pasinetti's nomenclature. So long as the growth factors in γ^* are not "too big," the matrix $(I - A - B\gamma^*)^{-1}$ will be non-negative and the price vector P' in (A.12) will make sense. We get a multisectoral mark-up formulation not far in spirit from equation (A.1) in appendix A.

A vector of "vertically integrated" labor coefficients or Marxian values can be defined as $V' = D'(I - A)^{-1}$. To express prices in terms of vertically integrated as opposed to hyperintegrated labor, we can write

$(I - A - B\gamma^*)^{-1} = (I - A)^{-1}(I + \Theta)$ where $\Theta = B\gamma^*(I - A - B\gamma^*)^{-1}$. These manipulations give $H' = V'(I + \Theta)$. The matrix Θ (with nonzero rows for all sectors producing capital goods) marks up the vertically integrated labor vector V' into its hyper-avatar H'. A sector's price depends on accumulation in all sectors,

$$P' = wV'(I + \Theta) = w(V' + \Lambda'),$$

where $\Lambda = V'\Theta$ is a vector with a typical element λ_i representing the labor tied up in capital goods going into new investment projects in sector i.

Pasinetti's relationship between labor and consumption parameters is

$$\Sigma(v_i + \lambda_i)c_i = 1. \tag{A.13}$$

It is easy to derive from the first rows of the SAM after prices are divided out to give the material balance equation $(I - A - B\gamma^*)X = cL$, where X and c are column vectors of output levels and consumption coefficients respectively. Premultiplying both sides of the output solution $X = (I - A - B\gamma^*)^{-1}c\,L$ by D' gives $D'X = H'cL$. Recognizing that employment $L = D'X$, we can divide out the (scalar) L terms to get $H'c = 1$, which is equivalent to (A.13).

REFERENCES

Aghion, Philippe, and Peter Howitt. 1992. A Model of Growth through Creative Destruction. *Econometrica* 60:323–51.

Amadeo, Edward J. 1989. *Keynes's Principle of Effective Demand.* Aldershot, Hants: Edward Elgar.

Amsden, Alice. 1989. *Asia's Next Giant: South Korea and Late Industrialization.* New York: Oxford University Press.

Arrow, Kenneth J. 1962. The Economic Implications of Learning by Doing. *Review of Economic Studies* 29:155–73.

Arthur, W. Brian. 1989. Competing Technologies, Increasing Returns, and Lock-in by Historical Events. *Economic Journal* 99:116–31.

Bacha, Edmar L. 1990. A Three-Gap Model of Foreign Transfers and the GDP Growth Rate in Developing Countries. *Journal of Development Economics* 32:279–96.

Bauer, P. T. 1972. *Dissent on Development.* London: Weidenfeld and Nicolson.

Becker, Gary S. 1964. *Human Capital.* New York: Columbia University Press.

Buchanan, James. 1980. Rent-Seeking and Profit-Seeking. In *Toward a Theory of Rent-Seeking Society,* edited by J. M. Buchanan, R. D. Tollison, and G. Tullock. College Station, TX: Texas A & M University Press.

Chakravarty, Sukhamoy. 1987. *Development Planning: The Indian Experience.* Oxford: Clarendon Press.

Chang, Ha-Joon. 1993. The Political Economy of Industrial Policy in Korea. *Cambridge Journal of Economics* 17:131–57.

Chenery, Hollis B. 1959. The Interdependence of Investment Decisions. In *The Allocation of Economic Resources,* edited by Moses Abramovitz et al. Stanford, CA: Stanford University Press.

Chenery, Hollis B., and Michael Bruno. 1962. Development Alternatives in an Open Economy: The Case of Israel. *Economic Journal* 72:79–103.

Collins, Randall. 1980. Weber's Last Theory of Capitalism: A Systematization. *American Sociological Review* 45:925–42.

Dixit, Avinash, and Joseph Stiglitz. 1977. Monopolistic Competition and Optimum Product Diversity. *American Economic Review* 67:297–308.

Dore, Ronald. 1986. *Flexible Rigidities: Industrial Policy and Structural Adjustment in the Japanese Economy, 1970–1980.* Stanford, CA: Stanford University Press.

Dutt, Amitava K. 1984. Stagnation, Income Distribution, and Monoply Power. *Cambridge Journal of Economics* 8:25–40.

Easterly, William. 1994. Economic Policies, Economic Shocks, and Economic Growth. Paper presented at a workshop on Endogenous Growth and Development, International School of Economic Research, Siena.

Ellman, Michael. 1975. Did the Agricultural Surplus Provide the Resources for the Increase in Investment during the First Five Year Plan? *Economic Journal* 85:844–64.

Evans, Peter B. 1992. The State as Problem and Solution: Predation, Embedded Autonomy, and Structural Change. In *The Politics of Economic Adjustment,* edited by Stephen Haggard and Robert Kaufman. Princeton, NJ: Princeton University Press.

Fanelli, Jose Maria, Roberto Frenkel, and Lance Taylor. 1993. The World Development Report 1991: A Critical Assessment. In *International Monetary and Financial Issues for the 1990s.* New York: United Nations.

Furtado, Celso. 1972. *Analise do "Modelo" Brasileiro.* Rio de Janeiro: Civilização Brasileira.

Gerschenkron, Alexander. 1962. *Economic Backwardness in Historical Perspective.* Cambridge, MA: Harvard University Press.

Gordon, David M. 1995. Putting the Horse (Back) Before the Cart: Disentangling the Macro Relationship Between Investment and Saving. In *Macroeconomic Policy after the Conservative Era,* edited by Gerald A. Epstein and Herbert M. Gintis. Cambridge: Cambridge University Press.

Harrod, Roy. 1939. An Essay in Dynamic Theory. *Economic Journal* 49:14–33.

Hayek, Freiderich von, ed. 1935. *Collectivist Economic Planning.* London: Routledge and Kegan Paul.

Heilbroner, Robert. 1991. *The Worldly Philosophers* (6th revised edition). New York: Simon and Schuster.

Hicks, John R. 1965. *Capital and Growth.* Oxford: Clarendon Press.

Hirschman, Albert O. 1958. *The Strategy of Economic Development.* New Haven, CT: Yale University Press.

Ingrao, Bruna, and Giorgio Israel. 1990. *The Invisible Hand: Economic Equilibrium in the History of Science.* Cambridge, MA: MIT Press.

Jones, Larry E., and Rodolfo Manuelli. 1990. A Convex Model of Equilibrium Growth: Theory and Policy Implications. *Journal of Political Economy* 98:1008–38.

Jorgenson, Dale. 1990. Productivity and Economic Growth. In *Fifty Years of Economic Measurement: The Jubilee of the Conference on Income and Wealth,* edited by Ernst R. Berndt and Jack E. Triplett. Chicago: University of Chicago Press.

Kaldor, Nicholas. 1940. A Model of the Trade Cycle. *Economic Journal* 50: 78–92.

Kaldor, Nicholas. 1957. A Model of Economic Growth. *Economic Journal* 67:591–624.

Kaldor, Nicholas. 1972. The Irrelevance of Equilibrium Economics. *Economic Journal* 82:1237–55.

Kalecki, Michal. 1971. *Selected Essays on the Dynamics of the Capitalist Economy.* Cambridge: Cambridge University Press.

Kennedy, Paul. 1987. *The Rise and Fall of Great Powers.* New York: Random House.

Keynes, John Maynard. 1930. *A Treatise on Money.* London: Macmillan.

Keynes, John Maynard. 1936. *The General Theory of Employment, Interest, and Money.* London: Macmillan.

Krueger, Anne O. 1974. The Political Economy of the Rent-Seeking Society. *American Economic Review* 64:291–303.

Krueger, Anne O. 1984. Comparative Advantage and Development Policy 20 Years Later. In *Economic Structure and Performance: Essays in Honor of Hollis B. Chenery,* edited by M. Syrquin, L. Taylor, and L. Westphal. New York: Academic Press.

Krugman, Paul. 1933. Towards a Counter-Counter-Revolution in Development Theory. *World Bank Economic Review* (supplement), 15–38.

Kuznets, Simon S. 1971. *Economic Growth of Nations: Total Output and Production Structure.* Cambridge, MA: Harvard University Press.

Lal, Deepak. 1983. *The Poverty of "Development Economics."* London: Institute of Economic Affairs.

Leibenstein, Harvey. 1954. *A Theory of Economic-Demographic Development.* Princeton, NJ: Princeton University Press.

Lewis, W. Arthur. 1954. Economic Development with Unlimited Supplies of Labor. *Manchester School of Economics and Social Studies* 22:139–91.

Lewis, W. Arthur. 1969. *Aspects of Tropical Trade, 1883–1965.* Stockholm: Almqvist and Wicksell.

Little, Ian M. D., Tibor Scitovsky, and Maurice Scott. 1970. *Industry and Trade in Some Developing Countries: A Comparative Study.* London: Oxford University Press.

Lorenz, Hans-Walter. 1989. *Nonlinear Dynamical Economics and Chaotic Motion.* Lecture Notes in Economics and Mathematical Systems No. 334. New York: Springer-Verlag.

Lucas, Robert E. 1988. On the Mechanisms of Economic Development. *Journal of Monetary Economics* 22:3–42.

Lustig, Nora. 1980. Underconsumption in Latin American Economic Thought: Some Considerations. *Review of Radical Political Economics* 12:35–43.

Marglin, Stephen A. 1984. *Growth, Distribution, and Prices.* Cambridge, MA: Harvard University Press.

Mises, Ludwig von. 1935. Economic Calculation in the Socialist Commonwealth. in *Collectivist Economic Planning,* edited by F. von Hayek. London: Routledge and Kegan Paul.

Murphy, Kevin M., Andrei Shleifer, and Robert Vishny. 1989. Industrialization and the Big Push. *Journal of Political Economy* 97:1003–26.

Myrdal, Gunnar. 1957. *Economic Theory and Underdeveloped Regions.* London: Duckworth.

Nelson, Richard R. 1956. A Theory of the Low-Level Equilibrium Trap in Underdeveloped Economies. *American Economic Review* 46:894–908.

Neumann, John von. 1938. A Model of General Economic Equilibrium. *Review of Economic Studies* 13:1–9.

North, Douglass C. 1981. *Structure and Change in Economic History.* New York: W. W. Norton.

Nurkse, Ragnar. 1953. *Problems of Capital Formation in Underdeveloped Countries.* Oxford: Basil Blackwell.

Olson, Mancur. 1982. *The Rise and Decline of Nations.* New Haven, CT: Yale University Press.

Pasinetti, Luigi L. 1981. *Structural Change and Economic Growth.* Cambridge: Cambridge University Press.

Polanyi, Karl. 1944. *The Great Transformation: The Political and Economic Origins of Our Times.* New York: Rinehart.

Prebisch, Raul. 1959. Commercial Policy in the Underdeveloped Countries. *American Economic Review* 49:257–69.

Preobrazhenski, Evgeny. 1965. *The New Economics.* Oxford: Clarendon.

Rebelo, Sergio. 1991. Long Run Policy Analysis and Long Run Growth. *Journal of Political Economy* 99:500–21.

Robinson, Joan. 1962. *Essays in the Theory of Economic Growth.* London: Macmillan.

Romer, Paul M. 1987. Growth Based on Increasing Returns Due to Specialization. *American Economic Review* (*Papers and Proceedings*) 77:56–62.

Rosenstein-Rodan, Paul N. 1943. Problems of Industrialization of Eastern and South-Eastern Europe. *Economic Journal* 53:202–11.

Rosenstein-Rodan, Paul N. 1961. Notes on the Theory of the Big Push. In *Economic Development for Latin America,* edited by H. S. Ellis and H. C. Wallich. New York: St. Martin's Press.

Rowthorn, Bob. 1982. Demand, Real Wages, and Economic Growth. *Studi Economici* 18:2–53.

Schumpeter, Josef A. 1934. *The Theory of Economic Development.* Cambridge, MA: Harvard University Press.
Schumpeter, Josef A. 1954. *History of Economic Analysis.* New York: Oxford University Press.
Schultz, T. W. 1963. *The Economic Value of Education.* New York: Columbia University Press.
Schultz, T. W. 1964. *Transforming Traditional Agriculture.* New Haven, CT: Yale University Press.
Scitovsky, Tibor. 1954. Two Concepts of External Economies. *Journal of Political Economy* 62:143–51.
Sen, Amartya K. 1963. Neo-Classical and Neo-Keynesian Theories of Distribution. *Economic Record* 39:54–64.
Sismonde de Sismondi, J. C. L. 1815. Political Economy. Edinburgh: *Sir J. D. Brewster's Edinburgh Encyclopedia.*
Solow, Robert M. 1956. A Contribution to the Theory of Economic Growth. *Quarterly Journal of Economics* 70:65–94.
Sraffa, Piero. 1926. The Laws of Returns under Competitive Conditions. *Economic Journal* 36:535–50.
Sraffa, Piero. 1960. *Production of Commodities by Means of Commodities.* Cambridge: Cambridge University Press.
Steindl, Josef. 1952. *Maturity and Stagnation in American Capitalism.* Oxford: Basil Blackwell.
Sylos-Labini, Paolo. 1984. *The Forces of Economic Growth and Decline.* Cambridge, MA: MIT Press.
Syrquin, Moshe. 1988. Patterns of Structural Change, in H. B. Chenery and T. N. Srinivasan (eds.) *Handbook of Development Economics* (Vol. I) Amsterdam: North-Holland.
Taylor, Lance. 1991. *Income Distribution, Inflation, and Growth.* Cambridge, MA: MIT Press.
Taylor, Lance. 1995. Pasinetti's Processes. *Cambridge Journal of Economics* 19:697–713.
Taylor, Lance, and Edmar L. Bacha. 1976. The Unequalizing Spiral: A First Growth Model for Belindia. *Quarterly Journal of Economics* 90:197–218.
Wade, Robert. 1990. *Governing the Market: Economic Theory and the Role of the Government in East Asian Industrialization.* Princeton, NJ: Princeton University Press.
Weber, Max. 1968. *Economy and Society,* edited by G. Roth and C. Wittich. New York: Bedminster Press.
Young, Allyn. 1928. Increasing Returns and Economic Progress. *Economic Journal* 38:527–42.

CHAPTER 3

Development Theory: Trends and Challenges

Pranab Bardhan

In the last two decades development economics has not merely survived quite a few premature obituaries written about it,[1] but has actually flourished and even branched out in important new directions. In this chapter I first discuss some of these recent advances in development theory and then explore what in my judgment are some of the important challenges facing development theorists today. Of course good theory has to be grounded in empirical reality, and there has been substantial progress in rigorous empirical work in development, but for the purpose of the present discussion I shall largely ignore it.

In the recent "lost" decade of development, particularly in Latin America and Africa, when external debt and general macroeconomic crises loomed large and the subsequent severe structural adjustment programs became imperative, development theory grappled with various topical problems arising from these crises, including a serious analysis of the implications and consequences of "sovereign risk" in connection with debt default, the various deterrents to default, and the credibility of sanctions.[2] The problem of the credibility and sequencing of reforms also got a great deal of theoretical attention as a by-product of the ongoing macroeconomic adjustment processes in Latin America and Eastern Europe. Partly on grounds of delimiting the scope of this chapter and acknowledging the constraints of my own areas of expertise, I shall in general desist from any further discussion of macroeconomic issues, except for those in the macro-dynamic literature on economic growth, with which we start.

In the last few years the so-called new growth theory has kindled theoretical interest in modeling development problems. Lucas (1988), pondering the questions of differential development performance of poor countries and what can be done about it, says: "The consequences for human welfare involved in questions like these are simply staggering: once one starts to think about them, it is hard to think about anything else." Coming from a leading economist in the mainstream, which has long marginalized development economics, this is indeed reassuring. But it is important to evaluate whether the advances made in the new literature on growth theory represent new and valuable insights in development economics, or primarily a rediscovery—with great fanfare—of some of the insights of the old development literature. I think it is a bit of both.[3]

Contrary to the claim sometimes made in the literature on the "new" growth theory, many of the growth models of the 1950s and the 1960s endogenized technical progress in significant ways: apart from Arrow's (1962) celebrated learning-by-doing model, in which learning emanated from the dynamic externalities of cumulated gross investment, the earlier related learning model of Haavelmo (1956), and Uzawa's (1965) model of investment in human capital generating technical change, there are several Kaldor models culminating in the Kaldor-Mirrlees model (1962) where investment is the vehicle of technical progress and Shell's (1967) model of inventive activity. Learning by doing, particularly in the form of acquisition of tacit knowledge and interfirm spillover effects of cumulated gross output, influenced development theory by providing a formal rationale for an old argument for support of "infant" industry producing import substitutes (or new exports), as in the models of Bardhan (1970) and Clemhout and Wan (1970). The acquired and sometimes policy-driven nature of dynamic comparative advantage, to which the East Asian challenge has awakened many developed country trade theorists, has been a persistent theme in the trade and development literature for decades. The old literature on the microeconomics of technological progress always emphasized the pervasiveness of externalities in the innovation process, in the transfer, absorption, development, and adaptation of new technologies; the discussion in development economics on the problems posed by the catching-up process in the developing countries reflected this. Thus the models of Romer (1986) and Lucas (1988), while helping in the formalization of these ideas of dynamic externalities in a perfect competition framework, do not provide any substantial breakthrough in development theory as such.

A much more substantive contribution of the "new" growth theory is to formalize endogenous technical progress in terms of a tractable imperfect-competition framework in which temporary monopoly power acts as a motivating force for private innovators. The leading work in this area of what has been called neo-Schumpeterian growth theory is by Romer (1987, 1990), Grossman and Helpman (1991), Segerstrom, Anant, and Dinopoulos (1990), and Aghion and Howitt (1992). Growth theory has now been liberated from the confines of the competitive market framework of earlier endogenous growth models in which dynamic externalities played the central role (even considering the models of Kaldor who repeatedly emphasized the importance of imperfect competition in the context of endogenous technical progress, the current models drawing on the advances in industrial organization theory are more satisfactory). In particular, the emphasis on new goods and the fixed costs in introducing them provides valuable new insights. The major impact of this literature on development theory has been in the area of trade and technological diffusion in an international economy.

The East Asian success stories have given credence to the belief of many economists in a positive relationship between "outward orientation" and economic development (although a rigorous empirical demonstration of the *causal* relationship between some satisfactory measure of outward orientation and the rate of growth is rather scarce). Standard neoclassical growth theory did not provide any such general theorem on the effect of trade on the long-run growth rate.

A major result in the new literature is to show how economic integration in the world market, compared to isolation, helps long-run growth by avoiding unnecessary duplication of research and thus increases aggregate productivity of resources employed in the R & D sector (characterized by economies of scale). But the presumption in many of the models of a common pool of knowledge capital created by international spillovers of technical information is sometimes not relevant for a poor country.

When knowledge accumulation is localized largely in the rich country, and the poor country is also smaller in (economic) size—particularly in the size of its already accumulated knowledge capital (which determines research effectiveness)—the rich country captures a growing market share in the total number of differentiated varieties, and the entrepreneurs in the poor country, foreseeing capital losses, may innovate less rapidly in long-run equilibrium with international trade than under autarky, as shown by Feenstra (1990) and Grossman and Helpman (1991, chap. 9). Trade reduces the profitability of R & D in the poor country, as it places local entrepreneurs in competition with a rapidly expanding set of imported, differentiated products. It may also drive the country to specialize in production rather than research, and within production, on traditional, possibly stagnant, industries that use its relatively plentiful supply of unskilled workers—thus slowing innovation and growth. For the lagging country, isolation would have been more advantageous for the pace of innovation.

Of course, slower growth does not necessarily mean that the

consumer loses from trade: apart from the usual static gains from trade, consumers may have access to more varieties innovated abroad. But trade may sometimes cause a net welfare loss, since in the poorer country it accelerates a market failure (underinvestment in research in the initial situation) by allocating resources further away from research.

One should note that the relevant R & D for a poor country is, of course, more in technological adaptation of products and processes invented abroad and in imitation. But even this kind of an R & D sector is usually so small that major changes in aggregate productivity and growth on the basis of the trade-induced general equilibrium type reallocation of fully employed resources into or away from the R & D sector, as emphasized by Grossman and Helpman, seems a little overdrawn if applied in the context of poor countries. In any case the ambiguity in the relationship between trade expansion and productivity growth in these general equilibrium models only confirms similar conclusions in careful partial equilibrium models, particularly when entry and exit from industries are not frictionless—see, for example, Rodrik 1992.

In the Grossman-Helpman model of the innovating North and the imitating South with all firms in Bertrand competition with one another, imitation has two opposing effects on the incentive to innovate in the North: on the one hand, imitation reduces the duration of monopoly profits of the innovator; on the other hand, it frees up Northern labor to produce more of the as yet unimitated products and to conduct more R & D.[4] In these models labor costs form the only component of the cost of entry into the imitative-adaptive R & D activity in the South. So, armed with cheaper labor the Southern firms can relentlessly keep on targeting Northern products for imitation, unhampered by many of the formidable real-world nonlabor constraints on entry (for example, those posed by the lack of a viable physical, social and educational infrastructure or that of organizational know-how in a poor country).

Most of the new models of trade and growth, by adopting the Dixit-Stiglitz-style consumer preferences, assume a uniform price elasticity and a unitary expenditure elasticity for each of the differentiated products that enter symmetrically in the utility function. This, of course, immediately rules out what has been a major preoccupation of the trade and development literature: to explore the implications of sectoral demand asymmetries for trade relationships between rich and poor countries. The Dixit-Stiglitz functional form also narrows the operation of scale economies to take the form of expansion of variety, rather than of scale of output. The assumption of monopolistic competition and contestable markets in the models also precludes any serious examination of the impact of trade on growth through the lowering of entry barriers in oligopolistic industries, industry rationalization, and reduction of the gap between actual and best- practice international technology that foreign competitive pressure may induce.

The slow diffusion of technology from rich to poor countries is often interpreted in the literature as reflecting the frequent laxity in the enforcement of patents in poor countries, thus compelling innovators in rich countries to protect their ideas through secrecy. This brings us to the controversial issue of intellectual property rights (IPR), which has sometimes divided the rich and poor countries, as notably in the recent Uruguay Round discussions. Rich countries often claim that a tighter IPR regime encourages innovations (by expanding the duration of the innovator's monopoly) from which all countries benefit. Poor countries counter this by pointing to their losses following on increased monopoly power of the larger companies of rich countries. Because the poor countries provide a very small market for many industrial products, the disincentive effects of lax patent protection in those countries may be marginal on the rate of innovation in rich countries, and as such attempts at free riding by the poor countries may make sense, as Chin and Grossman (1990) suggest. To this Diwan and Rodrik (1991) add the qualification that the disincentive effects may be very significant in the case of innovation in technologies or products that are particularly appropriate for poor countries (for example, drugs that combat tropical diseases). But both of these theoretical models use a static partial equilibrium framework. Helpman (1993) recently constructed a dynamic general equilibrium model of innovation and imitation to discuss the question of IPR. In the long-run equilibrium of his model, a tighter IPR (reducing the rate of imitation by the lower-wage poor country) increases the fraction of the total number of products produced (unchallenged) in the rich country, but *lowers* the long-run rate of innovation of new products[5] (this works through the rise in the price-earning ratio of the R & D firm in the rich country, consequent upon the general equilibrium labor reallocation effect of a larger range of manufactured products produced in the rich country).[6] Even apart from this effect on the rate of innovation, a tighter IPR, by shifting production from the lower-wage (and therefore lower-price) country to the higher-wage country, makes consumers in both countries worse off.

In another respect the new literature marks a substantial advance over the old. This relates to the dynamic economies of scale associated with learning by doing. An important extension of the models of Bardhan (1970) and Clemhout and Wan (1970) has been carried out by Krugman (1987) and Boldrin and Scheinkman (1988), where the learning effects (emanating from production experience measured by cumulated industry output) enhance over time the existing sectoral patterns of comparative advantage; this may call for a deliberate trade policy that can orchestrate a breakout from such a historical "lock-in."[7] An explanation of the reverse flow of capital and human skills from poor to rich countries in terms of the external effects of the higher average stock of human capital in rich countries, as suggested by Lucas (1990), is also an important corollary of these models of dynamic externalities and learning.

But these models of learning share with the earlier ones the unrealistic feature of continued learning at a given rate on a fixed set of goods. As Lucas (1993) comments, evidence on learning on narrowly defined product lines often shows high initial learning rates, declining over time as production cumulates, and for on-the-job learning to occur in an economy on a sustained basis workers and managers must continue to take on tasks that are new to them to continue to move up the quality ladder in goods. The major formulations that try to capture this in the context of an open economy are those of Young (1991) and Stokey (1991). On the basis of learning by doing that spills over across industries (although bounded in each industry) Young's model endogenizes the movement of goods out of the learning sector into a mature sector in which learning no longer occurs and thus gives a plausible account of an evolving trade structure. Stokey has a model of North-South trade, based on vertical product differentiation and international differences in labor quality; the South produces a low-quality spectrum of goods and the North a high-quality spectrum. If human capital is acquired through learning by doing and so is stimulated by the production of high-quality goods, free trade (as opposed to autarky) will speed up human capital accumulation in the North and slow it down in the South. A similar result is obtained by Young. The country that begins with a technological lead tends to widen that lead over time. (Of course it does not follow that the South would be better off under autarky.) It also indicates why a policy of subsidizing infant export industries is sometimes more growth promoting in the long run than that of protecting infant import-substitute industries, because in the former case the opportunities for learning spillover into newer and more sophisticated goods are wider than when one is restricted to the home market. Export growth encourages accumulation of technological capability not only in the producer firms but also in the specialized supplier firms through vertical linkage. A high level of skills in the labor force as in some of the East Asian cases facilitates this process. The rapid growth of exports also enabled these countries, as Pack (1992) points out, to overcome imperfections in technology markets, such as monopolistic licensing fees, that limit the diffusion of proprietary knowledge and hinder a move toward international best practice.

Going beyond these learning models, one can generalize and say that probably the most important contribution of the new growth theory is to formally draw our attention to the process of introduction of an ever-expanding set of new goods and technologies (in the case of developing countries, often imports of new types of produced inputs) and the large fixed costs usually associated with it. These fixed costs underline the fundamental importance of nonconvexities and imperfect competition in economic analysis. As Romer (1994) shows, the welfare costs of restrictions on the process of introduction of new goods (as, for example, in the case of trade or foreign investment restrictions in developing countries) are substantially larger than the static misallocation effects in the case when we deal with a fixed set of goods. I agree with Romer (1994) when he says: "New growth theory may not be *new,* but it is *about* newness. And newness, like history, matters." The new literature in some ways diverts our attention from the abiding concern of development economists with the problems of structural transformation and the reallocation of resources from traditional sectors to sectors with different organizational and technological dynamics. But it does serve a purpose in focusing attention on the serious nonconvexities involved in the process of diffusion and adoption of new goods and technologies in a developing country.

Although the emphasis in the new growth theory is to search for the factors that perpetuate growth, it is not directly concerned with an older question of development theory: given that underdevelopment tends to persist, how does a poor country get out of a poverty trap? Yet a fallout of the recent formalizations and explorations of dynamic externalities has been to revive interest in the older question. In the immediate postwar florescence of development economics, one particularly prominent idea was that of how coordination of investments across sectors is essential for industrialization. The literature that grew out of the famous paper of Rosenstein-Rodan (1943) emphasized that when domestic markets are small (and foreign trade is costly), simultaneous expansion of many sectors can be self-sustaining through mutual demand support, even if by itself no sector can break even (primarily because firms in a sector may not by themselves be able to generate enough sales to render profitable the adoption of modern increasing-returns technologies with large fixed costs). There was a presumption in this literature of multiple equilibria, and the essential problem was posed as one of escaping a "low-level equilibrium trap" to a higher-income equilibrium with industrialization.

To capture the full flavor of this problem of strategic complementarity of industries in terms of market size, one needs a full-scale model of plant-level economies of scale in production (with the associated imperfections in market competition), which can be tapped with large demand spillovers. This formalization was done in a recent model by Murphy, Shleifer, and Vishny (1989). One common objection to such models is that in an open economy where an industry faces the world market, the size of the domestic market cannot plausibly limit the adoption of increasing returns technologies. Such objections usually underestimate how the size of the domestic market matters even in an open economy. In any case the idea of intersectoral complementarities in investment can be reformulated for an open economy with tradeable final outputs, but where jointly used infrastructure (like roads, railways, power stations, or training facilities) and other nontraded support services and specialized inputs (like repair and maintenance, some ancillary parts and components, and financial communication or distribution services) are indispensable for the production and distribution of the final goods. One variant of the models in Murphy, Shleifer, and Vishny (1989) shows how in the case of shared infrastructure each industrializing firm that uses it contributes to the large fixed cost of building it and thus indirectly helps other users and makes their industrialization more likely. In one equilibria of the model, the infrastructure will make money on its first-period investment if the economy industrializes, but will incur a large loss if no industrialization takes place and there are no users of its services. Thus the infrastructure is not built lest an insufficient number of firms industrialize, and this in turn ensures that firms do not make the large-scale investments needed to industrialize. This is an underdevelopment trap caused by a coordination failure.

Alternatively, Rodríguez (1993) has a model of multiple equilibria arising from sectoral complementarity and cumulative processes generated by increasing returns in the production of support services and inputs. The tradeable final goods require that these nontraded intermediate inputs and services be readily available in close proximity. The domestic availability of a wide variety of such specialized inputs enhances the productive efficiency of the manufacturing sector, but the extent of input specialization (or division of labor in their production) is limited by the extent of the market. In such a situation the economy may get stuck in an equilibrium in which the division of labor in the input-producing sector is shallow and final goods production remains confined to the use of low-productivity techniques that do not require a wide variety of inputs.[8] The task of development policy here is to compensate for a historical handicap (in the form of a trap of low-productivity specialization), either by trade policy or a policy of subsidization of fixed costs or of other ways of encouraging appropriate linkages between the finals goods sector and the intermediate inputs sector. In the model of the preceding paragraph, on the other hand, coordination of investments between sectors is the key, and the role of expectations (about investment by other firms) and self-fulfilling prophecy become more important. The task of development policy is to coordinate expectations around high investment. This "history versus expectations" dichotomy in the dynamic processes of how a particular equilibrium gets established has been further analyzed by Krugman (1991) and Matsuyama (1991), and the relative importance of the past and expected future is shown to depend on some parameters of the economy (like the discount rate and the speed of adjustment).

The idea of strategic complementarities between sectors generated by increasing returns must be one of the early examples in the flowering of the general literature on coordination failures in economics. It was so central to the development economics of the 1950s. Yet it lost much of its intellectual force in the subsequent decades, not so much because it lacked, until recently, a firm anchoring in a formal model using tools of imperfect markets equilibrium analysis, as Krugman (1992) suggests, but more because at the policy level the difficulties of aggregate coordination were underestimated (particularly at the existing levels of administrative capacity and political coherence in the developing countries), and the incentive and organizational issues of micromanagement of capital were underappreciated. The resulting government failures diverted the profession's attention from what nevertheless remains an important source of market failure discovered by early development economics. From the policy point of view, the new literature on learning and strategic complementaries, like the earlier development literature on externalities, underestimates the difficulty of identifying the few sectors and locations where the spillover effects may be large and particularly difficult to internalize. It is sometimes overlooked that learning is often highly localized and project-specific. In addition, the extent of spillovers depends crucially on the nature of competition that the policy environment promotes and its interaction with the nature of the physical, social, and organizational infrastructure in the country.

Another by-product of the recent formalizations of market size, increasing returns, and imperfect competition has been in the area of economic geography, which throws some light on the problem of urban concentration and uneven regional development in the developing countries. Krugman (1994) has a model of the endogenous determination of agglomeration economies out of the interaction among economies of scale at the plant level, transportation costs, and factor mobility. (These economies may be particularly important in poor countries, where basic manufacturing using the transport system is still more important than the new footloose service industries and where the small market size makes the issue of scale economies significant.) The pattern of urban growth and regional inequality are shaped by a tension between centripetal forces that tend to pull population and production into agglomerations and the centrifugal forces that tend to break up such agglomerations. On the one hand, firms want to locate close to the large market provided by other firms' workers, and workers want to live close to the supply of goods provided by other firms; on the other hand, commuting costs and urban land rent (not to speak of congestion and pollution) tend to generate diseconomies of city size. Although this is no doubt a promising line of enquiry that invites more sophisticated formalization, here as in other aspects of the new growth theory the theoretical models have a long way to go before they can catch up with the complexity of the empirical reality, particularly in developing countries.

Another area where development theory has made great strides is in exploring the microfoundations of various economic-institutional arrangements, particularly in the field of agrarian relations. In the 1970s and 1980s, when microeconomic theory was going through a major overhaul to accommodate imperfect and asymmetric information and incomplete markets, development economics was often at the forefront in this changeover, since those information problems are particularly acute in the context of underdevelopment. The literature started with the analysis of sharecropping; in particular, Stiglitz's (1974) model of sharecropping, viewing this ancient institution as a compromise between risk-sharing and work-incentive effects, is one of the first fully worked-out principal-agent models in economics. The literature then went on to formalize models of labor tying (or two-tiered labor markets), interlocking of transactions in labor, credit and land-lease, credit market imperfections and credit rationing, and so on.[9] Radical economists have often cited some of these production relations as institutional obstacles to development in a poor agrarian economy, overlooking the microeconomic rationale of the formation of these institutions. Under a set of informational constraints and missing markets, a given agrarian institution (say, sharecropping or interlocking of contracts) may be serving a real economic function. Its simple abolition, as is often demanded on a radical platform, without taking care of the factors that gave rise to the institution in the first place, may not necessarily improve the conditions of the intended beneficiaries of the abolition program. There may be some important political lessons here from what may be called the economics of second best reformism.

A different area where development economists have been active relates to the theory of the state. Early development economics often displayed an unquestioning faith in the ability of the state to correct market failures and imperfections and to effectively direct the economic process toward development goals. In this literature the state was often left floating in some behavioral and organizational vacuum, permitting a blanket endorsement of indiscriminate state intervention, the adverse effects of which for both economic growth and income distribution are now painfully obvious in many countries. The neoclassical political economy literature that grew partly in reaction to this tendency drew pointed attention to how the regulatory state spawned an enormous waste of resources in rent-seeking activities, over and above the standard economic losses due to the misallocation effects of policy-induced distortions and the macroeconomic impotence of anticipated policies. There is also a growing literature on the incentive and organizational issues of industrial restructuring in the vast public sector of developing (as well as in formerly socialist) countries.

In this concluding section I shall enumerate, briefly and schematically, what I consider particularly important among the various challenges facing development theorists today:

1. In the preceding section I have mentioned how institutional economists have started explaining some of the preexisting economic arrangements in poor countries (particularly in agrarian relations) in terms of functions they serve under a set of informational constraints and missing markets (particularly of credit and insurance). In this context there is considerable scope for extending the concept of what Basu and Bell (1991) have called "fragmented oligopoly" in the rural credit markets as a more general theme describing the nature of many underdeveloped markets (where informational barriers to entry give some agents market power over some domain but at the same time they have to contend with other oligopolists in concurrent domains). A related issue is that of understanding how, as the network of economic transactions expands beyond the personalized confines of face-to-face local communities and costs of information and opportunism loom large, different societies devise (or fail to devise) relatively impersonal institutions of contracts and guarantees and the associated mechanisms of legal or social enforcement, so that the economies of specialization and gains from trade are realized without too high transaction costs. The assorted nonmarket mechanisms of kinship-based or state-provided means of enforcing

obligations and contracts in arm's length commercial transactions (like long-distance trade or credit provision) in the history of developing countries need to be aligned with development theory in the context of imperfect information and transaction costs. What Douglass North and others have done for Western economic history cries out to be done for developing countries in a possible collaborative attempt between economists, historians, sociologists, and legal scholars.

2. A related and vitally important issue is that of understanding institutional failures. Why do dysfunctional (social and economic) institutions persist in poor countries? What leads to frequent coordination failures in building developmental institutions and coalitions? In the usual account of the "new" institutional economics, more efficient institutions and governance structures evolve in response to new benefit-cost possibilities; suboptimal institutions are usually attributed to the rent-maximizing or predatory state that, for reasons of maintaining its support structures, may prolong socially inefficient property rights. It is often ignored that transaction costs, which form the rationale of nonmarket institutions, can themselves reduce pressures from any social selection process by raising barriers to entry and exit. Then there are the path-dependent, self-reinforcing forces, like increasing returns from adopting a particular institution that may turn out to be inferior in the long run; or like a mutually sustaining network of social sanctions on deviants.[10]

The "new" growth theory, as mentioned before, emphasizes fixed costs and nonconvexities in the process of introduction of new goods and technologies. But these fixed costs in the real world go much beyond the ordinary costs of starting new economic activities: they encompass, particularly in a developing country, massive costs of collective action in building new economic institutions and political coalitions and in breaking the deadlock of incumbent interests threatened by new technologies. These distributive conflicts, more than the efficiency-enhancing effects of new arrangements, are at the heart of institutional change or lack of change. Radical economists and sociologists inevitably refer to social power and class struggle in this context, but often in methodologically careless ways. The concept of power[11] is sometimes used in a question-begging way: differences in institutional arrangements are supposed to be explained by blanket references to differences in the power of the dominant class without an *independent* quantification of the latter, or without an adequate explanation of how individuals who could work out a beneficial arrangement under a new institutional dispensation are blocked in their efforts by the aggregative necessity of retaining control and status quo for the whole class to which they belong. These collective action problems are as important in bringing about technological change as in management of environmental resources and other public action programs. In resolving these coordination problems, we need to explore the various cases of frequency-dependent equilibria (or what Schelling has called "tipping equilibria") that go beyond the cases of strategic complementarities in investment emphasized in the new literature on growth theory and economic geography: in a multiperson game (say, in the context of management of local public goods including environmental resources), for example, how we "cooperate" when a critical mass of others "cooperate," and "defect" when they "defect"; or how we indulge in "corrupt" activities when we expect the others to do so, etc. The policy issue here is that of orchestrating the "tipping" in the right direction.

3. The gulf between left-leaning economists preoccupied with issues of equity (often, though not always, at the expense of efficiency) and mainstream economists preoccupied with efficiency (often, though not always, at the expense of equity) has to be bridged. The equity-efficiency trade-off is often a false issue. Theorists should pay more attention to egalitarian or redistributive projects that enhance productive efficiency, particularly in the context of various agency problems (when the owner-employer-creditor principal has to expensively monitor the tenant-employee-borrower agent), issues of work organization in firms, and those of building trust in resolving collective-action problems and coordinating sacrifices in macroeconomic adjustment (not to mention the case for public expenditure on basic health and education). In all these respects, persistent inequality in wealth distribution can be injurious to productive efficiency.

4. On the age-old political economy question of state versus market, there is now increasing awareness of the importance of the quality, rather than quantity, of state intervention, and of the complexity of market interactions on the one hand, and of the healthy disciplinary effects of market rivalry on the other. Sometimes it seems that the pendulum in our theories of the state has swung too much from the earlier naive presumption of a government optimizing social welfare to that of preoccupation with total malfeasance and the pork barrels of the predatory or rentier state. We should have a more nuanced theory consistent with cases of government successes as well as failures in achieving some institutional coherence in the pursuit of collective economic goals, and with the fact

that even in predominantly regulatory states riddled with rent seeking, there are some sectors (particularly the new, more dynamic sectors[12] where the bureaucracy has sometimes played a semi-entrepreneurial and development-promoting role). We should also look beyond the polar opposites of centralized state ownership or regulation and private ownership and appropriation to the many successful cases of local self-governing institutions (from the informal community-level organizations for management of water and other local public goods in different parts of the world to the village and township enterprises in South China owned by local governments), which seem to have resolved some of the agency and collective-action problems and harnessed local initiative, information, peer monitoring, and accountability. Development theorists, in collaboration with social anthropologists and political scientists, can contribute to a better understanding of when such local institutions work on a sustained basis and when they do not.

NOTES

1. For example, see Little 1982, Hirschman 1982, and Lal 1983.

2. The leading references here are those of Eaton and Gersovitz (1981), Kletzer (1984), and Bulow and Rogoff (1989).

3. For an elaboration of this argument, see Bardan 1995.

4. It may also be noted that in the Grossman-Helpman (1991, chap. 11) model of imitation, in which the poor country grows faster with imitation and trade than without them, it is the process of imitation rather than the integration of product markets per se that contributes to a more rapid pace of innovation in the poor country.

5. The result may not be robust for the case in which direct foreign investment as well as imitation acts as a channel of technology transfer, as Lai (1993) shows.

6. In a different context Mookherjee and Ray (1991) have shown that when a dominant firm decides on the adoption of a sequence of potential cost-reducing innovations with Bertrand competition in the product market, a faster rate of diffusion of the latest technology to a competitive fringe may, over some range, increase the competitive pressure on the leader, quickening the latter's pace of innovation.

7. A similar model of hysteresis, based on self-reinforcing advantages not of learning but of head starts in R & D, is developed in Grossman and Helpman 1991, chap. 8.

8. A low initial average level of human capital plays a similar trapping role in the model of Ciccone (1994), where the interdependence between individual human capital accumulation and the supply of specialized physical capital goods

may lead to equilibria with no potential for technical progress or growth. Earlier Azariadis and Drazen (1990) had emphasized the threshold effects of human capital and the multiple balanced growth paths induced by the externalities in the technologies of human capital accumulation.

9. For an overview of this whole literature on the theory of agrarian institutions, see Bardhan 1984 and 1989b, and Stiglitz 1988.

10. For an elaboration of these arguments, see Bardhan 1989a.

11. For an overview of the issues surrounding the concept of power, see Bardhan 1991.

12. For a comparative study of this new role of the state in informatics, see Evans 1995.

REFERENCES

Aghion, P., and P. Howitt. 1992. A Model of Growth through Creative Destruction. *Econometrica* 60:322–52.

Arrow, K.J. 1962. The Economic Implications of Learning by Doing. *Review of Economic Studies* 29:155–73.

Azariadis, C., and A. Drazen. 1990. Threshold Externalities in Economic Development. *Quarterly Journal of Economics* 105:501–26.

Bardhan, P. 1970. *Economic Growth, Development and Foreign Trade: A Study in Pure Theory*. New York: Wiley-Interscience.

Bardhan, P. 1984. *Land, Labor and Rural Poverty: Essays in Development Economics*. New York: Columbia University Press.

Bardhan, P., ed. 1989a. *The Economic Theory of Agrarian Institutions*. Oxford: Clarendon Press.

Bardhan, P. 1989b. The New Institutional Economics and Development Theory: A Brief Critical Assessment. *World Development* 17:1389–95.

Bardhan, P. 1991. On The Concept of Power in Economics. *Economics and Politics* 3:265–77.

Bardhan, P. 1995. The Contributions of Endogenous Growth Theory to the Analysis of Development Problems: An Assessment. In *Handbook of Development Economics*. vol. 3, edited by T.N. Srinivasan and J. Behrman. Amsterdam: North-Holland.

Basu, K., and C. Bell. 1991. Fragmented Duopoly: Theory and Application to Backward Agriculture. *Journal of Development Economics* 36:145–67.

Boldrin, M., and J.A. Scheinkman. 1988. Learning by Doing, International Trade and Growth: A Note. In *The Economy as an Evolving Complex System*, edited by P.W. Anderson, K.J. Arrow, and D. Pines. Reading: Addison-Wesley.

Bulow, J., and K. Rogoff. 1989. A Constant Recontracting Model of Sovereign Debt. *Journal of Political Economy* 97:155–78.

Chin, J.C., and G.M. Grossman. 1990. Intellectual Property Rights and North-South Trade. In *The Political Economy of International Trade: Essays in*

Honor of Robert E. Baldwin, edited by R.W. Jones and A.O. Krueger. Cambridge: Blackwell.

Ciccone, A. 1994. Human Capital and Technical Progress: Stagnation, Transition, and Growth. Stanford University, mimeo.

Clemhout, S., and H. Wan. 1970. Learning by Doing and Infant Industry Protection. *Review of Economic Studies* 37:33–56.

Diwan, I., and D. Rodrik. 1991. Patents, Appropriate Technology, and North-South Trade. *Journal of International Economics* 30:27–47.

Eaton, J., and M. Gersovitz. 1981. Debt with Potential Repudiation: Theoretical and Empirical Analysis. *Review of Economic Studies* 48:289–309.

Evans, P. 1995. *Embedded Autonomy*. Princeton: Princeton University Press.

Feenstra, R.C. 1990. Trade and Uneven Growth. NBER Working Paper No. 3276.

Grossman, G.M., and E. Helpman. 1991. *Innovation and Growth in the Global Economy*. Cambridge: MIT Press.

Haavelmo, T. 1956. *A Study in the Theory of Economic Evolution*. Amsterdam: North Holland.

Helpman, E. 1993. Innovation, Imitation, and Intellectual Property Rights. *Econometrica* 61:1247–80.

Hirschman, A. 1982. The Rise and Decline of Development Economics. In *The Theory and Experience of Economic Development*, edited by M. Gersovitz et al. London: Allen and Unwin.

Kaldor, N., and J.A. Mirrlees. 1962. A New Model of Economic Growth. *Review of Economic Studies* 29:174–92.

Kletzer, K. 1984. Asymmetries of Information and LDC Borrowing with Sovereign Risk. *Economic Journal* 94:287–307.

Krugman, P. 1987. The Narrow Moving Band, the Dutch Disease, and the Competitive Consequences of Mrs. Thatcher: Notes on Trade in the Presence of Dynamic Scale Economies. *Journal of Development Economics* 27:41–55.

Krugman, P. 1991. History versus Expectations. *Quarterly Journal of Economics* 106:651–67.

Krugman, P. 1992. Toward a Counter-Counterrevolution in Development Theory. Proceedings of the World Bank Annual Conference on Development Economics, 1992:15–38.

Krugman, P. 1994. Urban Concentration: The Role of Increasing Returns and Transport Costs. Proceedings of the World Bank Annual Conference on Development Economics, 1994.

Lai, E.L.C. 1993. International Intellectual Property Rights Protection and the Rate of Product Innovation. Unpublished.

Lal, D. 1983. *The Poverty of Development Economics*. London: Hobart Paperback.

Little, I.M.D. 1982. *Economic Development: Theory, Policy and International Relations*. New York: Basic Books.

Lucas, R.E. 1988. On the Mechanics of Economic Development. *Journal of Monetary Economics* 22:3–42.

Lucas, R.E. 1990. Why Doesn't Capital Flow from Rich to Poor Countries? *American Economic Review* 80:92–96.

Lucas, R.E. 1993. Making a Miracle. *Econometrica* 61:251-72.

Matsuyama, K. 1991. Increasing Returns, Industrialization and Indeterminacy of Equilibrium. *Quarterly Journal of Economics* 106:616–50.

Mookherjee, D., and D. Ray. 1991. On the Competitive Pressure Created by the Diffusion of Innovations. *Journal of Economic Theory* 54:124–47.

Murphy, K., A. Shleifer, and R. Vishny. 1989. Industrialization and the Big Push. *Journal of Political Economy* 97:1003–26.

Pack, H. 1992. Technology Gaps between Industrial and Developing Countries: Are There Dividends for Latecomers. Proceedings of the World Bank Annual Conference on Development Economics, 1992:283-302.

Rodríguez, A. 1993. The Division of Labor and Economic Development. Stanford University, mimeo.

Rodrik, D. 1992. Closing the Productivity Gap: Does Trade Liberalization Really Help? In *Trade Policy, Industrialization and Development: New Perspectives*, edited by G. Helleiner. Oxford: Clarendon Press.

Romer, P.M. 1986. Increasing Returns and Long-run Growth. *Journal of Political Economy* 94:1002–37.

Romer, P.M. 1987. Growth Based on Increasing Returns due to Specialization. *American Economic Review* 77:56–62.

Romer, P.M. 1990. Endogenous Technological Change. *Journal of Political Economy* 98:S71-S102.

Romer, P.M. 1994. New Goods, Old Theory, and the Welfare Costs of Trade Restrictions. *Journal of Development Economics* 43(1): 5–38.

Rosenstein-Rodan, P. 1943. Problems of Industrialization of Eastern and Southeastern Europe. *Economic Journal* 53:202–211.

Segerstrom, P.S., T.C.A. Anant, and E. Dinopoulos. 1990. A Schumpeterian Model of the Product Life Cycle. *American Economic Review* 80:1077–91.

Shell, K. 1967. A Model of Inventive Activity and Capital Accumulation. In *Essays in the Theory of Optimal Economic Growth*, edited by K. Shell. Cambridge: MIT Press.

Stiglitz, J.E. 1974. Incentives and Risk Sharing in Sharecropping. *Review of Economic Studies* 41:219–55.

Stiglitz, J.E. 1988. Economic Organization, Information, and Development. In *Handbook of Development Economics*, vol. 1, edited by H.B. Chenery and T.N. Srinivasan. Amsterdam: North-Holland.

Stokey, N. 1991. The Volume and Composition of Trade between Rich and Poor Countries. *Review of Economic Studies* 58:63–80.

Uzawa, H. 1965. Optimal Technical Change in an Aggregative Model of Economic Growth. *International Economic Review* 6:18–31.

Young, A. 1991. Learning by Doing and the Dynamic Effects of International Trade. *Quarterly Journal of Economics* 106:369-405.

CHAPTER 4

Saving, Investment, and Growth in Developing Countries: An Overview

Klaus Schmidt-Hebbel, Luis Servén, and Andrés Solimano

There is a clear resurgence of interest among economists in the themes of economic growth and development. This is certainly a welcome change from the 1980s, during which macroeconomics was dominated by a concern with short-term adjustment and stabilization issues, largely leaving aside the basic problems of growth, capital accumulation, and saving generation.

Material progress and improving living standards require sustained output expansion. Even though questions of capital formation, technical progress, and supportive saving have been at the core of economic analysis for two or three centuries, their links are far from being clearly understood. Causes and effects among them are not unambiguous, and several factors can start and support growth. The transformation of an initial growth spurt into a sustained process of output expansion and prosperity—a growth takeoff—requires accumulation of capital and its corresponding financing. This sets in motion a self-reinforcing process in which anticipated growth invites investment, actual investment supports growth, and saving flows are generated along the way to finance the accumulation effort as income rises.

These links, however, can be weak. As the Latin American experience of the 1980s has shown, the resumption of investment and growth after the debt crisis and a period of adjustment and depressed economic activity is far from automatic. Coordination failures, pervasive uncertainties, and irreversibilities in investment all make the recovery of growth a complex process. Booms are not problem free either, as they often generate unsustainable growth trajectories that lead to busts. These transitional problems are analytically exciting, but can constitute a nightmare for policy makers. The bliss of steady growth remains elusive. Historically, sustained growth paths have lasted at best a few decades, such as the golden-age growth period of 1950–73 in the industrial world. An encouraging example is provided by East Asia since the 1960s. In Latin America, the high growth enjoyed by Brazil and Mexico between 1940 and 1980 has been followed by persistently sluggish growth thereafter. Lately, a sustained path of high growth has been enjoyed by Chile since the mid-1980s.

This chapter provides a policy-oriented overview of recent theoretical and empirical work on saving and physical investment and their relationship with growth, with emphasis on developing countries. Because the research and policy agenda in these areas is quite broad, the paper focuses only on major issues and broad shifts in perspective highlighted in the recent literature. The discussion covers a variety of issues, such as the interaction between saving and investment, their links with growth, the determinants of saving and its sensitivity to policy measures like financial liberalization and pension system reform. The implications of uncertainty and instability for capital accumulation and GDP growth, the link between income distribution and capital accumulation, the practical importance of the externalities associated with physical investment, and the investment and saving response to policy reform are still far from being fully understood.

The chapter is organized in seven sections. First, it reviews recent world and regional trends in saving, investment, and growth. The chapter then reexamines the critical saving-investment-growth links in light of the recent theoretical and empirical literature. Next, the discussion turns to the behavior of saving, focusing on the links to fiscal policy, foreign saving, and financial and tax incentives. The chapter then examines the main features of investment behavior, highlighting new developments on the impact of irreversibility and uncertainty, political instability and institutional factors, and the links among income distribution, profitability, and investment. Next, the discussion addresses the saving and investment response to the different phases of adjustment and reform programs. Finally, the chapter's concluding section takes up the issue of appropriate policy interventions to foster accumulation and growth.

Facts and Puzzles: Long-Term Regional Trends

Saving, investment, and growth have shown in most world regions a thirty-year downward trend that is both puzzling and worrisome (see table 4.1).[1] World saving and investment rates have declined by some 3 percentage points of GDP during 1982–92 in comparison with 1974–81. Annual per capita world GDP growth shows a marked long-run decline

TABLE 4.1 World Saving, Investment, and Growth Rates by Major Regions and Subperiods, 1965–92 (Means and Standard Deviation)

	1965–73 (Mean)	1974–81 (Mean)	1982–92 (Mean)	1965–1992 (Mean)	1965–92 (Std. Dev.)
Gross National Saving (% of GNP, including transfers)					
Africa	10.7	8.3	4.8	7.7	8.7
Latin America and the Caribbean	16.8	18.6	13.0	15.8	6.0
East Asian Tigers	19.6	27.5	32.4	26.9	6.6
Other LDC	15.8	20.5	16.5	17.4	5.2
All LDC	14.1	15.0	11.4	13.3	7.1
OECD	25.7	23.5	21.2	23.3	3.1
World	16.6	16.8	13.3	15.4	6.3
Gross Domestic Investment (% of GDP)					
Africa	16.9	21.8	19.2	19.2	6.2
Latin America and the Caribbean	20.3	23.5	19.3	20.8	4.8
East Asian Tigers	22.8	30.4	32.6	28.8	6.2
Other LDC	18.7	23.4	21.9	21.3	4.6
All LDC	18.7	23.2	20.7	20.8	5.5
OECD	25.6	24.7	21.6	23.8	3.2
World	20.2	23.5	20.9	21.4	5.0
Current Account Balance (% of GNP, including transfers)					
Africa	6.7	14.4	15.2	12.3	9.3
Latin America and the Caribbean	4.2	5.6	7.9	6.1	5.3
East Asian Tigers	3.9	3.5	1.5	2.8	5.5
Other LDC	2.7	3.1	5.8	4.0	5.8
All LDC	5.0	8.9	10.3	8.2	7.3
OECD	−0.1	1.2	1.1	0.8	3.3
World	3.9	7.3	8.3	6.6	6.4
GDP Growth Rate (%)					
Africa	4.3	3.5	2.4	3.3	5.8
Latin America and the Caribbean	5.5	3.1	1.9	3.4	4.5
East Asian Tigers	8.0	6.6	6.2	6.9	3.3
Other LDC	5.0	2.9	3.3	3.7	4.7
All LDC	5.0	3.5	2.7	3.7	5.0
OECD	5.3	4.5	3.1	4.2	2.8
World	5.1	3.7	2.8	3.8	4.6
Per Capita GDP Growth					
Africa	1.2	1.1	−0.4	0.6	5.6
Latin America and the Caribbean	2.6	1.5	−0.7	1.1	4.6
East Asian Tigers	5.2	5.0	4.8	4.8	3.1
Other LDC	3.7	3.3	1.1	2.7	4.8
All LDC	2.4	2.0	0.2	1.5	5.0
OECD	4.0	2.2	1.7	2.8	2.9
World	2.7	2.0	0.5	1.8	4.6

Source: World Bank (see note 1).

from 2.7 percent in 1965–73 to 2.0 percent in 1974–81 and to a bare 0.5 percent in 1982–92.[2]

These negative trends are more marked in less developed countries (LDCs) than in OECD countries. And among developing regions, large disparities in saving, investment, and growth performance are observed, with Africa and East Asia providing the two extreme cases of regional divergence. While in Africa gross national saving rates were more than halved between 1965–73 and 1982–92—falling to a record low 3 percent of GNP in 1990–92—the East Asian tigers' national saving rates rose from 20 percent of GNP to 32 percent during the same period—actually reaching 35 percent in 1990–92. With massive increases in foreign saving inflows (from 6.7 percent of GNP in 1965–73 to 15 percent in 1982–92), Africa's investment performance did not suffer much despite the reduction in national saving; while lower than in the 1970s, Africa's recent investment rates exceed those achieved in 1965–73. The opposite trend in the contribution of foreign saving to financing domestic investment is observed among the East Asian tigers, where foreign saving has declined to a tiny 1.5 percent of GNP in 1982–92. This, however, does not make East Asia's investment performance any less impressive than its saving record: at 33 percent of GDP in 1982–92 (and 36 percent in 1990–92), East Asia's investment rate exceeds by twelve percentage points of GDP the rates prevalent in both OECD countries and other LDCs. It is not coincidental that East Asia's 1982–92 per capita GDP growth, at 4.8 percent per year, is ten times as high as the world's average of 0.5 percent. At the other extreme, Africa experienced an average annual 0.4 percent decline in per capita GDP during 1982–92.

Over the time periods examined, average Latin American and Caribbean (LAC) investment and growth performance is disturbingly similar to Africa's—both in magnitude and time pattern. In contrast, gross national savings rates are much higher (twice or more after 1974) in Latin America and the Caribbean and in Africa. Moreover, LAC's investment is financed to a larger extent by national saving than is the case for Africa, which results in lower current account deficits.

Another important aspect of countries' performance is the stability of their saving, investment, and growth patterns. The last column in table 4.1 reports regional averages of country standard deviations for 1965–92, which reflect the instability that countries have faced in their performance indicators during the last three decades.

Instability is much more acute in LDCs than in OECD countries—standard deviations of the five indicators are typically twice as large in the former as in the latter. While these measures of instability should be viewed with some caution,[3] their regional pattern does suggest that bad performance goes together with high instability. Africa is again the extreme case, with the largest standard deviations.

Higher instability in the poorer and worst-performing regions may well reflect their larger exposure to adverse foreign shocks, the higher incidence of various domestic shocks (ranging from wars to droughts), and their lower capability to cope with these shocks due to poor policy regimes and structural weaknesses in institutions. This inference is supported by annual figures for regional performance (not reported here), which reveal the importance of worldwide shocks for decade-long performance trends. Saving, investment, and growth suffered in all regions in the aftermath of the first (1973) and second (1980) oil shocks. But East Asia's performance suffered less and the region recovered more quickly from the adverse oil shocks than most other oil-importing developing countries.

We draw four conclusions from these facts. First, most world regions—including OECD countries but with the remarkable exception of East Asia—show a disturbing downward trend in their saving, investment, and growth performance during the last three decades. Second, the regional diversity within LDCs is growing: the poorest countries and regions (Africa) are getting even poorer while middle-income countries and regions (East Asia in particular) grow richer. Third, the poorer regions are not only affected by bad performance but also by much higher degrees of instability. This suggests that better policies and a mature institutional framework—encountered more often in East Asia than in Africa and most of Latin America—are paramount to overcoming spells of bad luck (e.g., adverse shocks) more rapidly and effectively. Finally, and perhaps most important, the facts strongly suggest the existence of both vicious circles of low saving and investment and deteriorating growth (e.g., Africa), along with virtuous circles of vigorous saving and investment and rapid growth (e.g., East Asia). The nature of these links is our next topic.

Saving, Investment, and Growth

The traditional wisdom of development theory since at least World War II has been that the long-run rate of economic growth is largely dependent on the saving rate: saving determines the financeable rate of capital accumulation, which in turn is the basic determinant of long-run growth.[4] Recent theoretical and empirical research has shed new light on this mechanism, and also uncovered some puzzles. In the following we draw from this work to examine three key questions that refer to each of the logical building blocks of the conventional wisdom: first, what is the relationship (and, specifically, the direction of causality) between growth and saving? Second, does countries' national saving really get translated into domestic investment—or, more generally, what is the saving-investment link? And third, what is the contribution of capital accumulation to growth—most important, is investment really the key to growth?

Saving-Growth Causality: Which Way?

The conventional wisdom would seem to be supported by the long-term patterns of saving and growth in developing countries described in the preceding section, which as noted earlier hint at the existence of a virtuous cycle between development and saving—as well as low saving and poverty traps—across countries and over time. Indeed, during the 1960s Asia and Sub-Saharan Africa had similar average gross domestic saving rates (12 percent of GDP); twenty years later Asian saving rates almost doubled to reach 22 percent of GDP, and African rates were halved to 6 percent of GDP. At the country level, Korean household saving rates started at levels close to zero in the mid-1960s and, after twenty years of high growth, rose above 20 percent of household income.

The apparent policy implication would be that raising domestic saving levels is of high priority to ensure a sustainable path of high growth. Yet recent research has shown that the relationship between private saving and income growth is a complex one. It is important to distinguish two aspects of the saving-income link: first, the saving response to income fluctuations; second, its response to trend income or output growth.

The Saving-Growth Link over the Cycle

Consider first income fluctuations. Ample evidence for industrial countries and empirical results for developing countries show that both public and private saving are strongly procyclical: most fiscal policies are countercyclical and private consumers tend to smooth consumption spending over the business cycle. If households are forward-looking and not credit constrained, and if temporary income fluctuations do not change permanent income much, consumption should respond only marginally to temporary income fluctuations. Even poor and credit-constrained households tend to smooth consumption in the short term by accumulating savings when times are good to be able to draw from their buffer stocks in bad times. When bad times last too long, buffer stocks are depleted and from then on consumption closely follows current income (see Deaton 1989, 1992). Households may be unable to distinguish between cycles and longer-term income changes; hence their perception of permanent income could be much affected by current shocks. This would imply that households will consume out of current income, saving less than predicted by conventional consumption theories and hence weakening the procyclical nature of private saving.

Few empirical studies of developing countries have looked closely at the effect of income fluctuations on saving. Exceptions are Gupta 1987 and Schmidt-Hebbel, Webb, and Corsetti 1992, which find that saving responds significantly and positively to temporary income shocks but by much less than what is predicted by the permanent-income hypothesis.

The Longer Term

Let us turn now to the relation between trend income and private saving, which is the more relevant one from the viewpoint of long-term growth. It is a bit ironic that while the strong correlation between saving and growth is a firmly established empirical fact, researchers have found it hard to identify the precise links between the two variables.

Most cross-country empirical studies that include income growth as a determinant of saving report a significant positive effect of growth rates on the saving rate. This result is obtained, for example, by Modigliani (1990) in a large study based on combined cross-country time-series data, performed separately for twenty-one OECD countries and eighty-five developing economies. Jappelli and Pagano (1994) for OECD countries, and Edwards (1994) for a sample of both OECD and LDC economies, confirm this finding. The same result arises in cross-country empirical work for developing economies—such as those by Collins (1991), Fry (1978, 1980), Giovannini (1983, 1985), Mason (1987, 1988), and Schmidt-Hebbel, Webb, and Corsetti (1992).[5]

From the viewpoint of textbook consumption theory, this poses a puzzle: both the conventional infinitely lived, representative-agent model and the overlapping-generations model (where growth takes place mostly within cohorts' lifetimes) would predict a negative effect of growth on saving, as individuals adjust their present consumption upward in anticipation of higher future income. The exception could be a life-cycle overlapping-generations framework where growth takes place between cohorts (rather than within each cohort's lifetime); in such conditions, growth increases aggregate saving for the simple reason that income of the active cohorts (and hence their saving) is larger than income (and dissaving) of the retired cohorts. However, Carroll and Summers (1991) show for three OECD countries, and Deaton (1989) for LDCs, that actual age-consumption profiles are not consistent with what is predicted by life-cycle theories, undermining the empirical importance of this mechanism.

A number of less conventional hypotheses on consumer behavior have been advanced to explain the positive saving-growth link—but have scarcely been tested (see the overviews by Carroll and Weil [1994] and Deaton [1995]). One is concentration of growth in households with high saving rates, such as rich or middle-aged households (Collins 1991). A related explanation is that growth pushes consumers beyond the threshold level of income under which they cannot save. Slowly changing consumption habits could also contribute to higher saving rates in the face of rapid growth (Carroll, Overland, and Weil 1994). Combinations of these approaches may also help explain the empirical evidence; Carroll and Weil (1994) suggest a mixture of habit formation with uncertain incomes (giving rise to precautionary saving) as a promising avenue for further research. A final unconventional hypothesis is that both consumption and wealth (or capital) enter the utility function—an idea advanced in different ways by "classical" economists (from Smith and Marx to Keynes and Schumpeter; see Zou 1993b) and which is resurfacing in some very recent literature (Cole, Mailath, and Postlewaite 1992; Fershtman and Weiss 1993; Zou 1993a, 1993b): higher growth raises wealth, but—due to wealth/consumption substitutability—increases consumption less than proportionately, thereby raising saving.

Of course, an alternative explanation would just go back to the Marshall-Mill tradition: saving is automatically translated into capital accumulation and thereby income growth, and this is simply the mechanism underlying the positive correlation between saving and growth observed in practice. Yet some empirical evidence that this may not be the whole story is provided by Carroll and Weil (1994), who argue that saving typically follows growth, rather than preceding it.

From the growth viewpoint, the likely conclusion is that causality between saving and growth runs both ways. Thus models that fail to take such two-way endogeneity into account likely overstate the contribution of saving to growth—and this even under the maintained hypothesis that saving is fully translated into investment. We now turn to this issue.

The Saving-Investment Relationship

Understanding the saving-investment link is important for at least two reasons: first, as just argued, it may hold the key to the positive correlation between saving and growth. Second, if capital accumulation is indeed the centerpiece of the growth engine, the interaction between saving and investment is crucial for assessing the validity of the traditional recipe that raising saving is the surest way to increase growth—

which involves the implicit assumption that each country's extra saving is necessarily translated into higher domestic investment.

Textbook macroeconomics emphasizes that the determinants of saving are different from those of investment. The former depends mainly on income and wealth, whereas the latter depends on profitability and risk.[6] As the result of two independent decisions, saving and investment can obviously differ ex ante, as emphasized by the Keynesian tradition, in which discrepancies between planned saving and investment are at the heart of macroeconomic fluctuations and growth crises. Indeed, Keynes's well-known "paradox of thrift"—according to which an ex ante increase in saving may lead via the multiplier effect on aggregate demand to an ex post decline in real output, investment and saving itself—illustrates that policies aimed at raising investment and growth by encouraging saving might actually yield the opposite result.

Nevertheless, in the closed economy national saving and domestic investment must be identically equal at least in an ex post sense, so that if saving effectively increases investment must rise as well. But matters are more complicated in the open economy, as capital flows introduce a distinction between national saving and domestic investment. National saving need not be used to invest domestically; it can also be devoted to finance investment abroad. Ideally, in a world of unrestricted capital mobility, each country's saving would flow to the most productive use in the world; thus an increase in national saving would be primarily reflected in an improvement in the current account balance, rather than in higher domestic investment and growth. And this mechanism seems all the more relevant in view of the substantial decline in barriers to international capital flows (especially among industrial countries) over the last two decades.

This reasoning, however, is in direct contradiction with the empirical evidence first reported by Feldstein and Horioka (1980), and recently updated by Feldstein and Bacchetta (1991), that in the long run saving and investment rates show a strong positive correlation. On a sample of industrial countries, Feldstein and Horioka find a correlation coefficient close to 0.9 (virtually the same found in Feldstein and Bacchetta's update). Other studies (Dooley, Frankel, and Mathieson 1987; Summers 1988) find a similarly strong correlation for LDCs, although somewhat lower in magnitude than for industrial countries. Still, an important argument for promoting national savings is that an excessive dependence on external savings makes the domestic economy exposed to volatility in global capital markets that in many cases can be destabilizing.

Low Capital Mobility or Omitted Factors?

Whether the previous result is empirical evidence of international capital immobility has been the subject of considerable debate. One view (defended by Feldstein and his associates) holds that international capital mobility is indeed far from perfect, and therefore national saving increases crowded-in domestic investment (albeit through unspecified mechanisms). The alternative view is that the observed saving-investment correlation says little about international capital mobility[7] and is mostly due to policy reactions and/or common factors that cause both saving and investment to move together in the longer term.

Along these lines, a wide variety of mechanisms have been proposed that could give rise to a strong saving-investment correlation even in the presence of high capital mobility (Obstfeld [1994] provides an extensive review; see also Dornbusch 1991a and Blecker 1994). For example, Frankel (1993) argues that, even under perfect capital mobility, shifts in saving alter the real interest rate, which in turn tends to move investment in the same direction as saving; however, this would imply that real interest rates differ across countries even in the long run—or, in other words, with uncovered interest parity real exchange rates would have to display long-run trends. A second explanation underscores the role of slowly changing demographic and technological factors affecting both saving and investment in the same direction (Obstfeld 1986; Tesar 1991; Taylor 1994). A third alternative attributes the saving-investment link to the operation of the economy's long-run budget constraint (Obstfeld 1986): in the long run, if the economy is close to a stationary foreign asset/GDP ratio, it is possible to show that saving and investment ratios cannot show much divergence.

An alternative view shifts the focus from international to domestic capital immobility, by underscoring the close link between corporate investment (which in industrial countries accounts for the bulk of private investment) and retained earnings empirically found in most OECD economies (and highlighted by Feldstein and Horioka themselves). Indeed, in industrial countries retained earnings typically represent the major source of corporate investment financing; the strong correlation between both variables (documented by Murphy [1984] for U.S. firms, and by Blecker [1994] for a sample of OECD countries) could be the key to the aggregate saving-investment correlation.[8] This type of mechanism seems particularly relevant for LDCs, in which capital market imperfections are widespread and borrowing constraints are the norm, not only for organized corporations but especially for households and firms in the informal sector, which in many developing economies account for the majority of private investment.

Finally, another leading explanation (first proposed by Summers [1988]) is based on the existence of restrictions on countries' ability to run current account imbalances, due either to lending constraints imposed by world capital markets on deficit countries, or to systematic (and successful) current account targeting by policy makers. In both cases, the result would be a strong ex post correlation between national saving and investment. In particular, under the extreme situation of a perfectly inelastic supply of foreign borrowing—as faced by many LDCs during the 1980s—national saving and domestic investment would be highly (indeed perfectly) correlated. Moreover, in such conditions the supply of foreign saving would play a causal role in affecting domestic saving and investment—in stark contrast with the textbook case of perfect capital mobility in which foreign saving is determined residually by the excess of domestic investment over national saving, and any extra gross capital inflows are completely offset by gross outflows. Along these lines, Argimon and Roldan (1994) find empirically that in EC countries enforcing capital controls (presumably to target the external balance), saving and investment display virtually one-to-one correlation, and the former appears to precede the latter.

To sum up, the saving-investment puzzle remains far from resolved. From the policy viewpoint, the key conclusion is perhaps that underlined by Dornbusch (1991a): unless the empirical saving-investment link is better understood, its existence does not justify very strong inferences about the investment and growth response to saving policies. As always, correlation must not be confused with causation.

The Investment-Growth Link

Growth and development theory have long regarded the accumulation of physical capital as the engine of growth. Indeed, the notion that raising the investment rate is key to increasing long-run growth has been at the heart of growth thinking since the time of David Ricardo.

The strong association between investment ratios and long-term growth performance is a well-established empirical fact (see, e.g., Kuznets 1973). Indeed, most country experiences of sustained growth tend to stress the link between capital accumulation and GDP growth. The case of East Asia, the most successful regional experience in terms of rapid and sustained growth of the last three decades, provides a good example. As documented in the preceding section, the East Asian economies have been able to maintain rates of GDP expansion on the order of 8 percent per year, supported by rates of capital formation around 30 percent of GDP. The Chilean growth experience of the last decade also confirms this empirical regularity. Clearly, high growth and high investment shares have gone hand in hand.

However, the key role of investment in the growth process was challenged in the 1960s and 1970s by neoclassical growth theorists. In the neoclassical model (Solow 1956), capital accumulation affects growth only during the transition to the steady state; in contrast, long-run growth is determined only by population growth and the rate of technical change, assumed exogenous. This view attracted considerable criticism from a number of authors (e.g., Kaldor [1957]; Robinson [1962]) on the grounds that the separation between investment and innovation (or technical change) was artificial, as most technical innovation tends to be embodied in new machinery and equipment.[9]

Growth-accounting exercises based on the neoclassical model (Solow 1957; Denison 1962, 1967) appeared to confirm that cross-country differences in investment ratios could explain only a limited portion of the differences in per capita growth performance over long periods, suggesting a crucial role for technological change (or, more honestly, unidentified residual factors) as a major source of long-run growth. The arithmetic of the Solow model, however, does not square well with the strong correlation between investment ratios and growth performance observed in practice (see Romer 1987). Recent research addressing this issue has brought capital accumulation back to center stage of the growth process, suggesting an enhanced—albeit more indirect—role for investment as a key growth determinant.

One line of research focuses on the complementarities between investment in physical and human capital: new and technologically advanced machines and equipment need to be operated by workers with adequate skills and education. Likewise, the identification and design of profitable and innovative investment projects requires also the existence of an entrepreneurial class with innovative skills and awareness of business opportunities. Along these lines, Mankiw, Romer, and Weil (1992) extend the Solow model to include human capital and, under the assumption that its accumulation is guided by that of physical capital, find that investment performance can account directly and indirectly (i.e., through the parallel accumulation of human capital) for the bulk of the variation in growth performance across countries.

A second line of research, that has featured prominently in the "new" growth literature (e.g., Romer 1986, 1987, among many others) emphasizes the close links between the accumulation of physical capital and technological change (a point already underscored by Allyn Young back in 1928, and also by Kaldor [1957] and Arrow [1962]). If productivity growth is endogenous rather than exogenous, and related to the accumulation of physical (or human) capital, then an increase in the rate of investment again raises the rate of growth in the steady state.

The strong correlation between technical progress and investment (or the capital stock) has been amply documented. Baumol et al. (1989), for example, show that in industrial countries technical change is highly correlated with capital-labor ratios. De Long and Summers (1993) estimate panel regressions of total factor productivity growth (TFP) for a large sample of developing countries. Consistently, their results show a positive and statistically significant correlation between the ratio of equipment investment to GDP and total factor productivity growth; they also find a negative coefficient for structures investment in the regressions.

If technical progress is driven by aggregate investment, then capital accumulation by any one firm benefits other firms in the economy, creating an externality that opens a gap between private and social returns to investment. In fact, De Long and Summers (1993) calculate a net social rate of return on equipment investment that is about 35 percent per year: 15 percent is the privately appropriated return on capital, and 20 percent corresponds to the external effects induced by the correlation between equipment investment and TFP growth. These figures, as the authors recognize, are probably on the high side but still provide an order of magnitude of the possible divergence between private and social returns to investment. Earlier work by Romer (1987) likewise estimated that the social marginal product of capital could be over twice as high as the private marginal return.

From Correlation to Causality

The strong investment-growth correlation referred to above has been extensively corroborated by a number of econometric studies. Levine and Renelt (1992) conducted extensive tests on the robustness of alternative specifications of the growth process. In particular, they looked for the specification least sensitive to changes in additional explanatory variables, the sample of countries, and the choice of time periods. Their main result is that the only robust regressor in the different growth equations—both across countries and over time—is the ratio of physical investment to GDP. Other variables, such as indices of external openness and price distortions, and indicators of fiscal and monetary policy stance, all are ultimately fragile as regressors. Moreover, this general result also holds in other empirical analyses of growth conducted for Latin America and East Asia.[10]

De Long and Summers (1991, 1993) advanced one step further by disaggregating investment into its structures and equipment components.

They present abundant empirical evidence, for both developing and developed economies, of a crucial nexus between investment in machinery and equipment and the rate of GDP growth. Estimating panel growth regressions for a sample of eighty-eight non-oil-exporting countries for the period 1960–85, De Long and Summers found a much higher contribution of machinery and equipment investment than structures investment to GDP growth. However, the robustness of their results has been challenged by Auerbach, Hassett, and Oliner (1994).

A related line of work is that of Easterly and Rebelo (1993), who explore the relationship with growth of different types of public investment. They gathered data on aggregate and sectoral public investment for nearly 100 countries. Subject to some reservations about the quality of their information, they find that central government investment is positively correlated with both output growth and private investment, while investment by public enterprises (which presumably competes more closely with private investment projects) is negatively correlated with growth. Sectorally, they also find that the strongest growth impact corresponds to public investment in infrastructure (transport and communications). These findings agree well with analytical and empirical results reported by Servén and Solimano (1993) on the complementarity between public and private investment. Public investment in ports, roads, telecommunications and the like, provides the basic infrastructure needed for private investment projects to operate profitably; thus such types of public projects are likely to have a maximum impact on growth. Empirical studies of private investment for Latin America (Servén and Solimano, chapter 7) and East Asia (chapter 8) show a positive and significant correlation between public and private investment.

Although all these empirical results underscore potentially important aspects of the investment-growth link, in principle they are less conclusive on the direction of causation. And, as with saving, it is necessary to distinguish between the cycle and the long term. In the short run, investment has been empirically shown to depend on the rate of output growth and/or the rate of capacity utilization, as indicators of future demand pressure and/or the severity of liquidity constraints faced by firms—two key variables in their decision to expand productive capacity. Thus, over the business cycle investment can be led by output in an accelerator-like fashion (see Servén and Solimano 1993, chapter 2 for further discussion and references).[11]

In the long term, the traditional wisdom of development economics has long been that capital accumulation is a fundamental cause of the growth process. Recently, however, this view has been challenged by several authors (e.g., Benhabib and Jovanovic 1991; King and Levine

1994) who argue that the comovement of investment ratios and growth rates may be largely due to the action of a third factor—technological innovation—driving both capital accumulation and output expansion. An extreme interpretation of this view would hold that capital accumulation is just a *consequence*, rather than a cause, of the growth process. Along these lines, empirical evidence recently provided by Blömstrom, Lipsey, and Zejan (1993) using a sample of 100 countries shows that growth Granger-causes investment, but not conversely.

Is Investment Sufficient for Growth?

While the extreme view just described seems rather implausible, the lesson to be drawn is that the investment-growth relationship is more complex than suggested by conventional wisdom. Indeed, the simplistic (albeit popular) view that capital accumulation is the only prerequisite for economic growth—a notion labeled "capital fundamentalism" by Yotopoulos and Nugent (1976)—is untenable as well. As the recent literature has emphasized, other complementary inputs—notably human capital and technical knowledge—are also paramount for growth. Expenditures on their acquisition are treated mostly as consumption in conventional national accounting, yet their economic role is similar to that of investment in physical capital. The role of human capital and technical knowledge in the growth process had attracted attention long ago (e.g., Arrow 1962), but has resurfaced as a central theme in the "new" growth theory. In fact, one view popular in the recent literature links long-term growth to the accumulation of a broad aggregate of "capital," which includes not only physical capital but also human capital and knowledge.

But even if these other inputs are available, the quality (i.e., productivity) of investment is a key determinant of its ultimate reward in terms of growth. Brute force capital accumulation in mindless pursuit of scale economies in a framework characterized by severe distortions is unlikely to have much of a growth payoff. Indeed, under extreme distortions massive capital accumulation can ultimately result in reduced growth and welfare when measured at shadow (i.e., distortion-free) prices—a proposition familiar from international trade theory (e.g., Johnson 1967; Brecher and Díaz-Alejandro 1977). Examples of this situation are not difficult to find among countries with heavily regulated investment regimes and/or extensive barriers to market forces; an extreme case is that of the former Soviet Union (see Easterly and Fischer 1994). In such an environment, additional investment tends to exacerbate the welfare cost of the distortions, because the extra capital is misallocated to socially inefficient activities. Thus an incentive framework free of major distortions is essential to realize the full growth potential of capital accumulation.

However, the conclusion that investment may not be the sole engine of growth does not alter the fact that capital accumulation remains a centerpiece of that engine. In general, it is hard to find countries that have been able to grow at high and sustained rates for long time periods without an important effort of capital formation—a fact noted long ago by economic historians such as Rostow (1958) or Gerschenkron (1962). In fact, one of the main merits of the recent literature lies perhaps in the renewed focus on technological change and external effects associated with physical investment as a major aspect of the growth engine—filling what Romer (1993) labels the "idea gap," as opposed to the "object gap" that can be filled just by accumulation of material inputs. As noted earlier, this notion that technical progress is largely embodied in new capital goods is hardly new in growth theory. From this perspective, the recent literature's emphasis on the major role of productivity gains in long-term growth contributes to enhance rather than lessen the importance of capital accumulation for the growth process.

Nevertheless, it is important to note that the experience of East Asia over the last two decades suggests that the recent literature's emphasis on "ideas" may have been overstated: as Young (1993) has convincingly argued, East Asia's stellar growth performance can be explained virtually in full by its unusually high investment ratios, and does not arise from any extraordinary productivity gains.[12] Indeed, Young estimates that over the last two decades productivity growth in East Asian countries proceeded at a rate close to the world average. This result is corroborated by De Long and Summers (1993), in whose framework East Asia's rapid growth is likewise unsurprising given its rapid pace of investment in machinery and equipment.

Saving

Regardless of whether saving is the chief force driving growth, ensuring adequate levels of saving remains a central policy concern in order to provide sufficient financing for investment and to avoid balance of payments disequilibria. Yet saving perhaps is the macroeconomic aggregate that is likely to be the most elusive to both the economist's understanding and the policy maker's influence. Whatever saving definition is used,[13] it shows massive dispersion throughout the world and over time. At the country level, for instance, while in Mexico gross domestic saving rates shrunk from 26.4 percent of GDP in 1980–87 to 20.7 percent in 1988–94 (thus contributing to the 1994–95 crisis), they grew from 17.0

percent of GDP in 1974–87 to 28.8 percent in 1994 in Chile (thus contributing to the latter's success). For the United States, many different explanations are offered for its secular reduction in net national saving rates from 8 percent in 1950–79 to 4.5 percent in the 1980s and to less than 2 percent since 1990, including budget deficits, population aging, and lower growth.

Having discussed the relations between saving and growth above, we focus next on three unresolved questions on the behavior of saving that are important for both research and policy design in developing countries.[14] They refer to the influence of public saving on national saving, the influence of foreign resource inflows on domestic saving, and the effectiveness of financial sector and pension system reform in raising private saving and increasing GDP growth.[15]

How Effective Is Fiscal Policy in Raising National Saving?

It is useful to distinguish between the transfer aspect of fiscal policy that affects overall consumer wealth (for instance, by raising taxes or cutting government consumption) from taxes or subsidies that aim primarily at changing the net rate of return on saving and hence the intertemporal allocation of life-long resources. Following this distinction we review next the intergenerational transfer aspects of fiscal policy, leaving the discussion of taxes and tax incentives and their effects on private saving to the following section.

At a theoretical level, the two dominant paradigms in modern neoclassical macroeconomics offer two strikingly opposing views on this issue.[16] According to the life-cycle overlapping-generations model, public saving affects national saving (and hence capital formation in a closed economy) because it shifts resources across generations that are only weakly (or not at all) connected to each other. In contrast, the infinite-horizon (or Ramsey) model predicts that when private consumers internalize the government's intertemporal budget constraint, changes in public saving are exactly offset by changes in private saving because of strong intergenerational linkages (the well-known Ricardian equivalence; see Barro 1974).

What does the evidence show? Most surveys of the empirical evidence for OECD countries reject Ricardian equivalence (Bernheim 1987; Hayashi 1985; Hubbard and Judd 1986; Leiderman and Blejer 1988); the notable exception is Seater (1993), who concludes that Ricardian equivalence holds approximately. Recent studies for developing countries also reject the Ricardian notion in its pure form (Haque and

Montiel 1989; Corbo and Schmidt-Hebbel 1991; Easterly, Rodríguez, and Schmidt-Hebbel 1994), but conclude that some offsetting of public saving by private savers occurs. Empirical rejection of Ricardian equivalence could imply that real-world consumption is bound by many features assumed away by Ricardian equivalence: weak intergenerational links, financial market imperfections (including borrowing constraints), consumer myopia, and precautionary saving under uncertainty.

However, the existing estimates of offset coefficients are few, too different from each other, and belong to widely differing samples. Even when using a common methodology, country estimates vary widely. For example, Corbo and Schmidt-Hebbel (1991) develop a nested-hypothesis framework that distinguishes between Keynesian, permanent-income, and Ricardian consumption hypotheses and apply it to a panel data sample of thirteen developing countries, rejecting each of these three simple hypotheses in their pure forms. In the overall sample, they find a public-private saving offset coefficient of 0.47; this result, however, conceals a large variation in individual country offset coefficients. The same is true for Bosworth's (1993) results for a panel of twelve OECD countries, with average offset coefficients in the 0.24–0.33 range (depending on the saving definition), but with a much wider range of offset coefficients among countries. Jappelli and Pagano (1994) report offset coefficients for a panel of OECD countries that vary between 0.38 and 0.48, and Edwards (1994) reports offset coefficients for a sample of OECD and LDC countries that vary similarly—between 0.43 and 0.58—depending on the regression specification.

The policy implication of the frequent rejection of Ricardian equivalence is that public saving is an effective tool in raising national saving, at least in the short to medium term.

Do Foreign Resource Inflows Crowd Out Domestic Saving?

While in the preceding discussion on public and private saving decisions causality runs from the former to the latter variable, foreign and national saving decisions can affect each other in either direction. As noted, the greater the international capital mobility, the larger the degree of endogeneity of foreign saving to domestic investment and saving decisions. What does the empirical literature say about the influence of foreign resource inflows on domestic saving (and investment)? We will start by referring to studies looking at the consequences of overall foreign saving, to summarize subsequently some results on the effects of foreign aid.[17]

With a non-econometric analysis, Chenery and Strout (1966) found a negative initial effect of capital inflows on domestic saving, although second-round effects on capacity growth tend to increase saving. Giovannini (1983) finds coefficients on foreign saving for LDCs to have mixed signs and to be insignificant in domestic saving regression equations. Fry (1978, 1980) and Giovannini (1985) find the effect significant and negative, although small. Schmidt-Hebbel, Webb, and Corsetti (1992) show a significant negative effect of foreign saving on household saving for a panel sample of ten developing countries. Gupta (1987) obtains the most extreme results: he reports crowding in (instead of out), as reflected by positive coefficients on foreign saving, which are significant for Asia and Latin America but not for Africa.

Studies on the effects of foreign aid focus typically on how it is spent on consumption and investment (i.e., on empirical estimates of the marginal propensities to consume [MPC] and invest [MPI] of foreign aid transfers). The cross-country literature on the relation between foreign aid and saving (and investment) was started by Griffin (1970, 1971), who found from ordinary least-squares (OLS) regressions for a cross section sample of LDCs a negative correlation between saving and aid, with an implied MPC of aid equal to 0.73. Subsequent studies by Weisskopf (1972), Papanek (1972, 1973), and Chenery and Eckstein (1970) generally found lower consumption propensities, implying that foreign aid was more effective in financing investment. However, Chenery and Syrquin (1975) found that on average 45 percent of an increase in foreign resources is translated into higher investment, while the remainder finances higher consumption. More recently, Levy (1988) found an MPC from (anticipated) foreign transfers equal to 0.4. For a sample of Sub-Saharan countries, the Global Coalition on Africa (1993) claims a negative and significant effect of foreign aid on domestic saving. The World Bank reports an MPC of 0.4 and a MPI of 0.6 for net transfers received by Sub-Saharan countries in the late 1980s (World Bank 1994a).

Much of this literature is haunted by biases stemming from data measurement error, misspecification, and simultaneity (including selectivity) as well as an inadequate treatment of resource fungibility (see Papanek 1972; Levy 1988; White 1994; and Obstfeld 1994 for methodological discussions). A recent study (Boone 1994) addresses and corrects for the more severe sources of bias and uses a large panel data base of ninety-seven developing countries to estimate marginal propensities to consume and invest out of foreign aid that differ radically from preceding work. When the sample is restricted to those eighty-two countries where aid is less than 15 percent of GNP—that is, most LDCs—all of aid is spent on consumption while nothing goes to investment. However, when the full sample is used (including the fifteen small Sub-Saharan African and island economies that receive aid equal to more than 15 percent of their GNP), Boone's estimated full-sample MPC drops to 0.45 and his MPI increases from zero to 0.35, suggesting that the lack of resource fungibility is severe in small and poor countries receiving massive aid financing primarily investment projects. His overall finding of a very high MPC in most other countries is consistent with his model that postulates a world comprised of heterogeneous countries that do not converge in income levels. In such a model the MPC of foreign aid is 1.0—but no convergence in income levels seems to be a rather stringent assumption.[18]

We draw three conclusions. First, empirical estimates of saving effects of foreign aid (and foreign saving at large) vary widely with samples, model specifications, and empirical methods. Second, the extent of external and domestic resource fungibility is the key determinant of the extent to which nonconcessional external resource inflows and foreign aid are channeled to higher domestic consumption and investment. Finally, and most important, very little is known about how to measure resource fungibility and how to identify its underlying causes. Until the latter issue is resolved, the relation between foreign resource inflows and domestic saving will be blurred.

Do Financial and Tax Incentives Raise Private Saving?

Governments have attempted to raise private saving through many means, including interest liberalization, direct tax incentives, and capital market reforms. Many of these attempts have failed, however (Gersovitz 1988; Deaton 1989), and this raises questions about the responsiveness of saving to such policies.

Is Private Saving Sensitive to the Real Interest Rate and to Tax Incentives?

There are two ways of looking at this question. One is by testing for the interest effect on saving or consumption levels. Along this traditional line of research, country and cross-country studies for OECD countries tend to show that saving is not much influenced by interest rates (see Deaton 1992, section 2.2). Increasing evidence for developing countries (Giovannini 1983, 1985; Corbo and Schmidt-Hebbel 1991; Schmidt-Hebbel, Webb, and Corsetti 1992) suggests that private saving (or consumption) typically does not respond to the real interest rate. Edwards (1994) confirms the insensitivity of private saving to the real interest rate for a cross-country sample of OECD and developing economies. In those exceptional cases where a positive response of saving to the interest rate is found (Gupta 1987; Fry 1988), it is quantitatively very small. There are many possible reasons for this finding.[19] For consumers not facing liquidity constraints, the substitution, income and human wealth effects of an interest rate rise roughly neutralize each other when the intertemporal elasticity of consumption substitution is close to 1, as has been found by Schmidt-Hebbel (1987) and Arrau (1989) for Southern Cone countries. Second, liquidity-constrained individuals do not respond much to changes in saving incentives—and liquidity constraints have a significant and positive effect on private and national saving rates in both OECD and developing countries (see Jappelli and Pagano 1994 for the former and Easterly, Rodríguez, and Schmidt-Hebbel 1994 for the latter). In addition, there could be a nonmonotonic relation between saving and interest rates arising from income concentration when interest rates increase. This would imply that at low and negative real interest rates, higher rates raise saving while at high interest rates the saving schedule bends backward.

A less conventional way of looking at this issue is to test how sensitive the rate of consumption growth is to the interest rate, following the Euler equation approach. This is equivalent to testing separately for the intertemporal substitution effect. Evidence reported by Deaton (1989) suggests a weak positive substitution effect across a large number of countries. Surprisingly, econometric studies for the United States fail to find significant positive effects. For developing countries Giovannini (1985) finds positive substitution effects for five countries and no effects in thirteen countries.

If on average private saving were insensitive to the (after-tax) real interest rate, three policy implications would follow. Fiscal stabilization, if it lowers the real interest rate, would not depress private saving through this channel. Financial reform, if it raises the real interest rate, would not raise the flow of private saving through this channel, although it may affect significantly the portfolio composition of the stock of savings, possibly from flight capital to domestically held financial assets. And tax incentives for saving would be ineffective in raising private saving.

On the latter point a sizeable literature has focused on the saving effectiveness of tax incentives in OECD countries, particularly in the United States, making use of cross-section household data typically unavailable in LDCs. The results of the studies for U.S. saving incentive plans (such as IRAs, 401(k) plans, and other schemes that offer tax deductions on contributions and accrual of interest but impose limits on annual contributions and withdrawals) are still inconclusive on their effects on overall national saving (see Gersovitz 1988 and Deaton 1989 for surveys). Among the more recent studies, Engen, Gale, and Scholz (1994) find that U.S. saving incentive plans have been ineffective in raising national saving although they may raise saving after two generations as a result of income shifts toward future generations.

Could Financial and Capital-Market Reforms Raise Private Saving?

Financial and capital-market reforms have potential effects on private saving—other than through changes in real interest rates—through various channels whose effects are of different signs. First, capital market reforms (and macroeconomic stabilization) could lead to reverse capital flight, raising the portfolio share of domestic assets and increasing measured income, measured net exports, and measured domestic saving, but without affecting overall (correctly measured) private saving very much. Second, financial liberalization and capital market deepening could raise the efficiency of intermediation, increasing growth and hence (indirectly) private saving (Easterly 1993; King and Levine 1993). Third, financial liberalization—and the consequent increase in geographical density of financial institutions, range of financial instruments, and quality of financial sector regulation and solvency-enhancing supervision—typically leads to financial deepening, reflected in a permanent increase in the stocks (and a temporary increase in the flows) of financial savings, such as financial and banking sector liabilities. Still, this increase in financial savings could simply reflect a portfolio shift without affecting overall private saving. Fourth, financial liberalization typically leads to expanded consumer lending and, more generally, less stringent constraints on consumer borrowing, affecting private saving negatively. It has been argued that, on balance, financial deepening has contributed to the growth in overall saving observed in East Asian economies (World Bank 1993).

Empirical studies have typically proxied financial deepening by a measure of broad money to output; but broad money could be negatively correlated with consumer borrowing constraints (and hence positively with consumption), and positively correlated with consumer wealth (and again with consumption as well). Hence its effect on saving is ambiguous—and so are the empirical results for cross-country samples. For instance, while Corbo and Schmidt-Hebbel (1991) and Schmidt-Hebbel, Webb, and Corsetti (1992) report negative effects of broad money on saving in LDCs, Edwards (1994) reports positive effects for OECD and developing economies.

Variables that reflect borrowing constraints more closely are reported to have less ambiguous effects on saving in empirical cross-country saving studies. Jappelli and Pagano (1994) found a significant negative effect of loan-to-asset-value ratios on net national saving in OECD countries and Edwards (1994) found a negative but insignificant effect of consumer credit on private saving in OECD and developing countries.

A final question arises about the potential effects on private and national saving of one important reform: the introduction of mandatory pension schemes and pension reforms that substitute pay-as-you-go (PAYG) systems by fully funded (FF) schemes. The saving effects of mandatory pension systems and reforms are typically analyzed in the framework of an economy that is an aggregate of different generations that save primarily for their own retirement and not for their offspring.

There are useful results from simulations of general equilibrium models that consider both the transfers across generations that result from pension systems and the factor market distortions of PAYG schemes. Simulation results for the United States by Auerbach and Kotlikoff (1987) illustrate that starting unfunded social security reduces long-term saving and output levels by modest amounts. Simulation results for representative economies show that the long-term effects of tax-financed pension reform transitions are small to moderate and reaped only in the very long run (see Arrau and Schmidt-Hebbel 1993 and Cifuentes and Valdés-Prieto 1995 for exogenous growth models). However, dynamic effects on saving and long-term growth through capital market deepening and labor shifts from informal to formal markets could be much more significant and reaped much earlier (see Corsetti and Schmidt-Hebbel 1995 for an endogenous growth model).

In contrast to the previous results, the large econometric evidence for OECD countries based on single-equation consumption or saving functions yields little or no effects of unfunded social security on contemporaneous personal or private saving levels (see World Bank 1994b). A major exception are Feldstein's (1974, 1995) results for the United States that suggest that Social Security programs reduce overall private saving by 40 to 60 percent. Econometric evidence for developing countries suggests that government social security benefits (typically through state-run PAYG schemes) have reduced private saving (Edwards 1994). Some evidence on Singapore's fully funded Central Provident Fund shows that it has boosted aggregate saving (World Bank 1993, 1994b) and econometric evidence on Chile's large increase in its private saving rate suggests that the substitution of FF for PAYG after 1981 has contributed to it (Corsetti and Schmidt-Hebbel 1995).

This evidence may reflect two points. First, leaving bequests could be a more important saving motivation than saving only for retirement, so that starting a mandatory PAYG system would not affect private saving by much. Indirect evidence on the importance of bequests is mounting, as recent household surveys from around the world show that saving rates of the elderly are as high or even higher than those of younger households (see Deaton 1995). Second, even if the bequest motive dominates the retirement motive, there seems to be a large number of households that are credit constrained, so that starting a FF scheme (as in Singapore) or substituting FF for PAYG (as in Chile) forces these households to save more than what they would voluntarily save, hence raising overall saving ratios.

Investment: New Developments

As noted previously, the analysis of investment decisions was pioneered by Keynes (1936), who challenged the then-prevalent view of the insepa-rability between saving and investment decisions. He emphasized the distinction between investors and savers, and viewed investment as a decision made under highly uncertain conditions that required unavoid-able guesses about prospective future returns and capital costs.

Since the 1960s investment theory has been in rapid evolution.[20] We begin this section by reviewing some recent developments in investment analysis. We focus on three issues: the implications of irreversibility and uncertainty for investment, the links between economic and political instability and investment, and the private investment consequences of ill-defined property rights and phenomena such as corruption.

Uncertainty and Irreversibility

Conventional investment theory focused on different variants of the cost of capital (Jorgenson) and the replacement versus market value of new capital goods (Tobin) as centerpieces of investment decisions. These theories provided useful insights about the decision to invest, but failed to fully consider three main features of investment deci-sions:[21] *(a)* the partial or complete irreversibility of most investment decisions—once the capital stock is installed it cannot be put to a new use without incurring a substantial economic cost; *(b)* most investment decisions face inherent uncertainty regarding future benefits and costs—the best investors can do is to attach (subjective) probabilities to the net returns of different investment projects; finally, *(c)* investors can control the timing of investment, waiting for relevant information that can reduce the uncertainty.

These crucial features have led to a new option approach that sees an investment opportunity as an option to buy an asset at different points in time, balancing the value of waiting with the opportunity cost (in terms of foregone returns) of postponing investment decisions.[22] Some empirical studies of investment both at microeconomic and aggregate levels confirm the importance of the value of waiting.[23]

Economic and Political Crises and Investment

Economic and political instability is an important field of application of the option view of investment. In particular, political and economic crises (a large external shock, a financial crash, a war, exacerbated social and political conflict) typically create considerable uncertainty about variables that are key in the decision to invest. The result can be a huge increase in the value of waiting for new information in order to revise the probabilities attached to the various possible events; this is turn causes an investment slump.

Political instability reflected in rapid government turnover may also hamper investment, if it leads to an unstable incentive and policy framework. An adverse investment impact is especially likely when the political change involves a redefinition of the basic "rules of the game" (investment codes, property rights, tax laws) and, in particular, when it raises expropriation risks (e.g., Chile in the early 1970s, Nicaragua in the 1980s). Empirically, recent studies (e.g., Alesina and Perotti 1993; Mauro 1993) confirm the important role of political instability as an investment deterrent.

Property Rights and the Cost of Doing Business

There is no question about the importance of property rights for investment. From the practical viewpoint, however, the formal definition of property rights needs to be complemented by other factors guaranteeing their effective enforcement. An important link in that enforcement are principal-agent relationships, which tend to be very complex. Monitoring of agents (managers, workers) by the principal (the owner) often has to face imperfect information and is costly. The mere existence of private property is no assurance that the agents will act in the best interests of the owners, a feature particularly relevant for investment.

Related to this is the issue of contract enforcement, whose effectiveness can be jeopardized by weak and inefficient judiciary systems. Yet without proper contract enforcement, property rights would be good only on paper. In the end, the lack of impartial mechanisms to resolve contractual disputes results in an increased cost of doing business, as the probability that contracts will be respected diminishes and/or expenses such as bribes become necessary.

This leads to the issue of corruption, which is critical for investment projects because their implementation—particularly in highly regulated economies—may involve many administrative steps: getting an investment permit, obtaining licenses to import critical inputs, gaining access to directed credit, assuring compliance with labor standards and environmental regulations, etc. The cost of doing business can rise substantially if the typical investor is forced to bribe government officials in order to complete or speed up these administrative steps. In this regard, corruption effectively amounts to a tax on investment. Recent cross-country empirical work by Knack and Keefer (1994) shows that higher measures of corruption, just like weaker property rights, tend to be associated with a significantly worsened investment performance.

The elimination of unnecessary regulation can reduce potential sources of rents for bureaucrats and thus corruption. Civil service reform, including competitive pay policies, career opportunities, and moral standards, is also an important aspect of institutional reform to boost investment and growth.

Profits, Income Distribution, and Capacity Utilization

A basic insight of Keynes (1936) is the dependence of investment on expected profits (relative to the cost of capital). The rate of profit (profits over capital) can be expressed as the product of the profit share (profits over output) times the rate of capacity utilization (output over capital). This brings out two key determinants of investment: income distribution and the level of aggregate demand (or phase of the business cycle). Functional income distribution essentially refers to the shares of capital, labor, and other factors in national income. However, the relationship between income distribution and capital accumulation is a complex one. On the one hand, a distribution of income biased toward capital can increase the profit rate through a higher profit share. On the other hand, if aggregate demand depends negatively on the profit share—because of a higher propensity to spend for labor than capital—then a redistribution of income toward capital will depress aggregate demand, lower the rate of capacity utilization, and depress the profit rate. In sum, the profitability effect can operate in an opposite direction to the demand effect, making the relationship between income distribution and investment ambiguous.

Other channels might be relevant too for the relationship between accumulation and distribution. Income distribution affects the choice of public policies and the degree of social and political stability: an uneven income distribution may encourage workers' demands and labor militancy, increasing the degree of political conflict. An uneven income distribution might also compel governments to seek populist policies of rapid redistribution of income that can be fiscally and macroeconomically destabilizing, as has been witnessed several times in Latin America during the last few decades (see Dornbusch and Edwards 1991). Redistributive policies in turn may be financed through higher taxes on capital, thereby discouraging investment and growth. The relationship between investment and distribution is filtered by political institutions and can be stronger in democracies than in nondemocracies (see Persson and Tabellini 1992 and Alesina and Rodrik 1992). Empirical evidence for a cross section of countries provided in Persson and Tabellini 1992 shows a positive and marginally significant correlation between equality in income distribution and the investment-to-GDP ratio.

Stronger results are obtained in Alesina and Rodrik 1992. In cross-section regressions using the ratio of total physical investment over GDP as the dependent variable and controlling for the type of political regime (democracies versus nondemocracies), they find a positive correlation between the degree of income equality and the investment ratio. A similar result arises when using average GDP growth rates as the dependent variable, thus suggesting that investment is an important channel through which income distribution affects GDP growth.

Adjustment, Reform, Saving, and Investment

This section discusses the main linkages between investment, adjustment, and overall systemic reform. Many adjustment programs seek to correct an excess of aggregate spending over real output that creates a deficit in the current account of the balance of payments and/or inflationary pressures. From simple national accounts identities the aggregate excess spending signifies an excess of investment over saving. A cut in investment spending often takes place during the first phase of an adjustment program. This is an adverse trend if the investment compression lasts too long, as was the case of Latin America in the 1980s after the debt crisis. In this case, productive capacities are impaired and so is the economy's ability to grow. If the productivity of investment is low, however, then some decline in investment will not be that harmful.

National saving also tends to follow a distinct pattern according to the different phases of an adjustment and reform program (of varying length, overlap, and partial recurrence). To understand the interactions between investment, saving, adjustment, and reform, it is useful to distinguish between the pre- and postreform situations.

The Prereform Situation

There is a wide variety in initial conditions for reform. Some countries might experience instability and large macro imbalances such as high and erratic inflation, exchange rate volatility, fiscal deficits, and balance of payments disequilibria. Examples abound, including Argentina, Brazil, Peru, Poland, and Russia in the late 1980s and the early 1990s. In contrast, other countries have initiated their reform programs from more stable macro conditions,[24] but with pervasive microeconomic distortions and an oversized state.[25]

When instability is rampant before reform, private investment is hurt. The key reason is that, as noted earlier, instability and uncertainty invite a delay in investment spending, as most investment outlays are irreversible. Empirically, evidence for five high-inflation countries in Latin America from 1960 to 1990 shows that private investment is negatively correlated with the level (and sometimes the variance) of inflation and with the variance of the real exchange rate, two indicators of macroeconomic instability. Interestingly, when the same equations for private investment are run for (low-inflation) OECD economies, investment is negatively correlated also with inflation and measures of exchange rate volatility (see Pindyck and Solimano 1993).[26] These results clearly support the hypothesis that instability is a powerful deterrent of private investment.

Prereform instability can also affect public investment, in particular if there is a fiscal crisis that forces governments to cut spending. In general, capital expenditures are cut before current expenditures, as the latter cuts often create less political resistance. Of course the costs show up in the future through lack of infrastructure and other productive capacities.

In the case of highly distorted but more "stable" macroeconomics, the problem is the low productivity of investment rather than too low a level of capital accumulation. The problem becomes one of "quality" rather than "quantity" of investment.

The Reform Period

Let us turn now to the situation in which reform policies are adopted. For analytical purposes we will identify three different phases of reform programs that are relevant in terms of their impact on investment and saving.

Phase I. Adjustment and Stabilization

In economies with large macro disequilibria, the first task of a reforming government is to restore basic macro balances and stabilize inflation. The typical package involves a combination of expenditure-reducing policies (fiscal and monetary restraint) along with expenditure-switching policies (depreciation of the real exchange rate). These policies are usually supplemented by the elimination of various subsidies and by foreign financing from multilateral institutions.

Austerity measures tend to reduce capital formation, at least in the short run, for several reasons. Fiscal adjustment often involves a cut of public investment, currency depreciation makes imported capital goods more expensive, and monetary tightening pushes up real interest rates, depressing private capital formation.[27]

On the saving side, during this first stage fiscal adjustment is also reflected in higher public saving. However, the contractionary effects of restrictive aggregate demand policies typically lead to a steep decline of private saving, as consumers attempt—as long as they are not credit constrained—to maintain their consumption levels during the recessionary phase. National saving often falls during this stage—a result of private saving cuts that exceed the increases in public saving. Depending on how strong the decline of domestic investment is, the ex ante demand for foreign saving—satisfied ex post only in the absence of a foreign borrowing constraint—could rise or fall during this period.

Phase II. Intensification of Structural Reforms and the Investment Pause

A second phase in reform programs comes after the basic macroeconomic disequilibria have been corrected. At this stage governments can accelerate the structural reforms comprising restructuring and liberalization. Of course, in practice there might be some simultaneity between macro stabilization and the structural reforms, as the latter will hardly consolidate if the macro fundamentals are not in place.

The response of investment in this second phase is mixed. In Chile private investment responded forcefully to the launching of reforms in the second half of the 1970s.[28] Likewise, private investment has surged in Argentina and Peru in the early 1990s after the launching of liberalization policies. By contrast, the response of private investment was modest in Israel, Mexico, and Bolivia in the aftermath of stabilization during the second half of the 1980s. A substantial deal of work has been done on the so-called investment pause after adjustment.[29] The combination of lack of confidence in the consolidation of structural reforms and the fact that investment is irreversible (in an economic sense) makes investors adopt a wait-and-see attitude in the aftermath of stabilization.

Public investment often suffers during the adoption of reform policies. In part this is a by-product of fiscal adjustment; however, the decline in public investment also reflects a deeper structural change. In the new development strategy that follows the adoption of market-oriented reform, a smaller role for the state is envisaged both as producer and provider of basic infrastructure. The privatization of state-owned enterprises typically leads to a decline in public investment. Also, the opening of new business opportunities to the private sector in activities that were formerly in the realm of the public sector—like power generation, roads, ports—leads to a decline in public investment in these activities. How does private saving respond to these structural reforms? If certain reforms—such as trade opening or liberalization of capital inflows—are not fully credible, they may spur a consumption boom to take advantage of temporarily cheap imported goods. And if they are credible and lead to an expectation of higher permanent income, consumers may spend today in anticipation of tomorrow's income gains. Moreover, trade liberalization frequently allows consumers to adjust their holdings of consumer durables toward desired levels after years of import deprivation. For all these reasons liberalization policies lead often to an initial decline in private saving that can be offset by an increase in public saving as fiscal adjustment is deepened in this phase.

Phase III. Maturity of Reforms and High Growth

The third phase of a reform program reflects consolidation of the measures taken before. This is a "happy period" as the fruits of reform start to accrue in terms of higher growth, enhanced stability and improvement in living standards. Examples of countries in this stage would be Chile in the late 1980s and 1990s and the rapidly growing economies of East Asia. At this stage the main problem is not how to get investment and growth under way, but rather how to preserve the dynamism already achieved. In this case, the sensible thing would be to maintain the fundamentals—low inflation, fiscal balance, external sustainability, adequate price signals, social stability—and monitor the sectoral composition of investment. In fact, during more advanced stages of the development process it becomes crucial to enhance the economy's infrastructure and support the physical investment effort with the provision of better education, training, and other forms of human capital accumulation.

On the saving side, once durable stock adjustment is well advanced and real growth is rising, private consumption tends to grow less than income, therefore generating a steady rise in private saving, as exemplified by the increase in Korean urban household saving rates from 3 percent of household income in 1965-70 to 23 percent in 1980–85 (Collins 1991) and by the rise in the private saving rate in Chile from 1 percent of GDP in 1979–81 to 12 percent in 1982–89 and to 17 percent in 1990–92 (Corsetti and Schmidt-Hebbel 1995).

Policy Issues and Final Remarks

We conclude by summarizing our discussion of the saving-investment-growth mechanism and deriving some policy implications for saving and investment. Two general lessons can be drawn from the recent theoretical and empirical literature. The first one is that, in spite of the virtuous circles of high saving and investment and rapid growth apparent in the empirical facts, the saving-investment-growth relationship is a complex one, in which causality runs in several directions. The second lesson is that investment and innovation remain the centerpieces of the growth process, and the close empirical association between saving and growth likely reflects the saving-investment correlation found in the data, whose causes are not well understood yet. In this regard, the new growth literature represents a decided (albeit perhaps unintended) return to the tradition initiated by Marx, Schumpeter, and Keynes.

Saving

Even if saving is not the chief driving force behind growth, ensuring adequate saving levels still remains a central policy concern in order to guarantee sufficient financing for capital accumulation and avoid an excess of investment over saving that can create inflationary pressures and/or balance of payments disequilibria. Moreover, encouraging private saving may be essential to expand investment in a framework of extensive capital market imperfections and liquidity constraints on firms and households, typical of many developing economies.

From our discussion of saving determinants and their empirical relevance in developing countries, we derive three lessons on the effectiveness of policies. First, since the evidence shows that public saving does not crowd out private saving one-to-one, raising public saving is an effective and direct way to raise national saving. The available evidence shows that the private sector offsets each dollar of additional public saving by dissaving an amount that ranges roughly from 25 to 55 cents.

Second, foreign saving inflows should be allowed and encouraged to support domestic investment—even if they help in part to finance consumption—as long as the domestic macroeconomic policy framework is sustainable, the domestic banking sector is effectively regulated and supervised, and the government does not provide guarantees on foreign credit flows. The historical literature has suggested that foreign aid finances consumption and investment roughly in equal proportions. However, more recent and systematic evidence estimates that most of aid is spent on consumption while little goes to investment—with exception of those countries that receive aid in excess of 15 percent of their GNP, where the effects on consumption and investment are again similar to each other. This shows that aid resources are more fungible the larger is the recipient economy relative to the amount of aid.

Third, one should not expect higher private saving in response to interest rate liberalization. The evidence shows that market-determined interest rates will improve financial intermediation, the quality of portfolio choices (hence avoiding or reverting capital flight and possibly raising measured saving flows), and the quality of investment, but will be ineffective in increasing overall saving flows. Likewise, financial deepening—as reflected by higher financial savings stocks—has ambiguous effects on private saving. Relaxation of constraints on consumer lending depresses private saving, sometimes contributing to unsustainable consumption booms such as in Latin America during the early 1980s and in Mexico during 1991–94. Pension system reform is one particular form of capital market reform, although it is also combined with important labor market and public finance reform dimensions. The econometric evidence on the effects of mandatory unfunded social security on private saving rates is mixed—possibly because leaving bequests is a stronger saving motive than accumulating for retirement. However, as large numbers of (poor and young) households are credit constrained and not saving much for retirement, starting a mandatory fully funded pension system could boost private saving significantly, as evidenced by Singapore and Chile.

Investment

If investment and innovation are the key to growth, an important policy question is whether an activist "investment policy" is needed to boost growth and, if so, which form it should take. In theory, the need for an activist policy could be justified by the existence of investment externalities—implied by the "public good" nature of technical innovation—which would result in socially insufficient private investment. To correct the externalities, the conventional policy response would involve subsidies and/or tax exemptions to capital accumulation. However, although this type of direct-intervention policy might theoretically boost growth, there are in practice serious limitations to the administrative and institutional capacities of government agencies to target the "right" investments and avoid rent seeking.

A less direct but perhaps more effective way to promote investment in the medium run, innovation, and growth is through the provision of a supportive policy and institutional framework. The recent investment literature suggests that such a framework requires several ingredients: macroeconomic stability, a relatively distortion-free relative price structure, well-defined (and effectively enforced) property rights, an environment conducive to a low cost of doing business, and adequate political institutions that foster social consensus and political stability. To complement all this, the government should ensure the provision of adequate infrastructure and human capital investment—be it in the form of public projects or with private sector participation.

NOTES

We thank Peter Montiel and Paulo Vieira da Cunha for detailed comments and discussions. We are also indebted to Felipe Larraín, Lance Taylor, and an anonymous referee for comments.

1. The data source for table 4.1 is the World Bank's BESD data base, which in turn is based on national accounts data published by country sources or by the IMF's International Financial Statistics. Regional means for each period are unweighted averages of country means for the corresponding period. Regional standard deviations for 1965–92 are unweighted averages of country standard deviations for 1965–92 (or the available period, if shorter). Note that the regional avarages of standard deviations reflect the average instability over time that countries face in any given region—and not the regional dispersion of country performance indicators. Sample sizes vary slightly by variables and years within the 1965–90 span, with the world sample varying between 99 and 104 countries, and declining more strongly for 1991 and 992 (when the world sample includes only between 87 and 102 countries). The main regions considered here are Sub-Saharan Africa, Latin America and the Caribbean, six East Asian countries (the "tigers" comprised by Hong Kong, Indonesia, Korea, Malaysia, Singapore, and Thailand), other developing countries (Middle Eastern and other Asian countries), all LCDs, and OECD countries. Former socialist countries are excluded from the sample.

2. One should be aware of the limitations of regional means and standard deviations: variable definitions are data quality vary across countries, some countries are excluded from each region, and the use of unweighted averages—while useful when treating each country experience as one distinct observation—is not representative of individual country (and regional) economic weights and is

inconsistent with world adding-up constraints (for instance, that the world's foreign saving should be zero).

3. Note that the standard deviation is larger when time trends or stepwise structural breaks are present—as actually is the case in many variables. Hence successful development—as reflected by uptrending saving, investment, and growth as in East Asia—could raise our measure of instability. Nevertheless, we prefer to report straightforward standard deviations instead of standard deviations from time trends, as the latter would be based on necessarily arbitrary trend estimates.

4. This notion rests on what is termed the "Marshall-Mill view" (adopted later by Solow as well; see Chakravarty 1993, chap. 3). For an alternative interpretation of post–World War II growth, see Marglin and Schor 1990.

5. Interestingly, Carroll and Weil (1994) show that this may be partly due to the outlying observations from fast-growing, high-saving East Asian countries: when these are omitted from their sample, the positive cross-country saving-growth correlation becomes much smaller and insignificant. This is corroborated by the results in Schmidt-Hebbel and Servén 1995.

6. This of course was one of the fundamental contributions of Keynes (1936). In the classical, pre-Keynes tradition, there was no independent investment function, and therefore investment just followed saving passively.

7. The validity of saving-investment correlations as a measure of international capital mobility has been extensively discussed by Frankel (1992, 1993), who examines three alternative measures: covered interest parity, uncovered interest parity, and real interest rate equalization. Frankel (1992) reports that the first of these is the most adequate, as it compensates for country risk; he reports a significant decline (nearly a complete disappearance) in covered interest differentials among industrial countries in the 1980s, which implies that capital mobility increased steadily over the same period. In turn, Montiel (1993) provides a comprehensive analysis of capital mobility in LDCs. More generally, the finding reported in the text that saving-investment correlations are typically lower for samples of LDCs than for industrial countries—despite the extensive capital controls and external borrowing constraints in many developing economies during the 1970s and 1980s—raises strong suspicions about their validity as measures of capital mobility.

8. However, as Obstfeld (1994) notes, this requires not only that firms finance their investment with corporate earnings, but also that households fail to pierce the "corporate veil," thus failing to offset a rise in firms' saving with a decline in household saving, and thereby allowing a rise in corporate investment to be matched with a rise in aggregate saving.

9. See also Schumpter (1934), who emphasized the fact that most innovations were embedded in the production of new capital goods and business practices.

10. See De Gregorio 1992, Corbo and Rojas 1993, and Lefort and Solimano 1993 for Latin America and Young 1994 for East Asia.

11. It is worth noting that this sensitivity of investment to cyclical variations in output (or other short-term factors) opens the possibility that short-term reces-

sions could have long-term effects, by causing a deep investment slump that leaves the economy "permanently" trapped in low-growth, low-investment equilibrium. In other words, the growth process could be path-dependent. See Bruno 1994 for further discussion and some country experiences.

12. It is important to recall, however, that East Asia's high rates of physical investment were also accompanied by an important effort at human capital formation.

13. Empirical work on saving is haunted by the low quality of saving data and the inadequacy of saving definitions. Aggregate saving data are often reported in national accounts statistics as a residual of another residual: consumption. Saving flows are typically inconsistent with changes in wealth stocks because of incomplete accounting, underreporting of capital income, and exclusion of capital gains. Saving does not have any identifiable deflator related to it, hence making it difficult to construct constant-price time series. Finally, researchers often fail to adequately correct raw saving data, for instance, for the inflation component of nominal interest payments.

14. Some of these unresolved puzzles have been pointed out by recent surveys of saving behavior in developing countries; see Gersovitz 1988; Deaton 1991; and Schmidt-Hebbel, Webb, and Corsetti 1992.

15. Issues related to the sectoral disaggregation of saving and differences in sectoral behavior are considered explicitly by the first and second questions. We will not discuss, however, a further disaggregation of private saving among households and firms, although some evidence exists that households are not able to "see through the corporate veil" (for instance, Bosworth 1993 estimates that out of nine OECD countries, the household saving offset coefficient for corporate saving is [not] significantly different from 1 in 6 (3) countries). However, there are very few saving studies for LDCs using household data, and only one using aggregate (national accounts) data for households (Schmidt-Hebbel, Webb, and Corsetti 1992).

16. See, for instance, Azariadis 1993, Blanchard and Fischer 1990, and Deaton 1992.

17. Two analytically essential (but seldom acknowledged) points should be addressed by empirical studies. First, a distinction should be made between nonconcessional foreign resource inflows (foreign investment plus nonconcessional lending) and foreign aid (unilateral transfers plus the grant component of concessional lending). While the former embody an external financing source, the latter implies a wealth transfer. Second, it is important to deal explicitly with resource fungibility at three different levels: external, domestic macroeconomic, and domestic microeconomic. External resource fungibility refers to the degree of international capital mobility. Perfect capital mobility is equal to extreme external resource fungibility and implies complete endogeneity of foreign resource inflows. Domestic macroeconomic resource fungibility implies that external resources lead to higher spending—in the absence of external resource fungibility—on both consumption and investment according to a domestic rationing mechanism (for instance, interest rates) that is independent

of the programmed resource use. Finally, domestic microeconomic resource fungibility implies that external resources lead to higher spending—in the absence of both external and domestic macroeconomic resource fungibility—on the broad spending category they are intended for (for instance, on consumption if intended for food consumption), but not necessarily on the specific project or sector they are targeted to.

18. Foreign aid could affect saving and investment indirectly through higher productivity growth. For instance, private investment and growth could rise when foreign aid conditionality is successful in promoting policy reforms and a better allocation of public expenditure, raising the productivity of private investment. However, Boone's cross-country growth regressions show that foreign aid does not play a positive role in most (eighty-two) developing countries—but aid helps growth in those fifteen small LDCs where it exceeds 15 percent of GNP.

19. One possibility is that the findings might be spurious due to severe aggregation problems assumed away by the representative-agent model. Following Deaton (1992, p. 70), consider a two overlapping-generations life-cycle model without bequests, where consumption at the individual level of each generation is flat along the life horizon, but where lifetime consumption of each generation is increased by productivity growth. Then aggregate consumption will increase over time, implying a biased estimate of the intertemporal elasticity of substitution of the presumed representative agent as obtained from the macro data.

20. See Servén and Solimano 1993 (chap. 2) for a survey of investment theories.

21. See Dixit and Pindyck 1994, chapter 1.

22. The option approach shows that the standard net present discounted value rule of investment (invest when the purchase and installation cost equals the expected return) must be modified. The correct rule is that the value of the new capital good must exceed the purchase and installation cost, by an amount equal to the value of keeping the investment option alive.

23. See particularly chapter 4 in Servén and Solimano 1993.

24. In these economies, the macro disequalibria (e.g., inflation) can be repressed. In turn, fiscal and balance of payments deficits can be financed by external aid granted for some specific geopolitical reasons.

25. See Solimano, Sunkel, and Blejer 1994 (chap. 1) for a discussion of initial conditions before reform in a broad variety of countries.

26. The relationship between investment and inflation is found to be nonlinear in Pindyck and Solimano 1993. Only when inflation rates exceed certain thresholds does a significant drop in investment take place; moreover, these thresholds are much higher in Latin America than in the OECD.

27. See Servén and Solimano 1993 (chap. 2) for a survey of the effects of fiscal, monetary, and exchange rate policies on investment.

28. This response was reversed in the crisis of 1982–83.

29. See Dornbusch 1991b, Solimano 1992, 1993, and Servén and Solimano 1993.

REFERENCES

Alesina, A., and D. Rodrik. 1992. Distribution, Political Conflict, and Economic Growth: A Simple Theory and Some Empirical Evidence. In *Political Economy, Growth, and Business Cycles,* edited by A. Cukierman, Z. Hercowitz, and L. Leiderman. Cambridge, MA: MIT Press.

Alesina, A., and R. Perotti. 1993. Income Distribution, Political Instability and Investment. NBER Working Paper 4486.

Argimon, I., and J. Roldan. 1994. Saving, Investment and International Capital Mobility in EC Countries. *European Economic Review* 38: 59–67.

Arrau, P. 1989. Intertemporal Monetary Economics: Evidence from the Southern Cone of Latin America. Ph.D. diss. University of Pennsylvania.

Arrau, P., and K. Schmidt-Hebbel. 1993. Macroeconomic and Intergenerational Welfare Effects of a Transition from Pay-As-You-Go to Fully-Funded Pension Systems. World Bank, June. Manuscript.

Arrow, K. J. 1962. The Economic Implications of Learning by Doing. *Review of Economic Studies* 29: 155–73.

Auerbach, A., and L. Kotlikoff. 1987. *Dynamic Fiscal Policy.* Cambridge: Cambridge University Press.

Auerbach, A., K. Hassett, and S. Oliner. 1994. Reassessing the Social Returns to Equipment Investment. *Quarterly Journal of Economics* 109: 789–802.

Azariadis, C. 1993. *Intertemporal Macroeconomics.* Cambridge, MA: Blackwell.

Barro, R. 1974. Are Government Bonds Net Wealth? *Journal of Political Economy* 82: 1095–1117.

Baumol, W. et al. 1989. *Productivity and American Leadership: The Long View.* Cambridge, MA: MIT Press.

Benhabib, J., and B. Jovanovic. 1991. Externalities and Growth Accounting. *American Economic Review* 81: 82–113.

Bernheim, B. B. 1987. Ricardian Equivalence: An Evaluation of Theory and Evidence. In *NBER Macroeconomics Annual 1987.* Cambridge, MA: MIT Press.

Blanchard, O., and S. Fischer. 1990. *Lectures on Macroeconomics.* Cambridge, MA: MIT Press.

Blecker, R. 1994. Policy Implications of the International Saving-Investment Correlation. Mimeo. American University.

Blömstrom, M., R. Lipsey, and M. Zejan. 1993. Is Fixed Investment the Key to Economic Growth? NBER Working Paper 4436.

Boone, P. 1994. The Impact of Foreign Aid on Savings and Growth. Manuscript. London School of Economics, June.

Bosworth, B. P. 1993. *Saving and Investment in a Global Economy.* Washington, D.C.: Brookings Institution.

Brecher, R., and C. Díaz-Alejandro. 1977. Tariffs, Foreign Capital and Immiserizing Growth. *Journal of International Economics* 7: 317–22.

Bruno, M. 1994. Short-Run Macroeconomic Management and Long-Run Economic Growth. Mimeo. World Bank.

Campbell, J. Y., and A. Deaton. 1989. Why Is Consumption So Smooth? *Review of Economic Studies* 56: 357–74.

Carroll, C., and D. Weil. 1994. Saving and Growth: A Reinterpretation. *Carnegie-Rochester Conference Series on Public Policy* 40: 133–92.

Carroll, C., J. Overland, and D. Weil. 1994. Saving and Growth with Habit Formation. Finance and Economic Discussion Series. Federal Reserve Board. Washington, D.C.

Carroll, C., and L. Summers. 1991. Consumption Growth Parallels Income Growth: Some New Evidence. In *National Saving and Economic Performance,* edited by B. D. Douglas and J. B. Shoven. Chicago: University of Chicago Press and NBER.

Chakravarty, S. 1993. *Selected Economic Writings.* Oxford: Oxford University Press.

Chenery, H. B., and W. Strout. 1966. Foreign Assistance and Economic Development. *American Economic Review* 66: 679–733.

Chenery, H. B., and P. Eckstein. 1970. Development Alternatives for Latin America. *Journal of Political Economy* 78 (4): 966–1006.

Chenery, H. B., and M. Syrquin. 1975. *Patterns of Development: 1950–1970.* Oxford: Oxford University Press.

Cifuentes, R., and S. Valdés-Prieto. 1996. Pension Reforms in the Presence of Credit Constraints. In *Pensions: Funding, Privatization, and Macroeconomic Policy,* edited by S. Valdés-Prieto. Cambridge: Cambridge University Press.

Cole, H. L., G. J. Mailath, and A. Postlewaite. 1992. Social Norms, Savings Behavior, and Growth. *Journal of Political Economy* 100 (6): 1092–1125.

Collins, S. M. 1991. Saving Behavior in Ten Developing Countries. In *National Saving and Economic Performance,* edited by B. D. Douglas and J. B. Shoven. Chicago: University of Chicago Press and NBER.

Corbo, V., and K. Schmidt-Hebbel. 1991. Public Policies and Saving in Developing Countries. *Journal of Development Economics* 36: 89–115.

Corbo, V., and P. Rojas. 1993. Investment, Macroeconomic Stability and Growth: The Latin American Experience. *Análisis Económico* 8.

Corsetti, G., and K. Schmidt-Hebbel. 1996. Pension Reform and Growth. In *Pensions: Funding, Privatization, and Macroeconomic Policy,* edited by S. Valdés-Prieto. Cambridge: Cambridge University Press.

Deaton, A. 1989. Saving in Developing Countries: Theory and Review. *Proceedings of the World Bank Annual Conference on Development Economics.* Washington, D.C.: World Bank.

Deaton, A. 1991. Saving and Liquidity Constraints. *Econometrica* 59: 1221–48.

Deaton, A. 1992. *Understanding Consumption.* Oxford: Oxford University Press.

Deaton, A. 1995. Growth and Saving: What Do We Know, What Do We Need to Know, and What Might We Learn. Manuscript. World Bank. March.

De Long, J., and L. Summers. 1991. Equipment Investment and Economic Growth. *Quarterly Journal of Economics* 106: 445–502.

De Long, J., and L. Summers. 1993. How Strongly Do Developing Economies Benefit from Equipment Investment? *Journal of Monetary Economics* 32: 395–416.

Denison, E. 1962. *Sources of Economic Growth in the United States and the Alternatives Before Us.* New York: Committee for Economic Development.

Denison, E. 1967. *Why Growth Rates Differ.* Washington, D.C.: The Brookings Institution.

De Gregorio, J. 1992. Economic Growth in Latin America. *Journal of Development Economics* 39.

Dixit, A., and R. Pindyck. 1994. *Investment under Uncertainty.* Princeton: Princeton University Press

Dooley, M., J. Frankel, and D. Mathieson. 1987. International Capital Mobility: What Do Saving-Investment Correlations Tell Us? *IMF Staff Papers* 34: 503–30.

Dornbusch, R. 1991a. Comment. In *National Saving and Economic Performance,* edited by B. Douglas Bernheim and J. Shoven. Chicago: University of Chicago Press.

Dornbusch, R. 1991b. Policies to Move from Stabilization to Growth. *Proceedings of the World Bank Annual Conference on Development Economics.* Washington, D.C.: World Bank.

Dornbusch, R., and S. Edwards, eds. 1991. *The Macroeconomics of Populism in Latin America.* Chicago: University of Chicago Press.

Easterly, W. 1993. How Much Do Distortions Affect Growth? *Journal of Monetary Economics* 32.

Easterly, W., and S. Fischer. 1994. The Soviet Economic Decline: Historical and Republican Data. World Bank Policy Research Working Paper 1284.

Easterly, W., and S. Rebelo. 1993. Fiscal Policy and Economic Growth: an Empirical Investigation. *Journal of Monetary Economics* 32: 417–58.

Easterly, W., C. A. Rodriguez, and K. Schmidt-Hebbel, eds. 1994. *Public Sector Deficits and Macroeconomic Performance.* New York: Oxford University Press/World Bank.

Edwards, S. 1994. Why Are Latin America's Saving Rates So Low?" Manuscript presented at the Conference on Growth Prospects in Latin America, Bogotá (Colombia), June.

Engen, E. M., W. G. Gale, and J. K. Scholz. 1994. Do Savings Incentives Work? *Brookings Papers on Economic Activity* 1: 85–151.

Feldstein, M. 1974. Social Security, Induced Retirement and Aggregate Capital Accumulation. *Journal of Political Economy* 82 (5): 905–26.

Feldstein, M. 1994. Tax Policy and International Capital Flows. *Weltwirtschaftliches Archiv.*

Feldstein, M. 1995. Social Security and Saving: New Time Series Evidence. NBER Working Paper 5054.

Feldstein, M., and P. Bacchetta. 1991. National Saving and International Investment. In *National Saving and Economic Performance,* edited by B. Douglas Bernheim and J. Shoven. Chicago: University of Chicago Press.

Feldstein, M., and C. Horioka. 1980. Domestic Saving and international Capital Flows. *Economic Journal* 90: 314–29.

Fershtman, C., and Y. Weiss. 1993. Social Status, Culture and Economic Performance. *The Economic Journal* 103: 946–59.

Flavin, M. 1981. The Adjustment of Consumption to Changing Expectations about Future Income. *Journal of Political Economy* 89: 974–1009.

Frankel, J. 1992. Measuring International Capital Mobility: A Review. *American Economic Review* 82 (2): 197–202.

Frankel, J. 1993. Quantifying International Capital Mobility in the 1980s. In *On Exchange Rates*. Cambridge, MA: MIT Press.

Fry, M. 1978. Money and Capital or Financial Deepening in Economic Development. *Journal of Money, Credit, and Banking* 10 (4): 464–75.

Fry, M. 1980. Saving, Investment, Growth, and the Cost of Financial Repression. *World Development* 8 (4): 317–27.

Fry, M. J. 1988. *Money, Interest, and Banking in Economic Development.* Baltimore: Johns Hopkins University Press.

Gerschenkron, A. 1962. *Economic Backwardness in a Historical Perspective.* Cambridge, MA: Harvard University Press.

Gersovitz, M. 1988. Saving and Development. In *Handbook of Development Economics,* edited by H. Chenery and T. N. Srinivasan. North Holland.

Giovannini, A. 1983. The Interest Elasticity of Savings in Developing Countries: The Existing Evidence. *World Development* 11(7): 601–07.

Giovannini, A. 1985. Saving and the Real Interest Rate in LDCs. *Journal of Development Economics* 18.

Global Coalition on Africa. 1993. Annual Report. Manuscript. November.

Griffin, K. 1970. Foreign Capital, Domestic Savings, and Economic Development. *Bulletin of the Oxford Institute of Economics and Statistics* 32: 99–112.

Griffin, K. 1971. Reply. *Bulletin of the Oxford Institute of Economics and Statistics* 33: 156–61.

Gupta, K. L. 1987. Aggregate Savings, Financial Intermediation, and Interest Rate. *Review of Economics and Statistics* 69 (2): 303–11.

Hall, R. E., and F. S. Mishkin. 1982. The Sensitivity of Consumption to Transitory Income: Estimates from Panel Data on Households. *Econometrica* 50: 461–81.

Haque, N. V., and P. Montiel. 1989. Consumption in Developing Countries: Tests for Liquidity Constraints and Finite Horizons. *Review of Economics and Statistics* 71 (3): 408–15.

Hayashi, F. 1985. Tests for Liquidity Constraints: A Critical Survey NBER Working Paper 1720.

Hubbard, R. G., and K. L. Judd. 1986. Liquidity Constraints, Fiscal Policy, and Consumption. *Brookings Papers on Economic Activity* 1: 1–50.

Jappelli, T., and M. Pagano. 1994. Saving, Growth, and Liquidity Constraints. *Quarterly Journal of Economics* 83–109.

Johnson, H. 1967. The Possibility of Income Losses from Increased Efficiency or Factor Accumulation in the Presence of Tariffs. *Economic Journal* 77: 151–54.

Kaldor, N. 1957. A Model of Economic Growth. *Economic Journal* 67: 591–624.

Keynes, J. M. 1936. *The General Theory of Employment, Interest, and Money.* London: Macmillan.

King, R., and R. Levine. 1993. Finance, Entrepreneurship, and Growth. *Journal of Monetary Economics* 32: 513–42.

King, R., and R. Levine. 1994. Capital Fundamentalism, Economic Development, and Economic Growth. Mimeo. World Bank.

Knack, S., and P. Keefer. 1994. Institutions and Economic Performance. Mimeo. University of Maryland.

Kuznets, S. 1973. *Population, Capital, and Growth: Selected Essays.* New York: Norton.

Lefort, F., and A. Solimano. 1993. Economic Growth after Market Based Reforms in Latin America: The Cases of Chile and Mexico. Manuscript. World Bank.

Leiderman, L., and M. Blejer. 1988. Modeling and Testing Ricardian Equivalence: A Survey. *IMF Staff Papers* 35 (1).

Levine, R., and D. Renelt. 1992. A Sensitivity Analysis of Cross-Country Growth Regressions. *American Economic Review* 82: 942–63.

Levy, V. 1988. Aid and Growth in Sub-Saharan Africa: The Recent Experience. *European Economic Review* 32(9): 1777–95.

Mankiw, G., D. Romer, and D. Weil. 1992. A Contribution to the Empirics of Economic Growth. *Quarterly Journal of Economics* 107: 407–38.

Marglin, S., and J. Schor. 1990. *The Golden Age of Capitalism: Reinterpreting the Postwar Experience.* Oxford: Clarendon Press.

Mason, A. 1987. National Saving Rates and Population Growth: A New Model and New Evidence. In *Population Growth and Economic Development: Issues and Evidence,* edited by D. G. Johnson and R. Lee. Madison, WI: University of Wisconsin Press.

Mason, A. 1988. Saving, Economic Growth and Demographic Change. *Population and Development Review* 14 (1): 113–44.

Mauro, P. 1993. Political Instability, Growth, and Investment. Manuscript. Harvard University.

Modigliani, F. 1990. Recent Declines in the Saving Rate: A Life Cycle Perspective. Frisch Lecture, Sixth World Congress of the Econometric Society, Barcelona (August).

Montiel, P. 1993. Capital Mobility in Developing Countries: Some Measurement Issues and Empirical Estimates. World Bank Policy Research Working Paper 1103.

Murphy, R. 1984. Capital Mobility and the Relationship Between Saving and Investment in OECD Countries. *Journal of International Money and Finance* 3: 327–42.

Obstfeld, M. 1986. Capital Mobility in the World Economy: Theory and Measurement. *Carnegie-Rochester Conference Series on Public Policy.* Amsterdam: North-Holland.

Obstfeld, M. 1994. International Capital Mobility in the 1990s. Board of Governors of the Federal Reserve System International Finance Discussion Paper 472.

Papanek, G. F. 1972. The Effect of Aid and Other Resource Transfers on Savings and Growth in Less Developed Countries. *Economic Journal* 82: 934–51.

Papanek, G. F. 1973. Aid, Foreign Private Investment, Savings, and Growth in Less Developed Countries. *Political Economy* 81(1): 121–30.

Persson, T., and G. Tabellini. 1992. Growth, Distribution, and Policies. In *Political Economy, Growth, and Business Cycles,* edited by A. Cukierman, Z. Hercowitz, and L. Leiderman. Cambridge, MA: MIT Press.

Pindyck, R., and A. Solimano. 1993. Economic Instability and Aggregate Investment. *NBER Macroeconomics Annual.*

Reynoso, A. 1988. Financial Liberalization and the Interest Elasticity of Savings in Developing Countries. Ph.D. diss. Massachusetts Institute of Technology.

Robinson, J. 1962. *Essays in the Theory of Economic Growth.* London: Macmillan.

Romer, P. 1986. Increasing Returns and Long-Run Growth. *Journal of Political Economy* 4, 1002–1017.

Romer, P. 1987. Crazy Explanations for the Productivity Slowdown. *NBER Macroeconomics Annual:* 163–202.

Romer, P. 1993. Idea Gaps and Object Gaps in Economic Development. *Journal of Monetary Economics* 32: 543–74.

Rostow, W. 1958. *The Stages of Economic Growth.* London: Macmillan.

Schmidt-Hebbel, K. 1987. Foreign Shocks and Macroeconomic Adjustment in Small Open Economies. Ph.D. diss. Massachusetts Institute of Technology.

Schmidt-Hebbel, K., and L. Servén . 1995. Saving and Income Distribution. Unpublished manuscript. World Bank.

Schmidt-Hebbel, K., S. Webb, and G. Corsetti. 1992. Household Saving in Developing Countries: First Cross-Country Evidence. *World Bank Economic Review* 6(3): 529–47.

Schumpeter, J. 1934. *The Theory of Economic Development.* Cambridge, MA: Harvard University Press.

Seater, J. J. 1993. Ricardian Equivalence. *Journal of Economic Literature* 31 (1): 142–90.

Servén , L., and A. Solimano. 1993. *Striving for Growth after Adjustment: The Role of Capital Formation.* Washington, D.C.: World Bank.

Solimano, A. 1992. Understanding the Investment Cycle in Adjustment Programs: Evidence from Reforming Economies. World Bank Working Paper 921.

Solimano, A. 1993. How Private Investment Reacts to Changing Macroeconomic Conditions: The Case of Chile in the 1980s. In *Reviving Private Investment in Developing Countries,* edited by A. Chhibber et al. North Holland.

Solimano, A., O. Sunkel, and M. Blejer, eds. 1994. *Rebuilding Capitalism*. Ann Arbor: University of Michigan Press.

Solow, R. 1956. A Contribution to the Theory of Economic Growth. *Quarterly Journal of Economics* 70: 65–94.

Solow, R. 1957. Technical Change and the Aggregate Production Function. *Review of Economics and Statistics* 39: 312–20.

Summers, L. 1988. Tax Policy and International Competitiveness. In *International Aspects of Fiscal Policies,* edited by J. Frenkel. Chicago: University of Chicago Press.

Taylor, A. 1994. Domestic Saving and International Capital Flows Reconsidered. NBER Working Paper 4892.

Tesar, L. 1991. Savings, Investment, and International Capital Flows. *Journal of International Economics* 31: 55–78.

Valdés-Prieto, S., and R. Cifuentes. 1993. Credit Constraints and Pensions. Manuscript, Catholic University of Chile, Santiago.

Weisskopf, T. E. 1972. The Impact of Foreign Capital Inflows on Domestic Savings in Underdeveloped Countries. *Journal of International Economics* 2: 341–78.

White, H. 1992a. The Macroeconomic Impact of Development Aid: A Critical Survey. *Journal of Development Studies* 28: 163–240.

White, H. 1992b. What Do We Know about Aid's Macroeconomic Impact? *Journal of International Development* 4: 121–37.

White, H. 1994. The Countrywide Effects of Aid: Report for the World Bank. Manuscript. Institute of Social Studies. The Hague.

World Bank. 1993. *The East Asian Miracle: Economic Growth and Public Policy.* Oxford: Oxford University Press.

World Bank. 1994a. *Adjustment in Africa: Reform, Results, and the Road Ahead.* Oxford: Oxford University Press.

World Bank. 1994b. *Averting the Old Age Crisis: Policies to Protect the Old and Promote Growth.* Oxford: Oxford University Press.

Yotopoulos, P., and J. Nugent. 1976. *Economics of Development: Empirical Investigations.* New York: Harper and Row.

Young, A. 1928. Increasing Returns and Economic Progress. *Economic Journal* 38: 527–42.

Young, A. 1994. Lessons from the East-Asian NICs: A Contrarian View. NBER Working Paper 4482.

Zou, Heng-fu. 1993a. The Spirit of Capitalism and Savings Behavior. Manuscript. World Bank.

Zou, Heng-fu. 1993b. The Capitalist-Spirit Approach to Growth: A Perspective from the History of Economic Analysis. Manuscript. World Bank.

CHAPTER 5

A Strategic Policy Approach to Government Intervention in Late Industrialization

Alice H. Amsden

Interpreting Successful Country "Models": Strategic Turning Points and Trade-offs

Given the impressive postwar development of some late-industrializing countries, their experiences are of interest to other countries still remaining poor. A specific object of curiosity—and contention—is the role played in the industrial transformation of successful cases by government. Contemplating the transfer of a specific country model necessitates moving logically from the very concrete to the more general, or from the details of a specific country experience to a level of generalization sufficient to create common points of comparative reference for many cases. Economists, however, are accustomed to reasoning deductively, starting with (and sometimes sticking with) highly abstract models.

This chapter attempts to work from the ground up to capture the experiences of successful latecomers while at the same time to suggest an analytical framework to process the information of successful cases for easier absorption by still-later industrializers. It tries to apply "strategy" to economic development theory as it relates to industrialization, analogous to the linkage of strategy with organization theory pioneered by Alfred Chandler (1962). The methodology of understanding the strategic decisions that governments in fast-growing countries have taken at key switching points in industrialization, with a given stock of competitive assets, is designed to enlighten aspiring emulators on what strategic policy decisions they themselves should take, given their own specific bundle of competitive assets, at comparable switching points.

Moving beyond a "Market Failure" Foundation

Deductive reasoning that starts from the abstract has tended to be marked even among innovative economists analyzing the developmental role of the state. Typically government intervention in markets, in the form of tariff protection, preferential credit allocation, or export subsidization, is analyzed to fit established ideas about market failures. To begin, the cause of underdevelopment itself is attributed to pervasive market imperfections. Then, government initiatives to reverse underdevelopment and spur industrialization are viewed in terms of overcoming market imperfections. A market failure approach is deductive because it observes governments intervening and then, ex post, interprets their behavior in a way that conforms with preexisting theories about how markets work (or fail to work).

This ex post approach, however, cannot explain very well why the intensity or nature of government intervention has differed even among successful late industrializers (for instance, Hong Kong versus Taiwan, or Thailand versus South Korea). This is because it does not make clear, empirically or logically, why market imperfections should differ across countries, all of which are underdeveloped, to a degree sufficient to explain significant variations in government's role. What, for instance, were the learning disabilities or information failures that were so much greater in Taiwan compared with Hong Kong (both of which benefited from the inputs of, say, Chinese overseas traders) that they created strikingly different patterns of government intervention? An inability to provide a cogent answer to such a question leaves emulating countries ignorant about which particular successful country to follow—in this example, Hong Kong or Taiwan. Moreover, the market failure approach, as now constituted, cannot pinpoint or prioritize the actual market imperfections that drove governments to intervene. Were they informational, for instance, or did they relate to price rigidities that prevented markets from clearing? If both, which was decisive? At minimum, a concrete knowledge of the priorities that drove successful governments to intervene is necessary for emulators to formulate their own sensible government policies.

On the other hand, a market failure framework for understanding government's role has many virtues, particularly when amended to incorporate imperfections related to information, learning, and coordination (see Stiglitz 1989). Therefore we take this framework as the starting point of this chapter. Then we attempt to reduce the deductiveness of the market failure approach by allowing actual historical conditions to explain the reasons behind the degree and nature of government intervention in fast-growing postwar late industrializers. By standardizing the nature of strategic turning points, and comparing the behavior of successful and unsuccessful cases, a theory of late industrialization begins to emerge to the extent that one can predict the developmental consequences of a government's strategic decisions about market imperfections given the bundle of competitive assets at its disposal.

At critical turning points in industrialization, governments face choices or trade-offs about how to create international competitiveness (defined as competing either in export markets or at home against imports). These turning points are generic and confront any industrializer, but depend specifically on time and place. We argue, however, that the postwar trade-offs that successful late industrializers faced, and that continue to confront aspiring latecomers, are similar enough even in their specifics to allow the lessons of successful countries to be digested at present by less successful ones. As discussed below, all "late" industrializers confront the same basic trade-offs because all operate within the same broad paradigm (Hikino and Amsden 1994).

The first turning point typically involves the behavior of an "allocatively correct," labor-intensive "leading sector" with potentially enough impact on the rest of the economy (owing to industry linkages or the accumulation of capital and foreign exchange) to start a growth momentum. A second turning point—for those countries that successfully navigate the first—involves a diversification of industrial activity. A third turning point, particularly for countries whose diversification path was problematic, involves a restructuring of existing industries and leading firms. Yet another turning point characterizes the attempt to move into industries where the opportunities to buy international technology are limited.

Turning points need not be sharp, in the sense of Walt Rostow's "take-off"; the creation of labor-intensive industry in late industrialization was, in fact, fairly drawn out in most countries (particularly in Latin America and South Asia, but even in East Asia, including Japan). Turning points may also differ in the number of industries they involve and hence in their partial or general analytical scope. Restructuring (for instance, as in Chile and China in the 1970s/1980s) tends to be economywide, whereas the first steps to industrialize or to move into science-based activity tend to be restricted to a limited number of sectors. Turning points must simply represent significant changes in the composition of output and employment, or in the way output is produced and employees are engaged.

We restrict our examination to one strategic decision and trade-off, which we illustrate with three successful countries: We consider the initial step toward industrial development, taking successes to be South Korea and Taiwan compared with Hong Kong (in the 1950s and 1960s).

Governments make decisions about which policy direction to follow that are "strategic" in the sense that they involve a "plan" and a "system" to carry out that plan. Beyond this, there are many meanings of the term "strategic." According to Von Neumann and Morgenstern (1947), a strategy is a series of actions that an agent chooses according to a particular situation. For Chandler (1962), strategy determines the long-term goals of the firm and the adoption of policies, along with an allocation of resources necessary to execute these goals. In the usage of Krugman (1986) and Brander (1986), "strategic trade theory" refers to any unorthodox theory of trade that attributes special importance, such as technological externalities, to particular industries such that special government policies may be warranted. In what follows, we more or less adopt the Chandlerian view of firm strategy and apply it to governments insofar as we are interested in long-term goals (related to industrialization) and the possible resources (subsidies or a social safety net, for instance) necessary to attain them. Long-term strategic decisions may involve "path dependence" such that to undo a decision may be difficult, and future strategic plans may be constrained by past ones. The Von Neumann and Morgenstern usage of "strategy" is inappropriate insofar as it relates to game theory, whereas the focus of this chapter is on the actions of government as a single actor, uninvolved in duopolistic or more complex games. Game theory may be relevant when it comes to analyzing the implementation of a strategic decision, but here we do not discuss implementation (an implication of which is noted in the conclusion).

Historically Incorrect Assumptions

The strategic policy approach we present differs from an orthodox free market approach in certain fundamentals. The picture of economic development envisioned in the free market approach is one of no trade-offs and no strategic choices for governments to make. All governments have to do to create international competitiveness is let markets find their own clearing prices and allow firms to follow their comparative advantage. This free market approach assumes one correct path and promises economic development to be socially costless. At most, income distribution may change (as Simon Kuznets observed) due to upward social mobility: as labor migrates from agriculture to industry, income inequality tends to rise. In the strategic approach, there are painful trade-offs because the assumptions underlying the free market theory are not upheld in practice (as argued further in the next section). The Heckscher-Ohlin-Samuelson model assumes that firms in the same industry in different countries enjoy equal levels of productivity such that a low-wage country is guaranteed international competitiveness in a labor-intensive industry. In fact, whether in the nineteenth or twentieth century, productivity has varied widely among firms in the same industry in different countries. Usually less productive countries have had to create international competitiveness either by "temporarily" lowering real wage rates, or by engaging in what is sometimes a lengthy process of raising productivity, possibly from the most aggregate level (involving infrastructure investment) down to the level of the firm.[1] Alternatively, in traditional Ricardian models devaluation is relied upon to create international competitiveness, also without any fall in real wages or rise in unemployment; income is merely redistributed from producers of nontradeables to producers of tradeables. Yet both in theory and in practice, exchange rate devaluations have been found to provoke macroeconomic contractions and large real wage declines.[2] Without the magic of radical new technology (or, as noted below, without flawless technology transfer to equalize international productivity differences), industrialization is not "free."

The nature of the choices or trade-offs that are necessary to create international competitiveness is thus key to understanding the postwar role of government in catching up. To create international competitiveness in a leading sector, latecomer governments typically have confronted the strategic decision of whether to cut real wages, and thereby reduce costs sufficiently to compete in world markets, or to lower costs (and possibly increase quality) by raising productivity. Due to capital market imperfections, the choice of raising productivity has invariably involved government subsidization of production. Governments have had to cover the interim costs of learning, with subsidies to boost profits typically involving tariff protection and preferential credit allocation, even in successful countries that have emphasized export growth (and have offered business additional export subsidies). A historical overview of trade-offs is the focus of the next section.

The more "competitive assets" a country possesses at the time it takes a strategic industrialization decision, the less need for its government to intervene.[3] A competitive asset is defined as something that raises productivity, measured as nominal value added per worker (Lary 1968). It is anything that contributes to the international competitiveness of raw labor power—for instance, natural resources, physical capital, and technological capabilities in the form of labor skills and managerial expertise. As we shall see, competitive assets also include monopolistic arrangements, such as export cartels, that allow firms to raise prices with the effect of raising value added per worker.

Proprietary technology in the form of new products and processes also raises value added per worker, but we define "late" industrialization as a process that proceeds in the absence of brand-new technology; late industrializers must borrow foreign technology that has already been commercialized. The absence of new technology, which was the hallmark of leading enterprises in the First and Second Industrial Revolutions, produces a convergence or homogenization in the competitive problems of all latecomers and provides a major reason why governments have, in general, intervened more in late industrialization than in previous industrial revolutions.

Macroeconomic variables condition the real policy choices governments face at any given moment, yet this chapter concerns decisions of government related only to industrial transformation, not macroeconomic management. We thus understate the importance of macroeconomic variables, although over relatively long stretches of time such variables cannot continuously dominate strategic industrial decisions, and therefore cannot be held responsible for them. Ultimately our focus is on how governments involve themselves in productivity growth at the firm level, where technology is specific rather than general and markets cannot instantaneously provide the know-how that firms need to compete internationally.[4]

Starting to Industrialize: The Trade-off between Lowering Real Wages and Subsidizing Learning

The inability of firms to compete internationally even in an "allocatively correct" labor-intensive sector is illustrated in figure 5.1, which assumes only one factor of production (labor). A competitive international incumbent, *A*, operates with higher wages than a latecomer, *B*, but also higher productivity, L/Y (for simplicity all values are expressed in a common currency). The relative wage and productivity differentials are such that unit labor costs, W/Y, are higher for the latecomer (W/Y_1) than for the incumbent (W/Y_0). This implies two possible market failures in country *B* (assuming no market failures in country *A*): international technology transfer to country *B* in the specific leading sector in question was imperfect and resulted in productivity variations compared with country *A*; wages in *B* are not sufficiently low because labor market imperfections or exchange rate rigidities (ignored in figure 5.1) prevent wages from falling further.

Figure 5.1 captures more or less the competitive plight of the South

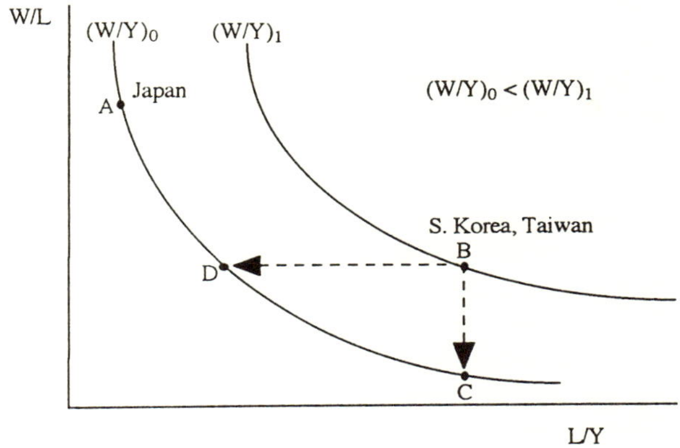

L = labor; Y = output; W/L = real wage per worker; W/Y = unit labor cost. Unit labor cost loci are rectangular hyperbolas, the product of the real wage and labor-output ratio. They, therefore, are constants. The same currency is assumed for all countries.

Figure 5.1 Subsidizing learning or cutting real wages

Korean and Taiwan "textile industries" (defined as spinning and weaving) in the 1950s, *B*, in relation to the Japanese textile industry, *A*, the world's most competitive exporter of textiles at the time. For want of data and volatility in Korea's and Taiwan's exchange rate, it is not possible to compare systematically either wages or productivity levels in these three countries in the 1950s. But clearly productivity in Korea and Taiwan was far below the Japanese level.[5] This was in spite of a long learning period for textile manufacture that began during the colonial period, and extensive technology transfers provided by textile machinery sellers beginning in the 1950s.[6] Machinery makers such as Platt (U.K.), Howa and Enshu (Japan), and Picarol (Belgium) sent their agents to Korea and Taiwan to set up new equipment and to troubleshoot erratic problems. In effect, technology transfer in the textile industry was "turnkey": foreigners initially all but ran the major mills, yet productivity was still relatively low.

Value added per worker can vary internationally due to two principal causes: differences in the vintage of equipment in use; or differences in production and operations management practices (including labor relations). The latter were largely at play in the Indian textile industry's rout by the Japanese textile industry in the nineteenth century (see Wolcott 1993 for a summary). Evidence from Korean textile companies in the 1970s–1980s also attests to the importance of production-related skills. In one company, for example, labor productivity related to ring spinning rose by a factor of 1.5 over a decade despite the fact that this technology was quite old and the addition of new capacity was negligible (Amsden 1989, pp. 252–53). Existing productivity differences with Japan were attributed by this company to technical skills related to: *(a)* maintenance and repair; *(b)* devising optimal machinery-operating conditions for the manufacture of different types of yarns or fabrics; and *(c)* mixing different types of fibers to achieve optimal blend. While equipment differences were probably also important in Japan's productivity edge (although Japan most likely had *older* equipment than Korea or Taiwan), so too were production differences, and these took time to learn and improve, especially when new vintages of machinery were introduced.[7]

As for wages in the textile industry in the 1950s and early 1960s, they were low by the standards of other manufacturing industries in Korea, Taiwan, and Japan; in all three countries the preponderance of the workforce in textiles was female. Given Japan's "low" wages during this period of surplus labor, coupled with its relatively high rate of productivity, Korean textile companies report that they had higher unit labor costs than Japan. Additionally, nonlabor costs were almost certainly strongly in Japan's favor: interest rates were higher in Korea and Taiwan than in Japan, and Japan's marketing (under the aegis of general trading companies) benefited from bulk raw material purchases. Assuming such cost differences, without government support the textile industries of Korea and Taiwan would have been overcome by Japanese competition even in their home markets.

In the heyday of foreign aid to Korea and Taiwan, the American government targeted many of its subsidized nonproject loans to the textile industry (Hong 1979).[8] For their part, the Korean and Taiwan governments were sensitive to the textile industry's needs both because of its importance in the economy and because of its politically powerful industrywide association (for Korea, see J. Kim 1966). Textile manufacturers were given protection from foreign imports as well as from Japanese foreign investors interested in establishing production in former colonies (for Korea, see Y.B. Kim 1980). When overcapacity emerged in the late 1950s and early 1960s, an array of export incentives was made available to textile manufacturers as well as to other industries (Frank, Kim, and Westphal 1975; B.L. Chen 1994; Liang and Liang 1982).

The Korean and Taiwan governments adopted policies in the 1950s and early 1960s whose effect was to lower (or freeze) real wages. Workers' demands were checked by martial law and repression of trade union activity and real wages were depressed by recurrent exchange rate devaluations. For instance, the Korean won was devalued by 50 percent in 1961, from 65 to 100 won for the dollar in January and from 100 to 130 won for the dollar in February (Frank, Kim, and Westphal 1975). The result, according to the Economic Planning Board, was inflationary:

> Many industries were hard hit by the revisions in the exchange rate, as well as overproduction capacity. This can be illustrated by observing the cotton textile industry, representing the largest portion of the entire industry, which is 99% dependent upon industry imports for the necessary supply of raw cotton. The price index of raw cotton increased by 11.5% in January of 1961 from the level of December 1960; reached 287.9 in February 1961, a 29.5% increase over the level of the previous month; and pressed even higher to 292.0 in March and to 299.8 in April . . . These increases in the price of raw cotton affected in turn the production costs of all cotton products and the price of cotton yarn (EPB 1962, p. 49, as cited in Amsden 1989, pp. 65–66)

A consequence of inflation was real wage decreases. The rate of growth of price-deflated earnings was 0 percent in 1962, −5.2 percent in 1963, and −5.8 percent in 1964 (Frank, Kim, and Westphal 1975, p. 222). Yet despite these measures (or because of them), the economy continued to stagnate rather than become internationally competitive.

Government policy only became unambiguously committed to increasing international competitiveness in textiles and other industries following the introduction of new supports to business in tandem with another devaluation. The government in Korea around 1965 (much as in Taiwan slightly earlier) substantially raised and expanded its export incentives (Frank, Kim, and Westphal 1975) and tightened and improved its export targeting system (Rhee, Ross-Larson, and Pursell 1984). It also extended the size and scope of its subsidized loans to selected industries (firms) and further *raised* tariff protection. Between 1963–67 and 1968–72, average tariff rates in Korea rose for yarns from 30 to 64 percent, for certain fabrics from 75 to 98 percent, and for other types of fabrics from 49 to 89 percent (Hong 1979, Table B16).

Along with greater profit-making opportunities, an export targeting system that began to tie access to long-term preferential credit to export performance, and rapidly rising real wages in Japan (due to the end of surplus labor [Minami 1973]), Korea's and Taiwan's exports soared and productivity rose. Yarns (kg) produced per employee in Korea increased from 20.62 in 1965 to 30.95 in 1971; fabrics (m) per employee rose in the same time period from 87.1 to 108.8 (Y.B. Kim 1980, p. 231). In terms of figure 5.1, after 1965 government strategic policies to increase international competitiveness became strongly committed to moving from *B* to a point like *D* rather than *C*.[9] Symbolically, in 1967 the Korean government became first among late industrializers to establish a ministry of science and technology, and the Taiwan government established something comparable to further productivity growth not long after. It can be said therefore that the market imperfections that both governments responded to most vigorously concerned information and learning.

Hong Kong's Competitive Assets

We may now also appreciate why it was possible for the Hong Kong government to intervene so much less than the Korean or Taiwan governments. When Taiwan and South Korea were in political disarray due to war in the 1950s, and investing in cotton textiles (with high sunk costs) to meet domestic demand (at a time when most people made their own clothes or had them made by tailors), Hong Kong was establishing its clothing industry. Thus Hong Kong's leading sector was not cotton spinning and weaving but rather apparel manufacture. As table 5.1 indi-

TABLE 5.1 Cotton Textiles (Spinning and Weaving) and Apparel Sectoral Share (%) in Exports and Employment Ratio, South Korea and Hong Kong[a]

	Textiles (A)			Clothing (B)		
South Korea						
Exports (Output)[b] (%)	15.1 (1963)	20.6 (1967)	17.1 (1971)	5.3 (1963)	18.5 (1967)	28.5 (1971)
Exports (Value Added)[c] (%)	23.7 (1960)	25.2 (1966)	26.4 (1970)	1.6 (1960)	12.5 (1966)	16.7 (1970)
Employment (A/B)[d]	17.3 (1955)	5.0 (1960)	3.1 (1966)	2.5 (1973)		
Hong Kong						
Exports (Output)[e] (%)	23.0 (1961)	14.0 (1967)	10.0 (1971)	29.0 (1961)	35.0 (1967)	40.0 (1971)
Employment (A/B)[f]	1.3 (1955)	1.6 (1962)	1.8 (1967)	1.5 (1971)		

[a]Years in parentheses.
[b]Park 1980, Table 16.
[c]Hong 1979, Table 8.7.
[d]Hong 1979, Table 8.13.
[e]Ho and Lin 1991, Table 6.6.
[f]Lin, Mok, and Ho 1980, Table 4.8.

cates, as early as 1961 exports of clothing from Hong Kong exceeded exports of textiles, whereas the reverse was true of Korea. The manufacture of apparel is considerably more labor intensive than the manufacture of textiles. Therefore international competitiveness depends relatively more on low wages in apparel production than in upstream textile manufacture, whose total unit cost determination is more sensitive to productivity and nonwage costs. Total labor requirements per dollar of output were roughly twice as great in clothing than in textiles in Hong Kong, while total capital requirements per dollar of output were approximately three times as great in textiles than in clothing (the data are for 1970, as discussed in Lin, Mok, and Ho 1980, Table 6.7; factor-intensity estimates for Korea may be found in Hong 1979).

Still, given our argument, it merits explaining how Hong Kong was able to export *any* textiles in the 1950s and 1960s without government support. The answer lies in Commonwealth preferences, which provided Hong Kong with a market protected from Japanese competition. In 1961, the West European market accounted for a greater share of Hong Kong's exports than the North American market (until the 1990s Korea's and Taiwan's exports to Europe were relatively inconsequential). What is more, because of its "first-mover" advantage in both clothing and textiles, "Hong Kong possessed larger export quotas than Taiwan and South Korea, and especially other LDCs" (Ho and Lin 1991, p. 277). Ironically, one of Hong Kong's major "competitive assets" derived precisely from a type of international cartel arrangement that Hong Kong's economic philosophy deplored. Given these quotas, and Hong Kong's extreme difference in population size compared with Korea or Taiwan, the share of clothing in its total exports and aggregate economy could be much greater. By virtue of its small size as well as trade orientation, Hong Kong's export concentration appears to have been extreme, and rose rather than fell as per capita income increased in the period 1961–73 (Lin, Mok, and Ho 1980).

Finally, Hong Kong was able to buttress its international competitiveness in manufacturing with virtually no government assistance (save the provision of mass subsidized housing) because it could regulate a flow of cheap labor from mainland China. By contrast, Korea and Taiwan maintained tight immigration policies. Thus while labor markets were "perfect" in all three countries (in the sense of being free from trade union pressures), they were more "perfect" in Hong Kong owing to immigration.[10] As late as 1987, clothing accounted for roughly one-third of Hong Kong's domestically manufactured exports and manufacturing employment, whereas the textile industries of Korea and Taiwan were in decline due to rising domestic wages and low-wage foreign competition (Ho and Lin 1991).[11]

Caveat Emulator

We may now provisionally conclude our comparison of government intervention in Korea and Taiwan relative to Hong Kong for the benefit of a hypothetical emulator, one still trying to create an efficient industrial nucleus in (or after) the 1990s.

For many such aspirants, the 1980s was comparable to the early 1960s in Korea and Taiwan insofar as endogenous policies and external circumstances drove key prices—including exchange rates, wages, and the prices of tradeables—closer to market-determined levels. In some countries real wages declined by as much as 50 percent (Amsden and Van der Hoeven, forthcoming). According to free market theory, a reduction in market "distortions" and the pursuit of comparative advantage should put the lowest-wage, most unindustrialized emulators in a strong position to compete internationally *without* subsidies. By contrast, our own analysis leads us to believe that a laissez-faire strategy is likely to succeed only to the extent that emulators have competitive assets comparable to those of Hong Kong in the 1950s.

In fact, at the end of the 1980s (the most recent data cover these years), almost ten years after many of the least industrialized countries had cut their real wages, devalued their exchange rates, and liberalized other prices, the preponderance of them still did not exhibit growth rates remotely comparable to those of Hong Kong in the 1950s. Clothing exports (standard industrial trade classification 84) continued to be dominated by *developed* countries (roughly 45 percent of the total, depending on the subcategory) and a small proportion of developing countries, with Hong Kong, Korea, and Taiwan heading the list with disproportionately large export shares (UNCTAD 1992). Clearly competitive assets other than low wages (such as quotas and trade barriers) were at play in this export distribution. Quotas are supposed to be phased out around the year 2005, ten years after the finalization of the Uruguay Round trade pact, giving the lowest-wage emulators more of a chance to compete internationally on free market terms. Nevertheless, there are some extremely low-wage clothing exporters (such as China and India) with relatively strong competitive assets in marketing, access to capital, and entrepreneurship, that make the competitiveness problems of the least industrialized countries vis-à-vis these competitors comparable to those of the textile industries of Korea and Taiwan vis-à-vis that of Japan in the 1950s and 1960s.

Some newcomers joined the list of clothing exporters in the 1980s—for instance, Bangladesh, Jamaica, and Nepal. Nevertheless, even in the smaller of these countries, such export activity had nowhere near the same economywide impact as it had in Hong Kong. Even ignoring Hong Kong's unusual economic structure and population size, what made clothing exports capable of exerting a large economywide impact was its integration with a domestic textile industry (which, as noted earlier, initially prospered by virtue of Commonwealth preferences). Backward integration was even more important in Korea and Taiwan, with larger initial spinning and weaving production capacities (and therefore a larger government presence).[12] By buying locally made fabrics, apparel manufacturers created mass employment and conserved scarce foreign exchange. In the absence of integration, a competitive clothing industry could be expected to generate jobs but not necessarily provide a nucleus for further growth.

Thus the strategic trade-offs facing the least industrialized emulators in the 1990s were more analogous to those confronting Taiwan and Korea in the 1960s than to those confronting Hong Kong in the 1950s. The choice was one of either creating international competitiveness by lowering real wages even further, as free market theory prescribes, or thoroughly revamping, streamlining, and making more efficient *and generous* the incentive system to subsidize learning.

There are, in fact, two other possible growth strategies for would-be emulators to follow that need to be discussed: one relates to relying on direct foreign investment to industrialize; another relates to building a leading sector in primary products (whose supply was inconsequential in the case of Korea, Taiwan, and Hong Kong). We turn briefly to these two strategies.

Direct Foreign Investment

In theory, direct foreign investment represents an instantaneous way for late-industrializing countries to equalize global levels of productivity without the need for government intervention to support local business. Such investment amounts to a perfect technology transfer and eliminates market imperfections related to knowledge. Since World War II, the attractiveness of direct foreign investment has increased in tandem with a rise in opportunities to compete internationally in labor-intensive niches created by high technology. Newly emerging industries such as electronics assembly give greater scope to low-wage comparative advantage and typically necessitate the overseas investments of multinational firms. In practice, a reliance by emulators on direct foreign investment to create international competitiveness is as problematic now (witness the experience of most "transitional" East European countries) as it was for most successful late industrializers in the early postwar years.[13]

The foremost problem associated with direct foreign investment (and the only one we discuss) is that it does not tend to flow *where* it is most needed, and *when* it is most needed. Unless they are very large, unindustrialized countries usually cannot attract foreign investment in their manufacturing sectors except in the most basic domestically oriented consumer goods industries (detergents, for instance). Export-oriented manufacturing investment tends to flow to countries that have already generated their own growth momentum; foreign capital accelerates growth further, but does not act as a catalyst. It also usually amounts to only a small fraction of total gross fixed capital formation.

According to an encyclopedic source on the subject of foreign direct investment: "From the perspective of multinational enterprises taken as a whole, most of the world is currently of little interest to them" (Dunning 1993, p. 21).[14] In the case of Hong Kong, where foreign investment accounts for as much as 30 percent of manufacturing output, such investment became important only after Chinese investors developed cotton textiles and clothing manufacturing facilities. Foreign investors in Korea and Taiwan also arrived after the government had triggered growth with a new incentive system.[15] Moreover, despite the importance of foreign investment, between 1967 and 1986 the average share of inward direct foreign investment in Korea or Taiwan never exceeded 2.0 percent of gross investment (data are unavailable for Hong Kong). The comparable maximum figure for Thailand was only 2.9 percent (ESCAP 1990, as cited in Amsden 1992).[16] Mexico and Brazil may be unusual for the amount and timing of their inward direct foreign investment, but until the 1980s such investment was inward oriented and its economic effects were controversial (see, for example, Fritsch and Franco 1992).

Thus, if for no other reason than scarcity, direct foreign investment cannot be relied on by the most needy countries to create an internationally competitive industrial nucleus to trigger economic growth.

Raw Material Processing and Diversification

A leading sector may comprise an industry that processes a natural resource (mineral or agricultural). In fact, the growth trajectories of many late-industrializing countries originated in such a sector (at one time called a "staple," as in Innis 1930); see figure 5.2. An example is

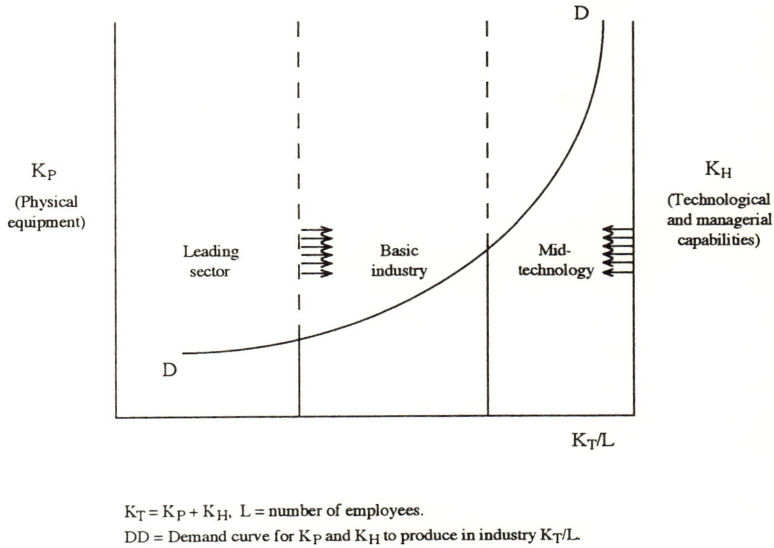

Figure 5.2 Industry diversification

the Argentine meatpacking industry or the Malaysian tin and rubber industries. Typically, moreover, such a sector was internationally competitive without any initial government subsidization (a natural resource constitutes a competitive asset by enhancing raw labor power and thereby raising value added per worker). The empirical question for emulators is whether a resource-based leading sector in successful postwar late industrializers such as Thailand, Indonesia, and Malaysia provided the basis for market-driven diversification into higher value-added industries, or whether diversification required government support.

In principle, the question of government intervention at the turning point of the diversification of the industrial base is comparable to what it was at the turning point of the initiation of industrial activity; it merely arises at a later stage. In fact, many of the issues related to diversification into new industries are distinct, with almost no established theory to guide their analysis. For instance, the diversification path in Albert Hirschman's linkage theory (1958) is driven by growth imbalances, but there is not much concrete about how imbalances are actually to be rectified. In Balassa's national "stages of comparative advantage" (1981), there is no specification of the mechanism whereby a country moves from stage to stage. Little has been written about the actual size or structure of the *agent* of diversification–whether it is a fresh start-up firm, a spin-off of an existing firm, or a diversified business group.[17]

It may be easier for a country to diversify in response to market signals, with no need for government incentives, than to initiate industrial activity because at the diversification stage, manufacturing enterprises already exist, some presumably with retained earnings, and laws and institutions to support industrial activity (such as schools and banks) are already in place. On the other hand, the severity of market failures associated with interindustry coordination and firm-specific learning tend to deepen as the industrial base becomes more capital- and then skill-intensive. The large economies of scale and huge investments associated with many mid-tech industries such as steel, shipbuilding, and automobiles involve governments in diversification in the capacity of planner, financeer, or owner. Finally, the trade-offs governments face in diversifying are different from those they face in triggering industrialization. Rolling back or retarding real wage growth is usually impractical at this stage of development (although it seems to regain popularity at a later stage of "restructuring"). Instead of a trade-off between reducing real wages or subsidizing productivity to create international competitiveness, strategic decisions at the diversification stage relate mainly to *timing:* as the government tries to accelerate accumulation faster than the pace set by the rate of saving of small-scale firms and their rate of technological capability acquisition determined by reverse engineering, different costs arise, such as those associated with monopoly power and industrial concentration.

Suffice it to say here that the degree of government intervention at the stage of diversification has differed among successful late-industrializing countries, just as it differed among them at the initial stage of industrial growth. Yet in virtually all cases, whether the initial leading sector was raw material-based or not, the scope and extent of government intervention has exceeded the import protection measures associated with infant industries in the nineteenth century. In Taiwan, state-owned enterprises were instrumental in developing basic industries such as steel, shipbuilding, heavy machinery, and petrochemicals, which provided inputs to small-scale, downstream firms. In South Korea, diversification was spearheaded by private conglomerates rather than state-owned firms, but the government's role as banker and planner in heavy industry was ubiquitous. In Thailand, which prospered initially on the basis of rice and other raw material-related exports, the government's role in diversification was less than in Malaysia or Indonesia, which initially also prospered on the basis of raw materials, but it was extensive nonetheless. As much as half of Thailand's non-agro-industrial exports in 1985 started out as heavily protected import substitutes in the 1960s (from industries that imported more than 10 percent of domestic consumption) and thereafter typically received special tax incentives (TDRI 1989, p. 61).

Conclusion: A "Necessitarian" View of Government

To understand successful cases of late industrialization for the benefit of aspiring emulators, this chapter proposes a strategic-policy approach to analyzing government economic intervention. Such an approach takes a market-imperfections framework as its starting point, but then uses historical evidence to determine which specific market imperfections successful country governments actually responded to at critical turning points in industrial development. Only one such turning point was examined in some detail, that of the establishment of a leading sector at the initiation of industrial growth. The trade-off governments had to face to create international competitiveness at this stage of development was either to cut real wages or subsidize firm-level learning. The greater the competitive assets a country has at its disposal (measured as value added per worker), the less costly is such a trade-off and the less need for a government to intervene.

The lesson for emulators that derives from how we analyze successful country experience is that if competitive assets do not warrant it (that is, if no trade-off exists), then governments should not intervene. Implicit in the strategic approach we develop is thus a "necessitarian" view of government market behavior. As Chalmers Johnson (1982) once observed about the Ministry of International Trade and Industry in Japan: "economic crisis gave birth to industrial policy" (p. 114). Given an emulating country's existing bundle of competitive assets, and given calculations of private profitability based on domestic import and export prices and interest rates approximating world prices, if private business enterprises, acting alone, can profitably initiate industrial development in labor-intensive industries, and thereafter diversify into more technologically complex sectors at relatively full employment, then in principle government intervention is unnecessary, as it tended to be in Hong Kong in the 1950s. If private investors cannot compete under these conditions, or diversify fast enough to generate a semblance of full employment, then a country must either accept the existing status quo (which may involve decreasing growth rates) or face strategic trade-offs, as most successful late industrializers, to varying degrees, have had to do. The less well endowed a country is with competitive assets, the more socially costly each strategic choice is and the more unfavorable a trade-off, as the experiences of successful late industrializers also suggest.

The postwar history of underdeveloped regions, of course, is strewn with examples of governments intervening in markets with subsidies of various sorts that are "unnecessary," as we have defined that term. Governments have intervened for reasons related to social welfare, corruption, and so forth. Such interventions may have been necessary for social or political reasons but not for economic reasons related to creating international competitiveness. A merit of analyzing government behavior in terms of competitive assets and strategic trade-offs is that the international competitiveness of an industry (firm) can, in theory, be calculated at a particular decision point (ex ante or ex post) such that from the viewpoint of competitiveness creation, the redundancy of government intervention, if any, can be determined. The good or bad results of such intervention can then also more easily be correctly attributed to economic (mis)management or other causes.

There are, however, many loose ends that must be tied together before a strategic policy approach can be of practical use to emulators and an analytical alternative to either the standard free market or market failure models. Among the looser ones is the concept of a "competitive asset," which has to be developed much further. Conditions have to be specified about the availability of assets at the time a strategic decision is made. The timing of strategic decisions also must be made less ad hoc and the condition of full employment made more explicit. Not least of all, the constraints as well as the competitive assets that successful countries experience at strategic turning points must be brought into the picture and systematized.

Still, because the historical evidence from East Asia suggests that most successful late industrializers at critical turning points typically could *not* create international competitiveness without government support, even in "allocatively correct" industries, the most sensible research agenda for the future does not involve working further with standard inductive models. The evidence for other countries needs to be accumulated and analyzed, although the information especially for nineteenth-century Latin America also strongly indicates that intervention, minimally in the form of tariff protection, was necessary for so basic an industry as cotton textiles to emerge in all major producing countries—Mexico, Brazil, and Argentina (see, for example, Platt 1973, chapters 5 and 8). A more promising course than to elaborate standard inductive models is to invest in formalizing the nature of the strategic policy choices that successful late industrializers confronted, and ultimately, to highlight what these cases had to do to implement their strategies effectively.

NOTES

I would like to thank the following people for helpful comments: Takashi Hikino, Helga Hoffmann, Felipe Larraín, Eva Paus, Andrés Solimano, Lance Taylor, and members of the Industrial Development Seminar in the Department of Urban Studies and Planning at MIT.

1. Pollard (1973) notes that "Right up to 1850 and 1860, continental centres frequently failed to achieve British productivity and economy even when using apparently similar equipment" (p. 182). For a careful post–World War II comparison of (vastly different) productivity levels internationally in the cement industry, see Diaz-Alejandro (1972).

2. For theory, see Krugman and Taylor 1979; for practice, see Taylor, ed., 1993.

3. In this respect, the strategic policy approach developed here differs from an approach that regards market failures as distortions from reality. In this specification of market failure, it is hypothesized that less government is needed the more perfect markets are. In the strategic approach, less government is needed the greater a country's competitive assets are, which may be characterized by high degrees of monopoly power.

4. The strategic policy approach we have outlined also differs from "new growth theory" if only because such theory accords no role to the firm and growth depends on aggregate variables such as investment in physical capital and primary education, rather than on firm-specific knowledge.

5. For an estimate of productivity differences in textiles in Japan, Korea, and Taiwan in the mid-1960s, see Woo 1978. Even in the early 1970s value added per worker in textile manufacture differed dramatically. Kuznets (1994) estimates that at prevailing exchange rates, value added per worker in Korea was only 35.9 percent as great as in Japan in 1970 and 36.1 percent as great in 1977 (p. 82).

6. The South Korean textile industry began under Japanese colonialism. One of the leading enterprises was Korean owned and received minor subsidies from the Japanese government (Eckert 1991). Many of the firms that were modernized in the 1950s (there were twelve major integrated spinning and weaving companies) originated as Japanese properties before the war (J. Kim 1966).

7. Patel and Pavitt (1994) document the continuous nature of improvements in mechanical technologies generally.

8. Korea and Taiwan had trouble competing initially in textiles despite the fact that they also benefited from U.S. foreign aid for education and physical infrastructure, both of which excelled by developing-country standards.

9. Around 1965 the textile industries of Korea and Taiwan also began to be transformed by the worldwide substitution of synthetic fibers for cotton fibers.

Among other advantages, such substitution raised product quality and increased the effectiveness of exchange rate devaluations by reducing dependence on imports. Both governments were proactive in providing subsidies to domestic firms to begin production of synthetic fibers.

10. By the 1990s, per capita income in Hong Kong was roughly twice that of South Korea, suggesting that the *average* wage level was also higher. But wage disparities across different sectors were probably higher as well, as suggested by Hong Kong's much more unequal income distribution than South Korea's (see Amsden 1991, Table 5.2).

11. There was also little need for the government to intervene in the next "strategic" turning point in Hong Kong's development—diversification. Owing to almost unique "competitive assets" by late-industrializing standards—political stability and excellent geographical location—Hong Kong was able to diversify into financial services. By the 1990s services accounted for as much as 70 percent of Hong Kong's GDP, one of the highest service ratios in the world (Ho and Lin 1991).

12. The importance of backward integration for economic impact is indicated by the following. In Korea (1970–71), when apparel exports are measured as output, they accounted for 28.5 percent of total exports, but when they are measured as value added, using input-output data, they accounted for only 16.7 percent of total exports (for input-output export measures, see Hong 1979).

13. The value of direct foreign investment flowing to Eastern Europe since 1989 has fallen far short of expectations. The investment that has occurred has been highly concentrated in Hungary, the Czech Republic, and Poland. It has been almost entirely oriented toward serving domestic market demand rather than exports (OECD 1993).

14. Multinational manufacturing investment has tended to cluster in some of the larger Latin American countries (Brazil and Mexico) and some of the fastest-growing East Asian countries (Hong Kong, Singapore, South Korea, Taiwan, and more recently Malaysia, Indonesia, Thailand, and China). The concentration of foreign investment has worsened over time: "No less than 88% of all the foreign direct investment stake in 1985 [including nonmanufacturing] was concentrated in the twenty wealthiest industrial market economies and upper middle income developing countries, compared to 75% in 1960" (Dunning 1993, p. 21).

15. There is a controversy over whether foreign investment led or lagged economic growth in Thailand. For the lead hypothesis, see Suehiro 1989. For the lag hypothesis, see Hewison 1989.

16. The maximum share for Malaysia, 13.7 percent in 1967–1986, was higher, but partially for political reasons. Roughly 30 percent of foreign investment in the mid-1980s was from Singapore, once a part of what is now called Malaysia. Had the two countries remained united, Malaysia's "foreign" investment would be lower (other things equal).

17. For a discussion of firm size in the early stage of industrialization in Taiwan, see Amsden 1991; for a recent discussion of the importance of conglom-

erate business groups as the agent of diversification in many late-industrializing countries, see Amsden and Hikino 1994.

REFERENCES

Amsden, Alice H. (in process). *The Rise of the Rest: Late Industrialization Outside the North Atlantic Region.*

Amsden, Alice H. 1992. A Theory of Government Intervention in Late Industrialization. In *State and Market: Rivalry or Synergy?* edited by Louis Putterman and Dietrich Rueschemeyer. Boulder, CO: Lynne Rienner.

Amsden, Alice H. 1991. Big Business and Urban Congestion in Taiwan: The Origins of Small Enterprise and Regionally Decentralized Industry (Respectively). *World Development* 19 (9): 1121–35.

Amsden, Alice H. 1989. *Asia's Next Giant: South Korea and Late Industrialization.* New York: Oxford University Press.

Amsden, Alice H., and Takashi Hikino. 1994. Project Execution Capability, Organizational Know-How, and Conglomerate Corporate Growth in Late Industrialization. *Industrial and Corporate Change* 3 (1): 111–47.

Amsden, Alice H., and Rolph van der Hoeven. 1996. Manufacturing Employment and Real Wages in the 1980s: Labour's Loss Towards Century's End. *Journal of Development Studies* (April).

Balassa, Bela. 1981. A Stages Approach to Comparative Advantage. In *The Newly Industrializing Countries in the World Economy*, edited by B. Balassa. New York: Pergamon.

Brander, James A. 1986. Rationales for Strategic Trade and Industrial Policy. In *Strategic Trade Policy and the New International Economics,* edited by Paul R. Krugman. Cambridge, MA: MIT Press.

Chandler, Alfred D., Jr. 1962. *Strategy and Structure: Chapters in the History of American Industrial Enterprise.* Cambridge, MA: MIT Press.

Chen, Been-Lon. 1994. Picking Winners and Industrialization in Taiwan. Discussion Paper, Institute of Economics, Academia Sinica, Nankang, Taipei, Taiwan.

Diaz-Alejandro, Carlos. 1972. Labour Productivity and Other Characteristics of Cement Plants—An International Comparison. In *Development and Planning: Essays in Honour of Paul Rosenstein-Rodan,* edited by Jagdish Bhagwati and Richard S. Eckaus. London: George Allen and Unwin.

Dunning, John H. 1993. *Multinational Enterprises and the Global Economy.* Wokingham, England: Addison-Wesley.

Eckert, C. J. 1991. *Offspring of Empire: The Koch-ang Kims and the Colonial Origins of Korean Capitalism, 1876–1945.* Seattle: University of Washington Press.

ESCAP (United Nations Economic and Social Council for Asia and the Pacific). 1990. *Restructuring the Developing Economies of Asia and the Pacific in the 1990s.* New York: United Nations.

Frank, Jr., Charles R., Kwang Suk Kim, and Larry E. Westphal. 1975. *Foreign Trade Regimes and Economic Development: South Korea.* New York: National Bureau of Economic Research.

Fritsch, Winston, and Gustavo H. B. Franco. 1992. Foreign Direct Investment and Patterns of Industrialization and Trade in Developing Countries: The Brazilian Experience. In *Trade Policy, Industrialization, and Development: New Perspectives,* edited by Gerald K. Helleiner. Oxford: Clarendon.

Hewison, Kevin. 1989. *Bankers and Bureaucrats' Capital and the Role of the State in Thailand.* New Haven: Yale University Press/Southeast Asian Studies.

Ho, Yin-ping, and Tzong-biau Lin. 1991. Structural Adjustment in a Free-Trade, Free Market Economy. In *Pacific Basin Industries in Distress: Structural Adjustment and Trade Policy in the Nine Industrialized Economies,* edited by Hugh Patrick. New York: Columbia University Press.

Hikino, Takashi, and Alice H. Amsden. 1994. Staying Behind, Stumbling Back, Sneaking Up, Soaring Ahead: Late Industrialization in Historical Perspective. In *Convergence of Productivity: Cross-National Studies and Historical Evidence,* edited by William J. Baumol, Richard R. Nelson, and Edward N. Wolff. New York: Oxford University Press.

Hirschman, Albert O. 1958. *The Strategy Of Economic Development.* New Haven: Yale University Press.

Hong, Wontack. 1979. *Trade, Distortions and Employment Growth in Korea.* Seoul: Korea Development Institute.

Innis, Harold A. 1930. *The Fur Trade in Canada.* New Haven: Yale University Press (rev. ed., Toronto: Toronto University Press, 1956).

Johnson, Chalmers. 1982. *MITI and the Japanese Miracle: The Growth of Industrial Policy, 1925–1975.* Stanford: Stanford University Press.

Kim, Yung Bong. 1980. The Growth and Structural Change of Textile Industry. In *Macroeconomic and Industrial Development in Korea,* edited by Chong Kee Park. Seoul: Korea Development Institute.

Kim, J.B. 1966. *The Korean Cotton Manufacturing Industry.* Ph.D. diss. University of California, Berkeley.

Krugman, Paul R. 1987. Introduction: New Thinking about Trade Policy. In *Strategic Trade Policy and the New International Economics,* edited by Paul R. Krugman. Cambridge, MA: MIT Press.

Krugman, Paul R., and Lance Taylor. 1979. The Contractionary Effects of Devaluation. *Journal of International Economics.*

Kuznets, Paul W. 1994. *Korean Economic Development: An Interpretive Model.* Westport, CT: Praeger.

Lary, Hal B. 1968. *Imports of Manufactures from Less Developed Countries.* New York: National Bureau of Economic Research.

Liant, Kuo-shu, and Ching-ing Hou Liang. 1982. Trade and Incentive Policies in Taiwan. In *Experiences and Lessons of Economic Development in Taiwan,* edited by Kwoh-ting Li and Tzong-shian Yu. Taipei: Academia Sinica.

Lin, Tzong-biau, Victor Mok, and Yin-ping Ho. 1980. *Manufactured Exports and Employment in Hong Kong.* Hong Kong: Chinese University Press.

Minami, R. 1973. *The Turning Point in Economic Development: Japan's Experience.* Economic Research Series Number 14, Institute of Economic Research, Hitotsubashi University, Tokyo.

OECD (Organization for Economic Cooperation and Development). 1993. Investment Patterns of Companies from OECD Member Countries into Central and Eastern Europe and the Newly Independent States: A Study Prepared for the OECD by Arthur Andersen. OECD, Paris.

Park, Chong Kee, ed. 1980. *Macroeconomic and Industrial Development in Korea.* Seoul: Korea Development Institute.

Patel, Parimal, and Keith Pavitt. 1994. The Continuing, Widespread (and Neglected) Importance of Improvements in Mechanical Technologies. *Research Policy* 23: 533–47.

Platt, D. C. M. 1973. *Latin America and British Trade, 1806–1914.* New York: Harper and Row.

Pollard, Sidney. 1973. Industrialization and the European Economy. *Economic History Review* 26 (4).

Rhee, Y-W, B. Ross-Larson, and G. Pursell. 1984. *Korea's Competitive Edge: Managing the Entry into World Markets.* Baltimore: Johns Hopkins University Press.

Stiglitz, Joseph. E. 1989. Markets, Market Failures, and Development. *American Economic Review* 79 (2).

Suehiro, Akira. 1989. *Capital Accumulation in Thailand 1855–1985.* Tokyo: Centre for East Asian Cultural Studies.

Taylor, Lance, ed. 1993. *The Rocky Road to Reform: Adjustment, Income Distribution, and Growth in the Developing World.* Cambridge, MA: MIT Press.

TDRI (Thailand Development Research Institute). 1989. Year-end Conference "Thailand in the International Economic Community," Background Paper No. 4: Trade in Manufactured Goods and Mineral Products. Prepared by P. Wiboonchutikula, R. Chintayarangsan, and N. Thongpakde. Bangkok, Thailand Development Research Institute.

UNCTAD (United Nations Conference on Trade and Development). 1992. *Handbook of International Trade and Development Statistics, 1991.* New York: United Nations.

Von Neumann, J., and Morgenstern, O. 1947. *Theory of Games and Economic Behavior,* 2d ed. Princeton: Princeton University Press.

Wolcott, Susan. 1993. Efficiency or Exploitation?: The Interwar Indian and Japanese Textile Industries. Paper presented at the Economic History Association Meetings, Tucson.

Woo, K.D. 1978. Wages and Labor Productivity in the Cotton Spinning Industries of Japan, Korea, and Taiwan. *Developing Economies* 16: 182–98.

Part II
Country and Regional Experiences

CHAPTER 6

Old and New Growth Theories: Some Illustrations for Latin America and East Asia

Vittorio Corbo

In recent years many developing countries have introduced economy-wide reforms aimed at restoring fundamental macroeconomic balances, increasing their integration with the world economy, increasing the use of markets in the allocation of resources and the distribution of commodities, decreasing the role of the government in the production and distribution of private goods, and liberalizing labor and financial markets. The ultimate objective of these reforms has been to adjust to large external shocks and to prepare the basis for sustainable growth. After many years of adjustment, however, the growth performance has been below expectations, prompting discussion about what else is required to accelerate the rate of growth on a sustainable basis.

The relationship between growth and its main determinants is complex. Empirical work in this area has usually moved ahead of development in growth theory. Thus, for a long time development economists thought that much more than factor accumulation was required to explain growth. Extensions of the Solow model, and the "new growth theories" years later, have given an important role to economic policies in the determination of the long-run growth rate, especially in creating a policy framework that facilitates innovation and the adaptation of technology. In particular, opening up to foreign competition contributes to increased productivity by providing access to better intermediate inputs and machinery and incentives for technological innovation.

Recent empirical work in this area assumes that long-term growth rates are determined by factor accumulation, and the efficiency with which factors are used. An appropriate policy framework, macroeconomic stability, and the reduction of distortions create the conditions for firms to undertake initiatives conductive to long-term growth through restructuring, capital accumulation, labor training, and technological innovation.

The purpose of this chapter is to provide a short update of the recent work on growth and then to examine the main determinants of growth in Latin America and East Asia. To accomplish this, the chapter reviews the recent record of Latin America and East Asia with respect to growth, investment, and saving. The rest of this chapter is divided into five sections. To set the stage, the following section reviews what has been learned from the recent empirical and theoretical work on the determinants of economic growth. The third section reviews recent work on the determinants of growth differentials in Latin America. The fourth section reviews recent studies on growth in East Asia. The fifth section examines the channels through which saving could affect investment and growth and discusses the determinants of saving rates. Finally, the sixth section presents some concluding remarks.

Explaining Growth: Old and New Growth Theories

Explaining differences in growth across countries and for the same country over time has long been a concern of economists. This is not surprising, as small differences in the rate of growth—when they persist for a long period of time—could make a large difference in output levels. A country that starts with an income per capita of $1,000 that grows at 2 percent per annum takes thirty-five years to double its income per capita. If the rate of growth is of 3 percent per annum, however, it takes only twenty-three years to double its income per capita.

The post–World War II work on growth was much influenced initially by the Harrod-Domar and then by the Solow growth models. In the Harrod-Domar non-steady-state version, for an economy with a large pool of unemployed labor, the investment rate and the technologically given capital-output ratio are the two key factors determining growth. Policy options in this model were concentrated on how to finance an increase in the investment rate, and in particular in assessing the growth effects of foreign aid through its effect on capital accumulation. Indeed, an extension of this model gave origin to the two-gap model of aid effectiveness developed by Chenery and his associates (Chenery and Bruno 1962). Most of the work on planning models of the 1950s and 1960s was based on the much simpler Domar version of this model.

The main limitations of the Harrod-Domar model are its long-run properties. If labor and labor productivity are growing at a constant rate, then unemployment will grow indefinitely or the economy will run out of labor (except in the rare case in which the ratio of the investment rate to the capital-output ratio is equal to the sum of the exogenously given rate of growth of the labor force and rate of change in labor productivity).

The Solow growth model of the late 1950s provided a solution to the long-run problem of the Harrod-Domar model by making the capital-output ratio an endogenous variable. The Solow growth model, in turn, also has a very strong implication. The long-term steady-state rate of growth of output per capita is entirely determined by the rate of exogenous technical progress plus the rate of growth of the labor force. Furthermore, in Solow's model the rate of technical progress is an exogenous variable unconnected to saving behavior or economic policies.

A surprising implication of the Solow model is that a change in the investment rate will cause only transitory deviations of the observed growth rate from the long-term (steady-state) growth rate, but it does not affect the long-run steady-state growth rate of per capita income.

Empirical work on growth in a cross section of countries carried out in the 1960s and 1970s, using a Harrod-Domar framework with surplus labor, found that using the investment rate as the only regressor left a large proportion of the variance in the growth rate unexplained. It has also been found that the wide and persistent dispersion of national growth rates observed in a cross section of countries could hardly be attributed to transitory deviations from the long-run steady-state growth rate of the standard Solow model. These findings led researchers to question the existing theory, and to consider in their empirical work a host of other factors that could be related to growth. The most systematic and influential work in this area was carried out at the World Bank by Hollis Chenery and his associates. This line of work extended the regressors suggested by the standard Harrod-Domar and Solow models to include human capital factors and variables related to technological change and the stance of policy (Chenery et al. 1986). However, this work did not receive much recognition in academic circles because it lacked a theoretical framework to link growth to the policy stance.

The work of Chenery and his associates incorporated the insights of many researchers who were working on development policies and issues from the early 1950s to the middle 1980s. Indeed, most development practitioners have long emphasized the role of economic policies and the formation of human and physical capital in growth. Díaz-Alejandro (1976) used this type of analysis to interpret the poor long-term growth performance of Argentina. Similar lines of argument had been used by Krueger (1978) and Little (1982).

Barro (1991) unleashed an explosion of empirical work on cross-sectional studies of growth. Barro tried to explain conditional convergence of growth rates across countries using an equation that can be considered an extended version of the transitional dynamics of a neoclassical model and also an empirical implementation of the new growth theories. Barro used the data base prepared by Summers and Heston, but extended to incorporate human capital and political variables.

On the theory side, the most important contributions have been made in the context of what is now known as "endogenous growth theories." In these new theories, the links among policy, investment, and long-term growth have been captured in simple analytic models (Romer 1986, 1990; Lucas 1988; Easterly 1993; Rebelo 1991). In these new theories, factor accumulation and efficiency improvements affect not only the level of income per capita but also its rate of growth. The ideas underlying these models—economies of scale, endogenous investment in human capital, externalities, and public goods—and the policy recommendation that the removal of distortions promotes growth, have been familiar in the development literature for a long time. Indeed, this theory can be interpreted as an extension of the Solow model by endogenizing the rate of technical progress. The increasing returns emphasis of this theory has already been considered within the Solow model (Solow 1994).

The empirical work on growth of recent years have followed two approaches that it is sometimes difficult to distinguish. The first approach has extended the Solow model by including another factor of production, human capital, and by also considering other variables that could explain changes in efficiency and the rate of technical progress (Mankiw et al. 1992). The second approach has introduced strong increasing returns in the production function through externalities in capital accumulation or other channels (Romer 1986).

The new work on growth highlights a number of channels through which public policies can affect growth. The promotion of human capital accumulation, through education and improvements in health and nutrition, can foster growth. So can investment in R & D. The models also point to the possibility of economies becoming stuck in a poverty trap: a situation in which low income and low human capital levels create incentives for high population growth and low human capital investment, thus perpetuating the state of poverty. Policies that stimulate investment in physical and human capital can help the economy break out of the trap. At a minimum, the new models provide a framework that may improve understanding of the operation of growth-promoting policies that have been proposed in the past; perhaps they will also improve the quality of future policies.

Most of the cross-section regressions that have been estimated use an equation of the form:

$$GQ - GL = F[I/K, GL, Z], \tag{6.1}$$

where GQ is the rate of growth of GDP, GL is the rate of growth of employment, I/K is the investment rate, and Z is a vector of other characteristics—macroeconomic stability, terms of trade shocks, degree of openness to trade, human capital level etc.—that also affect the rate of growth in per capita income. This type of regression suffers from simultaneity problems as some of the right-hand variables are not truly exogenous, and therefore the results obtained can at best be interpreted as indicative of some regularities. To partially avoid these problems, the investment rate can be taken as an endogenous variable when estimating the growth equation.

The work that has been done using an equation like (6.1) to examine the relation between macroeconomic stability and growth in per capita income has found that, controlling for other factors, there is a negative relationship between the inflation level or its standard deviation and income growth (Fischer 1991; Levine and Renelt 1992). Along the same line, work linking trade policy and growth has found that, after controlling for factor accumulation, countries with more open economies have had higher rates of growth (Easterly and Wetzel 1989; de Melo and Robinson 1992; Nishimizu and Page 1991; Dollar 1992; Levine and Renelt 1992; Edwards 1992).

There are many reasons why the increase in the degree of openness should be associated with higher growth (Dornbusch 1992). In particular, the new growth theories suggest a link between openness and the long-run rate of growth of output rather than a rise in the level of output. Grossman and Helpman (1992) and Romer (1986) suggest that this can occur through the favorable impact of openness on technological change. For example, openness to trade increases the growth rate because it provides access to a variety of imported inputs that embody new technology. On the other hand, Krugman (1987) maintains that greater openness expands the size of markets facing domestic exporters, thereby raising returns to innovation and thus enhancing the country's specialization in research-intensive production. However, the new growth theories also show that growth can be lowered by increased foreign competition, or it can be increased by import protection if protection promotes investment in the research-intensive sectors of the relevant country. Thus for Krugman the direction of the openness-growth relationship is an open question for empirical research rather than a theoretical given.

Fiscal policy can also have an effect on the long-term rate of growth. In general, government spending can enhance or hinder growth. Government spending may promote growth by providing essential public goods, but it could create negative growth effects by wasting resources on programs with a low rate of return or through the standard crowding out of private investment for a country with restricted access to foreign financing.

Accounting for Growth Differences in Latin America

The growth record of Latin American[1] deteriorated substantially in the 1980s, which some have called the lost decade. Indeed, the rate of growth of every major country but Chile decreased between the periods 1970–80 and 1980–91 (table 6.1). At the beginning of this decade a combination of terms of trade shocks and a sudden reduction in foreign borrowing combined with the cumulative effects of weak national policies and institutions unleashed a debt crisis. The rest of the 1980s was spent adjusting to the crisis and in some cases laying the foundation for the recovery of sustainable growth. Chile progressed the most in this

Table 6.1 Growth in the World Economy

	Real GDP Growth Rates				Real Per Capita Growth Rates	
	1960–70	1970–80	1980–91	1980–85	1965–90	1980–91
Low- and Middle-Income Countries	—	5.3	3.3	—	2.5	1.0
Latin America	5.0	4.9	2.0	−0.4	1.2	0.0
Argentina	4.2	2.2	−0.4	−1.4	−0.3	−1.5
Brazil	5.4	8.4	2.5	1.3	3.3	0.5
Chile	4.5	2.8	3.6	−1.1	0.4	1.6
Colombia	5.1	5.9	3.7	1.9	2.3	1.2
Mexico	7.2	5.2	1.2	0.8	2.8	−0.5
Uruguay	1.2	3.5	0.6	−3.9	0.8	−0.4
Costa Rica	6.5	5.8	3.1	0.5	1.4	0.7
East Asia	8.2	7.8	6.6	5.5	5.6	5.4
Japan	10.9	5.0	4.2	3.8	4.1	3.6
Korea	8.6	9.5	9.6	7.9	7.1	8.7
Singapore	8.8	8.5	6.6	6.5	5.3	
Hong Kong	10.0	9.3	6.9	5.9	6.2	5.6
Taiwan					6.8	
Indonesia	3.9	7.6	5.6	3.5	4.5	3.9
Malaysia	6.5	7.8	5.7	5.5	4	2.9
Thailand	8.4	7.2	7.9	5.1	4.4	5.9

Source: Jaspersen et al. (1994) and *World Development Report* 1993.

direction. In the second half of the 1980s, Chile started a period of sustainable growth that has resulted in an average growth rate of 6.6 percent for the years 1984–93. Starting in the second half of the 1970s, Chile introduced five types of reforms: *(a)* public sector reforms, to attain macroeconomic stability and improve efficiency; *(b)* trade policy reforms to open the country to foreign competition and to obtain the static and dynamic gains from trade; *(c)* goods and labor market reforms, to facilitate the needed drastic reallocation of resources; *(d)* financial sector reforms, to improve the efficiency of investment allocation and to facilitate the reallocation of resources; and *(e)* social sector reforms to reduce poverty and improve the income-generating capacity of the poorest groups within the population.

Later on in the decade, many countries in the region started to carry out reforms along the lines of the Chilean model with the purpose of creating the conditions to resume sustainable growth, but this time with much less dependence on foreign financing.

The examination of the growth record of Latin America requires the use of a richer model than the standard factor accumulation specification to account for the long-run effects of sharp terms of trade shocks, and for the potentially growth-deteriorating effects of macroeconomic instability. In recent years, "new growth theory" insights have been used to study the differences in growth performance across Latin American countries. This work has used cross-country regressions of the type reviewed in Levine and Renelt 1992. Recent work in this area includes De Gregorio 1992, and Corbo and Rojas 1992 and 1993. A summary of the main findings of Corbo and Rojas 1993 is presented here. Their findings are also compared with the results of other studies.

Using five-year period averages, Corbo and Rojas found that variations in the investment ratio is the most important single factor accounting for variations in the rate of growth of per capita income across Latin American countries: this factor alone accounts for 37 percent of the variation in the dependent variable. The addition of other new growth theory variables—such as the productivity gap with respect to the United States at the beginning of each period, the ratio of government expenditure to GDP, a measure of human capital at the beginning of each period, and two macroeconomic variables (the inflation rate and the ratio of the trade deficit to GDP)—raises the R^2 to 62 percent. The terms of trade, the inflation rate, the trade deficit ratio, and the human capital variable at the beginning of each period were the most significant of these additional variables. At a deeper level, investment is also an endogenous variable, and it too needs to be explained. Thus economic policies affect growth both directly and through their effect on the investment rate.

Corbo and Rojas found that the investment rate is a function of the rate of growth of per capita GDP, through the accelerator effect, the level of human capital at the beginning of each period, the saving rate, and a set of political and macroeconomic stability variables. This result is consistent with the new work on investment. In particular, political instability has a highly negative effect on investment rates, while macroeconomic instability has a direct negative effect on growth. The negative effect of political instability on investment is consistent with the view that investment is much affected by uncertainty. This result confirms recent theoretical work on the role of uncertainty and the credibility of policies on investment (Dornbusch 1990; Servén and Solimano 1992; Rodrik 1991; and Pindyck and Solimano 1993)

The main results of Corbo and Rojas are presented in tables 6.2 and 6.3. Table 6.2 presents the estimates for the growth differences, and table 6.3 the estimates for the investment equation. The estimation procedure used is panel data with random effects. To avoid the possibility of endogeneity, all the regressions were estimated by the instrumental variable technique. Additionally, all the standard errors were computed using White's (1980) heteroskedasticity-robust procedure.

GDP Per Capita Growth Differences

In general, the most robust determinants of growth are the investment rate, the relative productivity gap with respect to the United States at the beginning of each period, the government expenditures to GDP ratio, the primary school enrollment rate at the beginning of each period, the growth rate in terms of trade, and the two measures of macroeconomic stability (the inflation rate and the trade deficit to GDP ratio). In most of the regressions the coefficients of these variables appeared to be statistically significant regardless of the inclusion of other variables. The black market premium rate also appeared to be negatively correlated with growth, but this result was more sensitive to the specification used. The overall fit of the regressions is quite good, and the regressions explain up to 55 percent of the variability of the five-year average rates of growth of per capita GDP.

The addition of the terms of trade variable increases the explanatory power of the regression from 0.43 to 0.52. In all the specifications presented in table 6.2, the coefficient of the terms of trade variable was positive and highly significant, indicating that improvement in terms of trade will induce faster growth.[2] A possible explanation for this result lies in the fact that many of the Latin American countries in our sample depend quite heavily on export earnings and their import capacity to buy intermediate inputs and capital goods. Therefore an improvement in the terms of trade increases capacity utilization, and it shows up in a higher rate of growth. A similar argument was advanced by Díaz-Alejandro (1976, p. 238).

All the regressions presented in table 6.2 show evidence of conditional convergence of per capita GDP growth. That is, holding everything else constant, the countries with the lower level of per capita income grow at a faster rate than countries with a higher level. Because the logarithm of the productivity gap has a more straightforward interpretation than the level of the productivity gap, in regression 2 the level of the variable is replaced by its logarithm; the overall fit of the regression and the significance of the rest of the coefficients, however, was marginally lower in this case.

The human capital variable (proxied by the primary school rate at the beginning of each period) shows a positive and significant effect on growth in all the regressions, confirming the results of Corbo and Rojas (1992). On the other hand, government spending to GDP has a negative and significant effect on growth in all the regressions of table 6.2.

Regression 3 assesses the effect on long-term growth of macroeconomic instability. A stable macroeconomic framework can be described as one in which inflation is low and predictable, real interest rates are positive but not too high, fiscal policy is stable and sustainable, the real exchange rate is competitive and predictable, and the balance of payments situation is perceived as viable (Corbo and Fischer 1992). Two measures of macroeconomic instability were considered by Corbo and Rojas: the inflation rate[3] and the trade deficit to GDP ratio. Both variables have negative and significant coefficients.

In general, the main channel through which macroeconomic stability matters for growth is through uncertainty. The literature has concentrated on two channels here. First, policy-induced macroeconomic uncertainty reduces the efficiency of the price mechanism. This uncertainty, associated with high inflation or instability of the budget or current account, can be expected to reduce the level of productivity, and, in contexts where the real location of factors is part of the growth process, also the rate of increase of productivity. Second, macroeconomic uncertainty reduces the investment in innovation and adaptation of technology as resources are redistributed toward the management of the financial situation. Third, temporary uncertainty about the macroeconomic situation tends to reduce the rate of investment, as potential investors wait for the resolution of uncertainty before committing themselves. This third channel suggests that investment would be lower at times when uncertainty is high. In other words, countries with high inflation rates are expected to present not only

TABLE 6.2 Pooled Regressions for Growth Rate in GDP Per Capita (Five-Year Averaged Data for Latin American Countries, 1960–88, Inst. Variable Estimation)

	(1)	(2)	(3)	(4)	(5)	(6)	(7)	(8)	(9)
Constant	−0.019	−0.079	−0.016	−0.012	−0.018	−0.01	−0.011	−0.026	−0.02
	(−0.643)	(−1.781)	(−0.436)	(−0.374)	(−0.497)	(−0.447)	(−0.274)	(−0.848	(−0.638)
Investment Ratio in *t*	0.291	0.273	0.34	0.319	0.346	0.281	0.333	0.325	0.316
	(1.517)	(1.309)	(1.967)	(1.798)	(1.976)	(1.360)	(1.959)	(1.772)	(1.761)
Investment Ratio in *t*-1	−0.258	−0.239	−0.307	−0.294	−0.311	−0.276	−0.309	−0.289	−0.291
	(−1.611)	(−1.367)	(−2.073)	(−1.926)	(−2.076)	(−1.579)	(−2.106)	(−1.835)	(−1.862)
Productivity gap	−0.056		−0.079	−0.083	−0.078	−0.083	−0.08	−0.081	−0.081
Vis-à-Vis United States	(−2.997)		(−3.805)	(−3.821)	(−3.686)	(−3.284)	(−3.757)	(−3.689)	(−3.663)
Log Productivity Gap		−0.016							
Vis-à-Vis United States		(−2.470)							
Government Spending (x10E-2)	−0.119	−0.123	−0.073	−0.078	−0.074	−0.101	−0.073	−0.083	−0.084
	(−4.457)	(−3.820)	(−2.350)	(−2.406)	(−2.345)	(−1.930)	(−2.374)	(−2.542)	(−2.575)
Primary School Rate	0.044	0.049	0.041	0.046	0.041	0.047	0.04	0.044	0.043
	(2.901)	(2.555)	(3.178)	(3.306)	(3.072)	(2.822)	(2.903)	(3.312)	(3.089)
Growth Rate in Terms of Trade	0.208	0.199	0.188	0.185	0.19	0.201	0.179	0.186	0.177
	(4.565)	(4.919)	(4.172)	(4.274)	(4.204)	(4.709)	(3.797)	(4.090)	(3.721)

Inflation Rate			−9.96E-04	−4.45E-03		−7.03E-04	−1.02E-03		
			(−2.575)	(−1.487)		(−1.773)	(−2.723)		
Trade Deficit			−0.185	−0.209	−0.172	−0.180	−0.192	−0.189	−0.197
			(−2.022)	(−2.202)	(−1.863)	(−1.705)	(−2.091)	(−1.960)	(−2.036)
Black-market Premium Rate				4.10E-04	−9.27E-05				
				(−1.233)	(−2.925)				
Trade Ratio						0.008			
						(0.549)			
Assassinations							−0.002		−0.002
							(−1.278)		(−1.176)
For high inflation countries									
Dummy for Investment Ratio in *t*								−0.066	−0.068
								(−2.505)	(−2.584)
Dummy for Investment Ratio in *t*-1								0.062	0.062
								(2.159)	(2.171)
Sample Size	100	100	100	100	100	100	100	100	100
Corrected R^2	0.518	0.502	0.539	0.537	0.536	0.53	0.538	0.553	0.552

Note: t-statistics in parentheses. The regressions also include time-period dummies for periods 1965–69; 1970–74; 1975–79; and 1980–84.

TABLE 6.3 Pooled Regressions for Investment Ratios (Five-Year Averaged Data for Latin American Countries, 1960–88)

	(1)	(2)	(3)	(4)	(5)	(6)	(7)	(8)	(9)
Constant	9.601	9.394	7.899	8.908	9.033	9.11	8.402	9.896	8.927
	(3.964)	(4.246)	(3.050)	(3.904)	(3.992)	(4.061)	(3.414)	(4.458)	(3.528)
Growth Rate in GDP	28.339	38.527	37.474	37.395	37.662	37.911	35.835	34.983	35.159
Per Capita	(2.846)	(4.354)	(4.120)	(4.276)	(4.291)	(4.304)	(4.157)	(3.996)	(3.858)
Productivity Gap	−9.326	−13.609	−12.485	−13.442	−13.487	−13.531	−13.067	−14.096	−13.203
Vis-à-Vis United States	(−1.178)	(−2.083)	(−1.937)	(−2.041)	(−2.052)	(−2.066)	(−1.945)	(−2.281)	(−2.164)
Government Spending	−0.368	−0.361	−0.362	−0.349	−0.349	−0.351	−0.358	−0.377	−0.39
	(−3.360)	(−3.507)	(−3.502)	(−3.345)	(−3.336)	(−3.351)	(−3.350)	(−3.549)	(−3.707)
Secondary School Rate	37.679	40.176	41.448	39.747	39.749	39.839	40.108	39.609	41.162
	(2.260)	(2.809)	(2.776)	(2.741)	(2.749)	(2.768)	(2.665)	(2.887)	(2.908)
Terms of Trade Index		0.016	0.014	0.0153	0.015	0.015	0.014	0.014	0.013
		(3.921)	(3.633)	(3.865)	(3.889)	(3.909)	(3.644)	(3.890)	(3.573)
Dummy for High Infl.			−1.358						−1.301
			(−1.825)						(−1.817)
Inflation Rate				−0.115			−0.879	−0.111	
				(−1.549)			(−1.954)	(−1.676)	
Variance of Inflation					−0.058				
					(−1.543)				
Black-market Premium Rate						−0.009	0.084		
						(−1.504)	(1.772)		
Assassinations								−3.487	−3.456
								(−6.302)	(−6.508)
Sample Size	120	120	120	120	120	120	120	120	120
Corrected R^2	0.272	0.305	0.315	0.304	0.303	0.301	0.308	0.356	0.364

Note: t-statistics in parentheses. The regressions also include time-period dummies for periods 1960–64; 1965–69; 1970–74; 1975–79; and 1980–84.

low level of investment rates but also a low efficiency of their investment. This last point is assessed in regressions 8 and 9 through the inclusion of interaction effects on investment rate variables in countries with average inflation rates in the period 1960–88 of more than 30 percent per year. In both regressions the coefficients are significant, with the expected signs that, together with the direct effect of the investment rates on growth, indicated that the Latin American countries with lower average levels of inflation have showed faster growth.[4]

Regressions 5 and 6 assess the effect on long-term growth of trade openness. Two measures of openness were considered: the GDP share of total trade and the black market or parallel market premium. The first one tries to use a proximate effect of openness as a proxy for openness itself. The black market premium is directly related to changes in trade restrictions or in openness basically because the premium reflects the excess demand for tradable and for foreign assets that is not satisfied by the official foreign exchange market. Thus the greater the controls on the use of official foreign exchange, the larger the premium on the black or parallel market exchange rate. The estimates of regression 6 show that the coefficient of the share of total trade in GDP is positive but not significant. In the case of the black market premium rate, however, its coefficient in regression 5 is significant and negative, indicating that those Latin American countries with more foreign exchange restrictions have presented slower output growth.

The significant effect of the black market premium rate on growth depends on the presence of the inflation rate in the regression. When both variables are included in the specification (regression 4), both variables are not significant and the sign of the black market premium is positive, indicating that this variable could also represent some degree of macroeconomic instability more than the degree of openness of the economy. This caveat to use of the black market premium as a proxy for openness arises from the fact that the demand for foreign exchange assets is also a function of the degree of political and macroeconomic instability. Thus when the premium changes because the portfolio excess demand for foreign assets is affected by political or economic news or internal civil disturbances, it undermines the usefulness of the premium as a measure of openness. Then the premium may change due to speculation, even when there is no change in the degree of restrictiveness of the trade regime.

Finally, the roles of political variables on growth are investigated in regressions 7 and 9. Both regressions add as a growth determinant the index of assassinations taken from Barro and Wolf (1989). The estimates indicate that the coefficient of this variable is negative but not significant.[5] A possible explanation of this result can be found in the fact that the role of political variables is confined to its possible negative effect on investment.

Investment Rate Determinants

The second channel through which economic policies could affect growth is by their effect on investment rates. Table 6.3 presents estimates of a number of pooled investment regressions. In all these regressions the dependent variable is the share of investment in GDP for each of the periods also used for the growth equations. Regression 1 presents the results of the simplest model. In this model the investment rate is explained in terms of an accelerator model augmented by a human capital variable, the share of government spending in GDP and the productivity gap with respect to the United States. In this equation the coefficient of the relative productivity gap with respect to the United States and all the other coefficients are significant and with the expected signs. In particular, the significant coefficient on the growth rate in GDP per capita is consistent with the usual finding that the accelerator-type investment function performs well.

Similar to the results obtained on growth, both the human capital and the government expenditure on GDP present significant effects on investment rate in all the regressions of table 6.3. Both effects on investment not only present the expected signs, but also are significant at the 1 percent level.

In regression 2, we add the terms of trade variable. The terms of trade variable has a highly statistically significant coefficient; the inclusion of this variable not only indicates that improvements in the terms of trade are likely to make investment more attractive at home but also leaves the relative productivity gap as another variable that is significant at the 1 percent level. The importance of the terms of trade variable in the investment specification is shown in the increment of explanatory power (more than 3 percentage points) obtained when it is added to the equation.

Regressions 3, 4, and 5 assess the effect on the investment rate of macroeconomic instability reflected by three inflation measures: the inflation rate, the variance of the inflation rate, and a dummy variable for high-inflation countries.[6] Both the inflation rate and the variance of the inflation rate have similar negative effects on the investment rate; however, the negative relationship between inflation rate (or variance of the inflation rate) and the share of the investment is significant only at the 10 percent level. For observations with average inflation for a period of over 50 percent per year, the estimate of the dummy variable in regression 3 shows a more significant negative relationship with investment rate than that obtained with the other two measures of inflation. High inflation rates are associated with macroeconomic instability, and this uncertainty tends to reduce the rate of investment as potential investors wait for the resolution of the uncertainty before committing themselves. Thus investment would be lower at times when uncertainty is high, or countries with high inflation rates are expected to present low levels of investment rates. The results shown in regression 3, 4, and 5 tend to sustain the hypothesis that the effect of uncertainty, reflected by high inflation rates, on investment rates is stronger in countries that have experienced periods of higher inflation, especially at rates of more than 30 percent per year.

As another measure of economic uncertainty, which also provides a measure of expectation of depreciation of the currency and a crude index of distortions, regressions 6 and 7 add the black market premium rate. According to Fischer (1992), the expectation of a depreciation may affect investment through several channels: first, it is more attractive to hold foreign assets when depreciation is expected; second, economic uncertainty is higher under such conditions; but third, for those who can obtain foreign exchange at the official rate, foreign capital goods are cheap to import. Thus, while the first two channels suggest a negative relationship between the black market premium and the investment rate, the third suggests the opposite. On the other hand, as a general index of distortions the black market premium could be a signal that the balance of payment situation is unsustainable and that an adjustment of unknown character is about to take place. The uncertainty with respect to the type of adjustment measures that will be introduced would have a negative effect on investment. Then it is likely that the black market premium would be negatively correlated with investment.

In regression 6, the black market premium rate is the only measure of uncertainty or macroeconomic instability included. In this case its coefficient is negative and significant only at the 10 percent level. The coefficients of the other variables in the regression are significant and stable with respect to the estimates obtained from regressions 2 to 5. When another measure of macroeconomic instability, the inflation rate, is added together with the black market premium, both the inflation rate and the black premium rate are statistically significant; however, only the inflation rate presents the expected negative relationship with investment. This fact can be explained by the high collinearity between both variables, because high-inflation countries are also countries that show high levels of black market premium, reflecting the level of uncertainty and instability of the economy.

Finally, regressions 8 and 9 include additional variables to control for constitutional changes and political stability. The coefficient of these variables were negative and strongly significant, helping to improve the explanatory power of the regression by around six percentage points. As Barro (1991) maintains, this negative relationship between investment and political instability (proxied by figures on number of coups, index of political rights, and political assassinations) could involve the adverse effects of political instability on property rights and the linkage between property rights and private investment. However, the correlation could also reflect a political response to bad economic outcomes. From tables 6.2 and 6.3, it can be observed that the political instability variable is both strongly negative correlated with investment, and does not appear to affect significantly the rate of growth on GDP per capita significantly. The explanation would seem to be simple: political instability affects the rate of investment directly and thereby the rate of growth indirectly. Political instability (proxied in tables 6.2 and 6.3 by an index of political assassinations) can be interpreted as affecting the rate of investment. This result confirm recent theoretical work on the role of uncertainty and the credibility of policies on investment (Dornbusch 1990; Servén and Solimano 1992; Rodrik 1991; and Pindyck and Solimano 1993).

Using the estimated growth and investment equations, it is found that in a scatter of the residual of the growth regression and the residual of the investment regression—the latter run on the same set of regressors as the growth equation—the residual of the growth equation for Chile, Costa Rica, and Jamaica was positive in the last two periods, while the residual for the investment rate equation in the last two periods for Dominican Republic, Ecuador, El Salvador, Guatemala, Haiti, Mexico, Peru, and Trinidad and Tobago was negative.

Accounting for Growth Differences in East Asia

Since the beginning of the 1960s the growth performance of the East Asian countries has been remarkable in comparison with other developing countries in general and with developing countries when they were in similar stages of their economic development. The comparison with the rate of growth of countries in Latin America shows the dramatic differences in performance, specially in the last decade (table 6.1). Not surprisingly, in recent years much interest has emerged on learning the secret behind the East Asian success. Two representative pieces of this literature are World Bank 1993, and Fishlow et al. 1994. There is much agreement that macroeconomic stability with a competitive real exchange rate and a high level of human capital formation are part of the reason for the success, but there is much controversy on the role played by the extensive government intervention that one observes in some of these countries.

World Bank 1993 estimated a standard cross-country growth regression for 113 countries to examine the factors accounting for East Asian growth. The equation was estimated for three different samples: the period 1960–85, and then the subperiods 1960–70, and 1970–85. The data base used is also the one generated by Summers and Heston (1991). The fit of the regression is markedly better for the whole sample of years and for the period 1960–70. The study then uses the residual of the estimated regressions to estimate the productivity performance of each of the eight East Asian economies listed in table 6.1. A relation between the residual of the regression and the residual of a regression of investment rate on the same regressors that enter the growth equation shows that the East Asian countries are all positive outliers. That is, all the countries have a productivity performance superior to that of the average country in the sample and also an investment rate higher than that predicted by the investment equation.

Jaspersen et al. (1994) also use Barro-type regressions estimated for 114 countries with observations for the period 1960–85 to examine the productivity performance of East Asia in comparison with that of Latin American countries using the same methodology as the World Bank study. They find, as did the World Bank study, that in a scatter of the residual of the growth regression and the residual of the investment regression—the latter run on the same set of regressors—the residuals of both equations for the East Asian countries were positive. They also found that among the Latin American countries, all but Colombia, Mexico, and Brazil had negative residuals, and the three exceptions were all close to the line with residuals near zero.

Jaspersen et al. also present regressions in which the rate of growth of real GDP per capita is regressed against a larger set of regressors that include the initial GDP per capita, the investment rate, primary enrollment in 1960, the rate of growth of population in the period 1960–85, government expenditures (net of defense and education) to GDP, the number of coups per year, and two regional dummies (one for Latin American countries and one for East Asian countries). They find, as did Barro (1991), that both dummy variables are significant with the one for Latin America negative and the one for East Asia positive.

Easterly (1994) also compares the growth record of East Asia and Latin America in a growth equation framework. He then uses the estimated equation to gauge the differences in growth performance between East Asia and Latin America due to differences in the average value of a set of policy variables included as explanatory variables in its growth equation. Easterly finds that although the two regions started with the same level of per capita GDP in 1965, by 1989 a large gap had emerged, with the level of per capita income in East Asia more that twice the level of Latin America. Among the policy variables that he considered, price distortions, financial depth, budget deficits, political instability, and schooling accounted for the largest share of the difference in per capita GDP levels. Lately Young (1992) has convincingly argued that capital accumulation rather than efficiency gains (technical progress) is the main factor accounting for the high growth rate of the East Asian countries.

From this review of the recent empirical and theoretical work on growth we conclude that growth is much more than investment in physical capital.[7] However, for countries with an enabling policy environment and adequate investment in human capital, increases in investment rates have a large effect on growth. A larger investment rate could also be the vehicle to provide for the incorporation of new technology (De Long and Summers 1991). To achieve a sustainable increase in investment rates, however, it is not sufficient just to have a better policy framework, but an increase in national saving is also required. This is discussed in the next section.

The Role of Saving in Economic Growth

In principle, for a given increase in the demand for investment, the whole increase in the investment rate could be financed by borrowing on the international capital markets. Even for industrial countries, however, national saving provides most of the financing for domestic investment. The work initiated by Feldstein and Horioka (1980) and much reviewed during the rest of the decade has clearly shown that there is a very high correlation between saving rates and investment rates. The correlation is higher the less open the capital account of the balance of payments (Feldstein and Bacchetta 1991; and Frankel 1992).

Three factors could account for the high correlation between investment rates and saving rates. First, saving and investment rates respond to real interest rates, and even in perfectly integrated capital markets—with nominal interest rate parity—real interest rate parity will not follow due to expectations of changes in the real exchange rate (Frankel 1986). Second, investors' risk aversion would create a gap between domestic and foreign interest rates even in a world of fixed real exchange rates (Feldstein and Bacchetta 1991; Frankel 1991). Third, government policy could be geared to achieve a foreign saving to GDP target to avoid a deterioration in country solvency or, in a small open economy, to avoid a too sharp appreciation of the real exchange rate. Along this line Summers (1988) has suggested that governments have a reaction function whereby the size of the public sector deficit is adjusted to achieve a target foreign saving rate for different levels of the gap between the private saving rate and the private investment rate. Most IMF- and World Bank-supported adjustment programs also have a foreign saving rate target, with domestic policy adjusting to achieve the target (the latter determined by the availability of external financing). This last argument is closely related to the macroeconomics of the transfer problem that suggests putting an upper limit to the foreign saving rate. Heavy reliance on capital inflows in the early stages of an adjustment program could lead to a premature real exchange rate appreciation working at cross purposes with the objective of achieving sustainable, export-led growth. Thus it is difficult to disagree with Krugman's conclusion that it is rare that as much as 5 percent of GNP can be borrowed on a sustainable basis (Krugman 1993).

To provide some empirical evidence on the proportion of the investment rate financed through domestic saving, we study the relation between the investment rate and the gross domestic saving rate for a cross section of Latin American countries. The unit of observation is a single country, and the observation for that country has been averaged over a number of years.

The model estimated is given by

$$I_t/Q_t = a_0 + a_1\, S_t/Q_t,$$

where I_t is gross investment (including the change in inventories), Q_t is gross domestic product, and S_t is gross domestic saving. The model is estimated using data for twenty-two Latin American countries for different time periods.

The results of the estimation for the whole 1970–90 period, and for five-year intervals, are presented in table 6.4. The results indicate that the saving retention factor is much smaller in Latin America than what has been found in industrial countries. The higher value for the coefficient of saving is achieved in the 1981–85 period when the capital account was tightened during the depths of the debt crisis. The empirical result indicates that there is a large autonomous component of investment, whose level is fairly independent of the saving rate.

For the low-income countries that rely on aid-financed foreign saving, there is an additional argument for increasing the national saving rate. Because aid prospects appear to be worsening, the countries in this group that want to increase their investment rates will have to increase national saving, as the foreign saving rate that they can obtain will most likely decrease over time.

Thus the only way to finance a sustainable increase in the demand for investment is through a sustainable increase in the national saving rate. National saving is the sum of private saving and public saving. The weight of the empirical evidence suggests that private saving rates are not very sensitive to policy variables, and in particular to real interest rates (Giovannini 1985; Corbo and Schmidt-Hebbel 1991; Dornbusch and Reynoso 1989). In the extreme case of a negative and unpredictable real interest rates, however, real interest rates probably discourage saving—certainly they reduce the amount and efficiency of financial intermediation and encourage capital flight. Increased public saving will contribute to increasing national saving, provided it is not offset by a decrease in private saving through Ricardo equivalence effects. Empirical evidence presented in Corbo and Schmidt-Hebbel 1991, shows that changes in public saving generally are not greatly offset by the response of private saving. This evidence on saving highlights the central importance of fiscal balance as an instrument to achieve a higher national saving rate.

Most empirical work shows that the most important determinant of saving rates is the growth rate of income. Therefore there is a virtuous circle, as a higher saving rate makes possible a higher investment rate, a higher investment rate in a less distorted policy environment results in a

TABLE 6.4 The Impact of Domestic Saving on Domestic Investment

	Coefficients	
Period	a_0	a_1
1970–1990	0.10	0.537
	(0.020)	(0.102)
1970–1975	0.099	0.583
	(0.019)	(0.088)
1976–1980	0.121	0.544
	(0.028)	(0.122)
1981–1985	0.073	0.633
	(0.023)	(0.120)
1986–1990	0.085	0.517
	(0.026)	(0.137)

Note: Terms in parentheses are the estimated standard errors.

higher growth rate, the higher growth rate results in a higher saving rate, and so on (Collins 1991; Carroll, Weil, and Summers 1993). The challenge is to get the process started.

Institutional developments in the financial system could also have an effect on the saving rate and certainly on financial savings. The creation of an appropriate regulation and supervision system is a precondition for the deregulation of the financial system. But this is not all. Transaction costs in dealing with small savers could be too high to make this type of business attractive to commercial banks, and the development of other type of financial intermediaries could have a positive effect on saving. In this connection it has been claimed that the creation of postal savings institutions by the public sector is one of the reasons for the high saving rate of the Asian countries (World Bank 1993).

Another institutional reform that could have a positive effect on saving rates is a pension reform. In particular, the shift from a pay-as-you-go to a private, fully funded individual capitalization pension scheme would most likely result in an increase in the personal saving rate. Furthermore, if the pensions of the retirees of the old system are suspended or financed out of an increase in taxes or a reduction in public expenditures, rather than through an increase in public debt, the total saving rate would also increase (Valdés and Cifuentes 1990). Once an individual capitalization system is created, the pressures for a more transparent, less regulated, and better supervised financial system would increase as the holders of individual pension accounts demand less risk and more return from their investments.

Financial developments in the form of a wider monetization and financial deepening could result in higher saving through lower transaction costs for potential savers, and most likely would result in a more efficient use of savings through the pooling of resources, the creation of a richer portfolio of financial instruments, a better screening of projects, and by partially overcoming problems of adverse selection in credit markets. In a new growth theory framework these efficiency effects, directly and through their impact on innovations, would have positive effects on the long-run growth rate (King and Levine 1993).

Conclusions

The empirical work reported in this chapter provides some clues on the impact of policy on growth. A brief summary of the main findings follows. Examining the growth process for Latin American countries, it was found:

- Economic policies affect growth directly, through the transitional dynamics of the growth process, and indirectly through their effect on investment rates.
- The change in terms of trade has a significant positive effect on growth in real per capita GDP.
- Human capital variables have a positive effect on growth, both through the growth equation and through a higher rate of investment. This result shows that public policy has an important role in promoting growth by enhancing the human capital base. The latter could be done through the direct provision of human capital for low-income groups of the population and the creation of an enabling environment for the accumulation of human capital.
- Controlling for other factors, the share of government expenditures in GDP has a negative effect on growth and investment rates.
- Political instability has a negative effect on growth through lower investment rates.
- In the case of the Asian countries, all have a productivity performance above the average for a large sample of countries.
- Finally, to sustain a growth process it is necessary to accompany the endogenous increase in the investment rate with an increase in the saving rate. The most direct route to achieving an increase in the national saving rate is through an increase in the saving rate of the public sector.

APPENDIX

Overview of the Data

The data required to generate the trade openness variable, the inflation rate variable, and the direct foreign investment variable are taken from the World Bank Data Base; the black market premium data are taken from the *World Currency Yearbook*; the terms of trade data are taken from ECLAC statistics, and all the other time series data are taken from Summers and Heston 1991. These two authors have compiled internationally comparable annual figures on output and its composition, prices, and exchange rates for 134 market economies from 1950 to 1988. Data for the time-invariant variables are taken from the data base of Barro and Wolf (1989).

Given the characteristics of the data, we can choose their organization, ranging from averaging each country's experience into one data point and estimating a single cross-sectional equation to pooling cross-sectional and time-series data and estimating a panel equation.

The single cross-sectional equation has been the alternative most used in the empirical growth literature. However, averaging over the entire sample period eliminates the information contained in the sample about the effect of changing conditions of growth in individual countries and allows only cross-country variation to inform the estimates. Therefore, trying to obtain as much as possible from the data, a panel estimation using subperiod averages was considered for the period between 1960 and 1988. Because we are interested in secular growth patterns, some amount of averaging was required to net out irregular fluctuations in the annual data. For this purpose, the data were pooled using five-year averages and one four-year average. The periods are: 1960–64, 1965–69, 1970–74, 1975–79, 1980–84, and 1985–88.

NOTES

1. This section draws on Corbo and Rojas 1993.

2. This result differs from the finding of De Gregorio (1992) that terms of trade changes did not have a significant effect on growth in Latin American countries. The main difference between ours and De Gregorio's work is that we work with change in terms of trade and he works with the level. A result similar to Corbo and Rojas has been found in Easterly 1994.

3. The variance of the inflation rate was also included as an explanatory variable, with a negative and significant effect on growth. Since the general results do not change with respect to the results obtained using the inflation rate, we do not report the results for the variance of inflation in table 6.

4. F-tests were carried out to test the null hypothesis that the investment rates and interaction effects coefficients were not significantly different from zero. The levels of significance of the F-test for regressions 8 and 9 were 0.13E-5 and 0.15E-5 respectively, rejecting strongly the null hypothesis.

5. We report only the result for the variable number of assassinations per million population per year (1960–85). Other variables were also considered and were found not to have a significant effect on growth. These variables were: index of civil liberties, index of political rights, and number of coups.

6. Average inflation rates of 50 and 30 percent per year in each five-year period were used as cutoff points. In both cases the coefficient of the dummy was significant; however, in the case of 50 percent cutoff point, the coefficient was more significant and the explanatory power of the regression was higher. In table 6.5, we report only the results where the dummy takes value of one when the country has an average inflation rate of over 50 percent per year.

7. Work by King and Levine (1993) shows that financial deepening and the expansion of a financial system geared to the private sector through private banks, by improving the probability of successful innovation and the quality of

the financial system, accelerates growth. In particular, they show that three indicators of financial development—financial depth, the relative importance of banks as opposed to central banks, and the ratio of private credit to GDP—are positively and significantly related to a set of growth indicators. They conclude that "the predictable component of financial development tends to be very strongly associated with growth and the sources of growth" (p. 25). See also De Gregorio and Guidotti 1992.

REFERENCES

Barro, R. J. 1991. Economic Growth in a Cross Section of Countries. *Quarterly Journal of Economics* 106: 407–43.

Barro, R. J., and H. C. Wolf. 1989. Data Appendix for Economic Growth in a Cross-Section of Countries. Mimeo. Harvard University.

Carrol, C., D. Weil, and L. H. Summers. 1993. Savings and Growth: A Reinterpretation. *Carnegie-Rochester Public Policy Conference* 40: 133–92.

Chenery, H., and M. Bruno. 1962. Development Alternatives in an Open Economy: The Case of Israel. *Economic Journal* 57: 79–103.

Chenery, H., S. Robinson, and M. Syrquin, eds. 1986. *Industrialization and Growth: A Comparative Study.* New York: Oxford University Press.

Collins, S. 1991. Saving Behavior in Ten Developing Countries. In *National Saving and Economic Performance,* edited by B. D. Douglas and J. B. Shoven. Chicago: University of Chicago Press and NBER.

Corbo, V., and Klaus Schmidt-Hebbel. 1991. Public Policies and Saving in Developing Countries. *Journal of Development Economics* 36: 89–115.

Corbo, V., and S. Fischer. 1992. World Bank Supported Adjustment Programs: Rationale and Main Results. In *Adjustment Lending Revisited: Policies to Restore Growth,* edited by V. Corbo, S. Fischer, and S. Webb. Washington, D.C.: World Bank.

Corbo, V., and P. Rojas. 1992. Los Determinantes del Crecimiento Económico: Introducción. *Cuadernos de Economía* 29 (87).

Corbo, V., and P. Rojas. 1993. Investment, Macroeconomic Stability, and Growth: The Latin American Experience. *Analisis Económico* 8 (1): 19–35.

De Gregorio, J. 1992. Economic Growth in Latin America. *Journal of Development Economics* 39: 59–84.

De Gregorio, J., and P. Guidotti. 1992. Financial Development and Economic Growth. IMF Working Paper WP/92/101.

De Long, J. B., and L. H. Summers. 1991. Equipment Investment and Economic Growth. *Quarterly Journal of Economics* 106(2): 445–502.

De Melo, J., and S. Robinson. 1992. Productivity and Externalities: Models of Export-Led Growth. *Journal of International Trade and Economic Development* 1: 41–69.

Díaz-Alejandro, C. F. 1976. *Foreign Trade Regimes and Economic Development: Colombia.* New York: Columbia University Press.

Dollar, D. 1992. Outward-Oriented Developing Economies Really Do Grow More Rapidly: Evidence from 95 LDCs, 1976–85. *Economic Development and Cultural Change* 40: 523–44.

Dornbusch, R. 1990. Policies to Move from Stabilization to Growth. *World Bank Annual Conference on Development Economics:* 19–48.

Dornbusch, R. 1992. The Case for Trade Liberalization in Developing Countries. *Journal of Economic Perspectives* 6: 69–86.

Dornbusch, R., and A. Reynoso. 1989. Financial Factors in Economic Development. *American Economic Review* 79: 204–209.

Easterly, W. R. 1993. How Much Distortions Affect Growth. *Journal of Monetary Economics* 32: 187–212.

Easterly, W. R. 1994. Sorpresas, Ajuste y Crecimiento Económico. In *Crecimiento Económico,* edited by M. Aparicio and W. Easterly. Bogota: Banco Mundial—Banco de la República.

Easterly, W. R., and D. L. Wetzel. 1989. Policy Determinants of Growth: Survey of Theory and Evidence. World Bank Policy Research Working Paper 343.

Edwards, S. 1992. Trade Orientations, Distortions, and Growth in Developing Countries. *Journal of Development Economics* 39 (1): 31–57.

Feldstein, M., and C. Horioka. 1980. Domestic Saving and International Capital Flows. *Economic Journal* 90: 314–29.

Feldstein, M., and P. Bacchetta. 1991. National Savings and International Investment. In *National Saving and Economic Performance,* edited by D. Bernheim and J. Shoven. Chicago: University of Chicago Press.

Fischer, S. 1991. Growth, Macroeconomics, and Development. In *NBER Macroeconomics Annual 1991,* edited by O. Blanchard and S. Fischer. Cambridge, MA: MIT Press.

Fishlow, A., C. Gwin, S. Haggard, D. Rodrik, and R. Wade. 1994. *Miracle or Design? Lessons from the East Asian Experience.* Washington, D.C.: Overseas Development Council.

Frankel, J. A. 1986. International Capital Mobility and Crowding-Out in the U.S. Economy: Imperfect Integration of Financial Markets or of Goods Markets? *In How Open Is the U.S. Economy?* edited by R. Hafer. Lexington, MA: Lexington Books.

Frankel, J. A. 1992. Measuring International Capital Mobility: A Review. *American Economic Review* (May): 197–202.

Giovannini, A. 1985. Saving and the Real Interest Rate in LDCs. *Journal of Development Economics* 18: 197–217.

Grossman, G., and E. Helpman. 1992. *Innovation and Growth in the Global Economy.* Cambridge, MA: MIT Press.

Jaspersen, F., A. Estevadeordal, and I. S. Guerra. 1994. Growth of the Latin American and Asian Economies. Mimeo. Development Research Division, IDB.

King, R., and R. Levine. 1993. Finance, Entrepreneurship, and Growth. *Journal of Monetary Economics* 32 (3): 513–42.

Krueger, A. O. 1978. *Liberalization Attempts and Consequences*. New York: Ballinger Publishing Company and NBER.

Krugman, P. 1987. Is Free Trade Passé? *Economics Perspectives* 1 (2): 131–44.

Krugman, P. 1993. What Do We Need to Know about the International Monetary System? *Essays in International Finance* 190.International Finance Section. Princeton University.

Levine, R., and D. Renelt. 1992. A Sensitive Analysis of Cross-Country Growth Regressions. *American Economic Review* 82 (4).

Levine, R., and D. Renelt. 1991. Cross-Country Studies of Growth and Policies: Methodological, Conceptual, and Statistical Problems. World Bank Policy Research and External Affairs Working Paper 608.

Little, I. A. 1982. *Economic Development: Theory, Policy, and International Relations*. New York: Basic Books.

Lucas, R. E., Jr. 1988. On the Mechanics of Economic Development. *Journal of Monetary Economics* 22 (1): 3–42.

Mankiw, G., D. Romer, and D. Weil. 1992. A Contribution to the Empirics of Economic Growth. *Quarterly Journal of Economics* (May): 407–38.

Nishimizu, M., and J. Page, Jr. 1991. Trade Policy, Market Orientation, and Productivity Change in Industry. In *Trade Theory and Economic Reform North, South, and East,* edited by J. De Melo and A. Sapir. Oxford: Basil Blackwell.

Pindyck, R., and A. Solimano. 1993. Economic Instability and Aggregate Investment. In *NBER Macroeconomics Annual 1993,* edited by O. J. Blanchard and S. Fischer. Cambridge, MA: MIT Press.

Rebelo, S. 1991. Long-Run Policy Analysis and Long-Run Growth. *Journal of Political Economy* 99: 500–521.

Rodrik, D. 1991. Policy Uncertainty and Private Investment in Developing Countries. *Journal of Development Economics* 36: 229–42.

Romer, P. 1986. Increasing Returns and Long-Run Growth. *Journal of Political Economy* 94 (5): 1002–1037.

Romer, P. 1990. Endogenous Technological Change. *Journal of Political Economy* 98: s71–s102.

Servén, L., and A. Solimano. 1992. Private Investment and Macroeconomic Adjustment: A Survey. *World Bank Research Observer* 7: 95–114.

Solow, R. M. 1994. Perspectives on Growth Theory. *Journal of Economic Perspectives* 8: 45–54.

Summers, L. 1988. Tax Policy and International Competitiveness. In *International Aspects of Fiscal Policies,* edited by J. Frenkel. Chicago: University of Chicago Press.

Summers, R., and A. Heston. 1991. The Penn World Table (Mark 5): An Expanded Set of International Comparisons, 1950–1988. *Quarterly Journal of Economics* 106 (2): 327–68.

Valdes, S., and R. Cifuentes. 1990. Previsión Obligatoria Para Vejez y

Crecimiento Económico. *Documentos de Trabajo* 131. Instituto de Economía, Universidad Católica de Chile.

White, H. 1980. A Heteroskedasticity-Consistent Covariance Matrix Estimator and a Direct Test for Heteroskedasticity. *Econometrica* 48: 817–38.

World Bank. 1993. *The Asian Miracle*. Washington, D.C.: World Bank.

Young, A. 1992. A Tale of Two Cities: Factor Accumulation and Technical Change in Hong Kong and Singapore. In *NBER Macroeconomics Annual 1992*, edited by O. J. Blanchard and S. Fischer. Cambridge, MA: MIT Press.

CHAPTER 7

Economic Growth under Alternative Development Strategies: Latin America from the 1940s to the 1990s

Andrés Solimano

State dirigisme and import substitution provided the engine for growth in Latin America from the 1940s to the late 1970s. Although the growth performance of the region was respectable in that period, with annual growth of around 5 percent, the development model started to run out of steam in the 1970s and definitely collapsed in the 1980s under the pressure of the debt crisis and growing macroeconomic instability. Under these circumstances, governments altered their development strategies in the direction of opening up their economies, reducing the role of the state, and deregulating activities previously precluded for the private sector.

This chapter examines three propositions regarding Latin American growth and its links with policy transformation: *(a)* The postwar growth performance of Latin America, say from the 1940s to the onset of the debt crisis in the early 1980s, relied strongly on factor accumulation, with a declining contribution of total factor productivity growth over time (a sort of "extensive" growth pattern); *(b)* The accumulated experience of market-based reform shows that reform can be followed by either recessionary or expansionist output responses in the short term. The magnitude of initial disequilibria, external factors, and the response of exports and investment to the reform policies are the basic determinants of those growth outcomes; *(c)* The long-run growth impact of market reform is still an unsettled issue, and evidence suggests that a sustained acceleration of growth after reform may come with a long lag (a decade or so). The dominant view stresses an increase in total factor productivity growth as a main channel for an acceleration of growth after reform that improves the quality of resource allocation and the productivity of investment.

The critique of the traditional development model followed in Latin

America—based on import substitution and state dirigisme—focuses not so much on a failure of that model in delivering acceptable rates of output growth, but on the fact that this was an "extensive" pattern of growth relying on factor accumulation (capital and labor) with a reduced contribution of total factor productivity growth (associated with a policy regime based on import substitution and state dirigisme that brought a distortive structure of incentives in the economy). The empirical evidence reviewed tends to support this view on the sources of growth in traditional development model. It also shows that, macroeconomically, the growth process in several countries of the region was often accompanied by recurrent balance of payments crisis and inflationary pressures.

The contention that the short-term growth impact of reform is influenced besides other factors by the phase of the business cycle and the external conditions faced by the reforming economy is examined in a sample of countries starting reform from a variety of initial conditions in the 1970s, 1980s, and 1990s. In that perspective, Chile adopted market-based reforms in the second half of the 1970s in a context of increasingly abundant capital flows, existing spare capacity, and unemployed labor. As a result, growth rapidly accelerated after major reforms were undertaken. In contrast, reform programs adopted in the 1980s in Mexico and Bolivia did so under the hardship posed by the external debt crisis and the sharp cut-off of foreign financing to the region. These programs were followed by either stagnation or modest growth. More recently, in the early 1990s, reform programs have taken place in severely distressed economies such as Argentina and Peru and also in the more economically stable Colombia. Under a more favorable international environment than that of the 1980s, particularly regarding capital inflows, these programs have been followed almost immediately by renewed growth.

In evaluating the impact of reform on long-run growth, we face the problem of too few observations. Chile is the economy in the region with the longest experience—nearly two decades—with comprehensive market-based reform. Mexico and Bolivia also adopted comprehensive reform measures, but only since the mid-1980s. Empirical evidence for Chile points out a positive effect of reform on long-term productivity growth, but also shows a substantial lag in the impact of reform on capital formation—a key ingredient for sustainable, capacity-based output expansion.

The chapter is organized into four sections in addition to this introduction. The first section discusses conceptual issues surrounding the relationship between stabilization, reform, and growth. The second section looks at the historical and more recent growth record of seven Latin American economies that have adopted, to different degrees, programs of market-based reform in the last three decades. The third section presents econometric evidence of sources of growth from the 1940s to the 1980s for these reforming economies and then provides additional evidence on the long-run impact of reform on the rate of economic growth in Chile and Mexico. The last section contains concluding remarks.

Growth under Alternative Policy Regimes: Conceptual Issues

This section reviews the main features of growth under two main policy regimes: state dirigisme-cum-import substitution, the development model of Latin America between the 1940s and 1980s, and market-based development.

State Dirigisme and Import Substitution

Growth under state dirigisme and import substitution was driven mainly by capital-intensive investment. On the one hand, public investment was envisaged as a key policy device for mobilizing domestic savings, boosting growth, and avoiding the potential coordination failures of decentralized markets. Public investment focused on sectors such as energy, public utilities, telecommunications, and infrastructure—activities that tend to be capital intensive. On the other hand, private investment was stimulated through subsidized credit, tax rebates, and preferential exchange rates. The import tariffs structure favored the import of machinery and equipment and inputs; this apparatus of investment promotion tended also to make growth rely on the expansion of capital-intensive activities and the import of capital goods.

At the macro level the growth pattern suffered at different points in time from two main disequilibria: chronic inflation and recurrent balance of payments crises. The inflationary pressure came from two sources: first, the tendency for the state sector to expand led to increasing pressures on public spending which, giving rigidities of the tax system, was reflected in the appearance of fiscal deficits, financed in many cases by money creation.

A second source of inflationary pressure was associated with distributive conflicts among different groups (powerful urban labor unions, the industrialist-capitalist class, landowners) over their relative shares in national income. This gave rise to the traditional wage–price–devaluation spiral that under accommodative monetary policies produces inflation.

The recurrent balance of payments crisis in Latin America under import substitution is related to two main factors: one factor, endemic to the region, is linked to external vulnerability—particularly, international commodity price shocks that hit hard the economies whose export earning are concentrated on a few primary commodities. Another factor behind recurrent balance of payments crises was a tendency for real currency overvaluation associated with a protected tariff structure, which, in the end, increased the import content of output growth. Very often the balance of payments became a binding constraint to sustained growth, as expansionary cycles threatened balance of payment equilibrium, thus inviting stop-and-go macro policies.

Market-Based Development

The debt crises and macroeconomic turbulence of the 1980s made these underlying problems of the postwar development model of Latin America to emerge in full force. The disappointment with the traditional development model led to the adoption of a new policy regime that sought to couple macroeconomic stability with a smaller state, open foreign trade regimes and liberalized markets. Mapping and measuring the impact of these reforms on the rate of economic growth is a complex task. In fact, there are several methodological problems, among them: *(a)* The sample of actual country cases with a long experience with market reform is small. This is in contrast with the large sample of country experiences with import substitution and state dirigisme, a development strategy that lasted for several decades. *(b)* At the analytical level, there is ambiguity on whether the reforms affect the level and/or the rate of growth of output. *(c)* There is an implicit identification problem in determining the relative contribution of the different components of reform—macro stabilization and microeconomic and institutional reforms—in terms of their effects on the rate of economic growth. *(d)* We know little about how the time phasing and interaction between these two main components of overall reform affect economic growth. *(e)* Individual reform policies do not always produce a growth effect that goes in the same direction. *(f)* Identifying the relevant transmission mechanisms—consumption, investment, exports on the demand side; capital formation and productivity growth on the supply side—on how reform policies affect the rate of economic growth is not easy. *(g)* There are considerable lags in the effects of policies measures on capital formation, productivity and GDP growth. With these caveats in mind, we will briefly review the expected growth effects of the different components of a reform package.

Macro Stabilization

Many reform programs in Latin America started from deteriorated macroeconomic conditions characterized by high and/or erratic inflation, large fiscal deficits, and unsustainable current account disequilibria. This has been an important force propelling reform.[1]

Macroeconomic instability—inflation, exchange rate volatility, stop-and-go policies—hampers economic growth for several reasons[2]: *(a)* it discourages irreversible investment outlays; *(b)* a noisy and unpredictable macro environment reduces the informational content of price signals, worsening the quality of resource allocation and, possibly, productivity growth; *(c)* under inflationary conditions, entrepreneurs and firms devote an increasing portion of their time and effort to avoiding inflationary losses (or making inflationary gains) from assets management rather than actual production and innovation.[3] Therefore the restoration of macroeconomic stability is a basic precondition for fostering growth. Moreover, the type of stabilization program adopted to restore macro stability matters for determining the short-term growth impact of reform.[4]

Orthodox or money-based programs such as those applied in Chile in 1975, Bolivia in 1985, and Peru in 1990 centered on a permanent reduction in the rate of growth of the money supply and the fiscal deficit to reduce inflation. These programs tend to be recessionary in the short run because restrictive monetary policies push real interest rates up, depressing aggregate demand, output, and employment. The extent of output contraction depends on several factors, chiefly, the credibility of the program and the degree of wage and price rigidity and the existence of institutional mechanisms of indexation that "filter" the impact of slower money growth on the rate of inflation.

Exchange-rate-based stabilization (Southern Cone in the late 1970s, Argentina convertibility plan in 1991) rely on the exchange rate as the key nominal anchor for disinflation. These programs tend to be expansionary in the short term. Domestic absorption (consumption and investment) increases after slowing down the rate of devaluation (or fixing it altogether), for two reasons: first, the rise in real wages that often takes place at the beginning of the program stimulates current consumption; second, the initial drop in real interest rates associated with a slower pace of devaluation encourages investment and the consumption of durable goods. All these effects are expansionary.[5] However, this is not the full story. The real exchange rate overvaluation that often develops during these programs squeezes export- and import-competing industries, over time, on the supply side. Moreover, the real appreciation invites substitution of demand away from domestic goods toward (transitorily) cheaper foreign goods. Clearly, the initial expansion of economic activity gives way to a downturn later on. More dramatically, if the currency appreciation leads to a balance of payments crisis (as it happened in the Southern Cone in the early 1980s and Mexico in late 1994), then the downturn can turn into a full-blown recession to quickly reduce imports.

The effects of *multiple anchor programs or heterodox plans* (Israel in 1985 and the Mexican stabilization plans after 1988) on growth are more ambiguous. The main rationale for these programs is the coordinated use of several nominal anchors to avoid, or dampen, the often large recession that comes with orthodox stabilization and the undesired changes in key relative prices, associated with exchange-rate-based stabilization. In general one can expect these (multiple anchor) programs to be moderately restrictive as monetary and fiscal restraint is needed to support the anchors. In practice, the Mexican program of 1988–89 and the Israeli one of 1985 were moderately recessive in the early phases of implementation.

To summarize, in the long run the shift from inflationary conditions to more stable macro conditions has positive effects on long-term growth; however, the transition is more complex and depends largely on the type of stabilization program adopted, that is, the choice of nominal anchor(s) and the stance of the accompanying fiscal and monetary policies—all conditioned by the external environment under which stabilization takes place. In general no stabilization program can avoid some recession; the real difference across programs is between recession now or recession later during the course of disinflation.

Structural Reforms

The structural reforms of a program of market-based transformation have a longer-run horizon. The chief transmission mechanisms to growth are capital formation and the rate of total factor productivity growth. These reforms cover several areas. Let us start with *trade liberalization*. In general the effect of trade reform (measured as the degree of external openness, e.g., the share of exports plus imports over GDP or as an index of import tariffs and other trade restrictions) on output growth, capital formation, and productivity growth are subject to dispute. One argument for a positive correlation between the degree of external openness and the rate of total factor productivity growth is that the more open the economy, the more the country can adopt (or import) technical innovations developed in foreign countries.[6] Nevertheless, it is still an open question whether this is a level effect (once and for all) or a rate of change effect (more permanent).[7] The impact of trade reform on aggregate capital formation is also potentially ambiguous and depends on factors like the credibility of the foreign trade reform and the differences in capital intensity between export- and import-competing industries.[8]

Financial deepening is expected to generate a positive effect on capital formation and productivity growth by easing credit constraints, mobilizing savings, and enabling a better evaluation and screening of good investment and innovation projects. These effects, however, are of a long-run nature. In the short term, financial liberalization undertaken when macroeconomic stabilization is still incomplete tends to be accompanied by high real interest rates and possibly by financial fragility.[9] Empirical evidence such as Easterly 1993 and King and Levine 1993 suggests an adverse effect on growth of moderate-to-large negative real interest rates and of low coefficients of monetization (a proxy of financial repression) for a cross-section of developing economies. Two main arguments are used to rationalize these findings showing a negative effect of financial repression on growth: a depressing effect on the average rate of return on capital (Easterly) or a lower rate of technical innovation (King and Levine).

The effects of *privatization* on growth are more likely to operate in the long run, provided that total factor productivity growth is accelerated and private investment responds positively to the new business opportunities made available by privatization. In the short run, however, the effects are more ambiguous, as privatization tends to be accompanied by cuts in public investment that can be contractionary and by an often timid initial response of private investment.[10]

Summing up, the growth effects of structural reforms (trade liberalization, financial reform, privatization) may be ambiguous in the short run. The positive growth effects of market reform are more likely to come in the medium to long run as the new policy reform is consolidated and the private sector reacts more fully to the new opportunities provided by the reforms.

Country Experiences: Short- and Medium-Run Growth Effects of Policy Reform

The Latin American economies grew at an average rate near 5.0 percent (eight countries, table 7.1) or 5.5 percent (nineteen countries) between 1950 and 1980.[11,12] The best performers in that period were the two largest economies of the region, Mexico and Brazil, with annual rates of GDP growth between 6.5 and 7 percent. That dynamism exhibited by the region as a whole came to an abrupt end in the early 1980s, after the onset of the debt crisis that forced debtor countries to adopt stiff austerity measures. As a consequence of these shocks, average GDP growth for the group of eight economies declined to 1.1 percent between 1980 and 1990 (table 7.1) nearly one-fifth the average rate of growth of the period 1950–80. In 1990–94 the picture started to change (table 7.1), and GDP growth recovered to an annual average rate close to 4 percent. Interestingly, the fastest growing economies in the 1950–80 period, Brazil and Mexico, are among the slowest growers during most of the 1980s and early 1990s.

Table 7.2 presents GDP growth rates for countries that have undertaken programs of market-based reform in the 1970s, 1980s, and 1990s. It presents for each country the historical growth record (1950–80) and averages of growth rates for several years before and after the starting of market-based reforms.

In the 1970s, Chile launched the most comprehensive program of stabilization and reform in the region. On the stabilization front, the program comprised money-based stabilization in 1975, followed by an exchange-rate-based stabilization plan in 1979.[13] On the structural front, during the second half of the 1970s tariffs to trade were drastically reduced, the financial market liberalized, and public enterprises privatized. The average rate of growth three years before 1974–75 was very sluggish, and in 1975 the Chilean economy sharply contracted. Afterward growth resumed forcefully, helped by the existence of excess capacity and unemployed labor. Moreover, there were large productivity gains following the reforms. However, it is interesting to note that steady GDP growth in Chile—at annual rates of 7 percent—was achieved only since the late 1980s (and running through the 1990s), nearly a decade after reforms

TABLE 7.1 Rates of Growth of GDP in Eight Latin American Economies, 1950–94 (Annual Averages, %)

	1950–80	1980–1990	1990–94
Argentina	3.2	−1.1	6.2
Bolivia	3.4	−0.1	3.9
Brazil	6.9	1.5	1.0
Chile	3.4	2.8	6.1
Colombia	5.0	3.4	4.0
Mexico	6.4	1.6	3.0
Peru	4.5	−0.3	2.9
Venezuela	5.9	1.0	3.8
Average	4.8	1.1	3.9

Sources: Hofman 1991, Elias 1992, ECLAC (various issues).

TABLE 7.2 Rate of GDP Growth (Historical Averages, before and after Reform)

Country	Historical Period	Year(s) Starting Reform	Historical Period	3 Years before	GDP Growth Rates Year(s) Starting Reform	3 Years after	5 Years after	10 Years after
Programs of the 1970s								
Chile	1950–70	1974–75	3.9	0.7	−6.7	7.2	7.5	3.7/4.6[a]
Programs of the 1980s								
Mexico	1950–80	1983	6.4	5.2	−5.3	1.0	1.2	2.0
Bolivia	1950–80	1985	3.4	−3.7	−0.1	0.7	1.7	2.3[b]
Venezuela	1950–80	1989	5.9	6.0	−7.8	8.0	5.7[d]	
Programs of the 1990s								
Colombia	1950–80	1990	5.0	4.4	4.0	3.3		
Argentina	1950–80	1991	3.2	−2.8	8.9	7.3[c]		
Peru	1950–80	1991	4.5	−8.5	2.1	1.9[b]		

Source: Author's elaboration.

[a]18 years after.

[b]8 years after.

[c]2 years after.

[d]4 years after.

were launched. During the transition period leading toward high and sustained growth, the process was affected by policy failures, external shocks, and large economic fluctuations.

Comprehensive market-based reform in the 1980s comprised, mainly, Mexico and Bolivia. In Mexico reforms followed two stages: initial fiscal and external adjustment (1983–85) with trade liberalization, deregulation and privatization, and further stabilization taking place after 1985.[14] Oddly, the post-reform growth rate of Mexico has been less than a third of its average rate of the period 1950–80. Bolivia suffered mounting and explosive inflation and negative growth in the first half of the 1980s before adopting the stabilization plan of 1985 and other liberalization policies. These policies contributed to stop and revert the output collapse of the high inflation period. Afterward, per capita growth has been positive but low.[15] The general lesson of the reform programs initiated in the 1980s is that policy reform was not followed by any spectacular upsurge in the rate of economic growth. Beyond country-specific factors, the unsupportive external environment of most of the 1980s—particularly in terms of a negative external transfer—stands as an important common explanation for the sluggish post-reform growth performance in Mexico and Bolivia.[16]

In the early 1990s Argentina and Peru entered the club of comprehensive reformers after being hit by hyperinflation and dramatic economic decline. Both countries managed to stop hyperinflation and initiated programs of trade liberalization, financial reform, deregulation, and privatization. The growth response to these policies in the two countries was quite sizeable, denoting a considerable enthusiasm of the private sector (both national and foreign) for the new policies. Moreover, the recoveries took place from initially depressed output levels after the period of stagnation that characterized the high inflation years. In a way, the initial growth response in Argentina and Peru is similar to the strong Chilean recovery of the second half of the 1970s. Like the late 1970s, the early 1990s is a period of large capital inflows to Latin America.[17] Clearly the size and direction of capital inflows are important determining factors of the different growth response to the reform programs of the 1980s and 1990s.

Finally, it is interesting to mention the case of Colombia, a country with a long tradition of prudence in macro policies and gradualism in the adoption of structural reforms. In contrast to Argentina and Peru, macro conditions were relatively stable in Colombia before reform. The economy was growing at a rate of around 4 percent per year (see table 7.2)—certainly a respectable record for the stagnated 1980s. This of course made it more difficult to achieve a rapid acceleration of growth after the reforms.

Long-Run Growth under State Dirigisme and Market Reform: Econometric Evidence

We have observed that the overall growth record of the main Latin American economies in the pre-reform period, 1950–80, was quite respectable. As we document in this section, however, this growth pattern relied strongly on factor accumulation (labor and capital) with a declining contribution of total factor productivity growth to overall GDP expansion. Table 7.3 provides Elias's (1992) decomposition of sources of growth between factor accumulation and total factor productivity (TFP) growth for Argentina, Brazil, Chile, Bolivia, Mexico, Peru, and Venezuela for each decade from the 1940s to the 1980s.

From this growth decomposition we find that the average contribution of TFP growth to GDP growth—across countries and decades—was 20 percent. This is a relatively low number when compared with a larger sample of developing countries and developed economies. In fact, Chenery, Robinson, and Syrquin (1986) report, for a similar period, a share of TFP growth in total value-added growth of 31 percent for developing countries and 50 percent for developed economies. In the first two decades of import substitution and state dirigisme, the 1940s and 1950s, the contribution of total factor productivity growth was sizeable, particularly in the three largest economies of Latin America: Argentina, Brazil, and Mexico. However, as table 7.3 and figure 7.1 show, a declining rate of TFP growth took place since the 1960s in most of these economies, a trend that further deepened in the 1970s.

Importantly, this evidence shows that the traditional development model in Latin America was displaying clear signs of exhaustion and dynamic inefficiency (in terms of declining productivity growth) well before the debt crisis of the 1980s when growth rates sharply fell or turned negative.[18]

Evidence for Chile

Let us look in more detail at the econometric evidence on the impact of the reforms on long-run growth in Chile. A sources of growth regression for the period 1951–89 (see Lefort and Solimano 1993), with a dummy for post-1974 reform shows:

TABLE 7.3 Sources of Growth, 1940–80 in Selected Latin American Economies (Average Rate of Change per Year)

	GDP Growth (%)	Contribution Factor Accumulation (%)	Total Factor Productivity Growth (%)
Argentina			
1940–50	5.1	2.0	3.1
1950–60	3.3	2.5	0.8
1960–70	3.8	3.6	0.2
1970–80	2.7	3.0	−0.3
Average (1940–80)	3.7	2.7	1.0
Brazil			
1940–50	5.5	N.A.	N.A.
1950–60	6.8	3.2	3.6
1960–70	5.9	4.5	1.4
1970–80	8.2	7.1	1.1
Average (1940–80)	6.6	4.9	2.0
Chile			
1940–50	3.3	1.4	1.9
1950–60	3.5	2.8	0.7
1960–70	5.0	3.7	1.3
1970–80	3.1	2.1	1.0
Average (1940–80)	3.7	2.5	1.2
Colombia			
1940–50	4.1	3.0	1.1
1950–60	4.6	3.7	0.9
1960–70	5.2	4.4	0.8
1970–80	5.8	5.2	0.6
Average (1940–80)	4.9	4.1	0.8
Mexico			
1940–50	6.0	1.6	4.4
1950–60	5.6	4.6	1.0
1960–70	7.1	5.9	1.2
1970–80	6.2	6.1	0.1
Average (1940–80)	6.2	4.6	1.6
Peru			
1940–50	4.4	3.9	0.5
1950–60	3.9	6.5	−2.6
1960–70	5.3	4.3	1.0
1970–80	3.7	4.2	−0.5
Average (1940–80)	4.3	4.7	−0.4
Venezuela			
1940–50	N.A.[a]	N.A.	N.A.
1950–60	7.9	5.7	2.2
1960–70	5.4	4.0	1.4
1970–80	3.9	5.6	−1.7
Average (1940–80)	5.7	5.1	0.6

Source: Elaborated from Elias 1992.
[a]N.A. = not available.

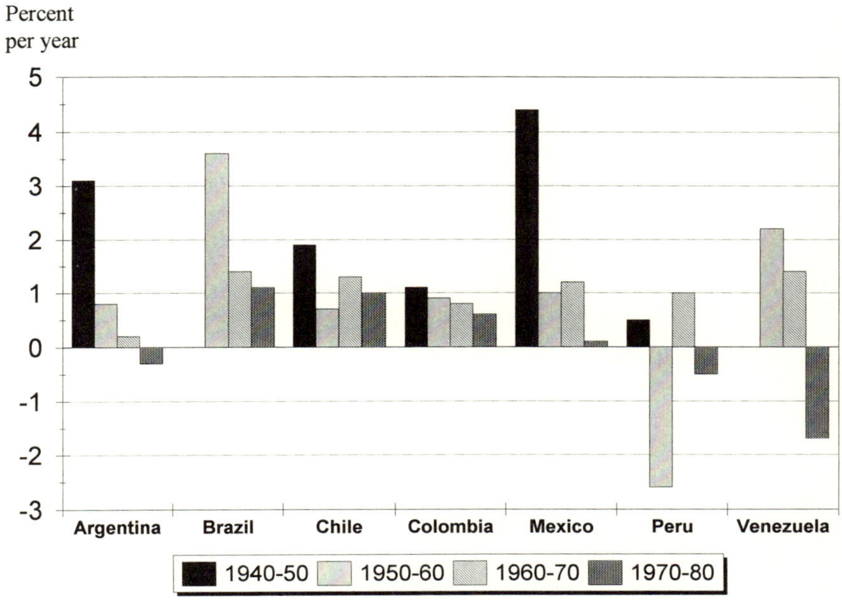

Figure 7.1 Total factor productivity growth

$$GY = \underset{(0.358)}{0.002} + \underset{(7.927)}{0.593}(GKNR) + 0.407(GL) - \underset{(-3.92)}{0.0698}(DREC)$$

$$+\underset{(1.96)}{0.016}(DREF)$$

Rsq (adj). = 0.82
DW = 1.81

Where *GY* stands for the rate of growth of real GDP, *GKNR* is the rate of growth of the stock of nonresidential capital, *GL* is the rate of growth of employment, *DREC* is a recession dummy taking values 1 for 1975 and 1982–83 and zero for the other years. *DREF* is a reform dummy activated after 1974. The *t*-statistics are in parentheses. It is interesting to note that the reform dummy shows a statistically significant increase in the rate of growth of total factor productivity after the adoption of the reforms.[19]

A similar result is obtained when running separate regressions for before-and-after reform samples:
Before reform (period 1951–73):

$$GY = -0.001 + 0.701\,GKNR + 0.297\,GL$$
$$\quad (-0.136) \quad (6.65)$$

Rsq (adj.) = 0.734
DW = 1.93

After reform (period 1974–89):

$$GY = 0.016 + 0.52\,GKNR + 0.479\,GL - 0.065\,DREC$$
$$\quad (2.27) \quad (4.731) \qquad\qquad\qquad (-3.22)$$

Rsq (adj) = 0.874
DW = 1.26

It is interesting to note that the constant of the regression in the period 1951–73 is slightly negative and statistically insignificant, suggesting almost nil average TFP growth. In contrast, the constant goes up to a rate of 1.6 percent per year in the period 1974–89 and is statistically significant. Again, this provides evidence of an acceleration in the rate of growth of total factor productivity after the reforms.

This trend is shown also in table 7.4, which portrays a change in the relative contribution of factor accumulation and TFP growth to the observed rates of growth of GDP after 1974. Of the 3.5 percentage points of average GDP growth in the period 1951–73 (pre-reform period), 0.2 percentage points are explained by total factor productivity growth, with the rest being explained by capital accumulation and labor growth. In contrast, in the period 1974–92 (post-reform), of the average annual rate of GDP growth of 3.8 percent, the contribution of TFP growth is roughly 1 percent. That represents a substantial increase in the relative contribution of TFP growth in the later period.

Table 7.4 also provides a supply and demand decomposition of GDP growth in the post-1974 period. Interestingly, the results show that TFP growth accelerated more both in 1976–81, right after the implementation of the main structural reforms, and in 1989–92, a period of sustained growth. Table 7.4 also shows that exports have almost doubled their contribution to GDP growth in the period 1974–92 in comparison with 1951–73. Clearly, Chilean growth after the reforms has been driven mainly by exports.

An important question posed at the outset of this chapter is the relative contribution of macro stabilization vis-à-vis structural reforms to GDP growth and the transmission mechanisms at work. Lefort and Solimano (1993) run partial regressions for explaining capital formation,

TABLE 7.4 Decomposition Analysis of Sources of Growth, Supply and Demand Factors, Chile 1951–92 (Average Annual Change, %)

								Demand Factors[a]		
	GDP Growth	Rate of Growth of Labor	Total Labor Contrib.	Rate of Growth of N-R Cap.	Rate of Growth of Cap. Util.	Total Capital Contrib.	TFP Growth	Rate of Growth Consump.	Rate of Growth of Invest.	Rate of Growth of Exports
1951–92	3.64	2.48	1.01	3.46	0.05	2.08	0.54	3.05	4.38	8.94
1951–73: Prereforms	3.49	2.00	0.81	4.57	−0.36	2.49	0.18	3.91	1.11	6.06
1974–92: Reform period	3.82	3.06	1.25	2.12	0.55	1.59	0.98	2.45	6.62	10.92
1974: Normalization	0.97	−0.14	−0.06	1.54	4.92	3.83	−2.80	−18.27	19.11	45.95
1975: Stabilization and recession	−12.91	−7.98	−3.25	1.22	−9.87	−5.13	−4.53	−11.42	−22.77	2.35
1976–81: Implementation of major economic reforms	7.20	3.77	1.54	2.10	1.74	2.28	3.39	7.96	12.25	11.16
1982–83: Recession and financial crisis	−7.40	−7.55	−3.07	1.48	−2.24	−0.45	−3.87	−7.76	−24.41	2.67
1984–88: Recovery and re-consolidation of reforms	5.51	9.29	3.78	−0.08	1.66	0.94	0.79	3.89	11.55	7.68
1989–92: Sustained growth	7.12	3.07	1.25	5.60	0.30	3.50	2.38	6.16	11.73	12.13

Source: Lefort and Solimano 1993.

[a]The rates of growth of the demand components for the whole sample and the prereform period correspond to 1961–92 and 1961–73.

productivity growth, and GDP expansion as a function of a set of macro structural reforms and external sector variables. The macroeconomic variables (inflation, the variability of the real exchange rate, the growth rate of public spending) had the highest explanatory value for the rate of GDP growth; in addition, the regressions show that these macro variables were also the most important group of determinants of capital accumulation. This confirms the presumption that investment is very sensitive to instability and that is probably the chief mechanism of transmission of macroeconomic disturbances into output growth. Another interesting result is that the two structural reform variables—an index of import tariffs and a variable of financial deepening—have a positive and significant impact on GDP growth, acting primarily through the rate of growth of total factor productivity.

Mexico

In Mexico, the effect of the reforms on GDP growth was tested with the dummy variables method. The results of a sources of growth equation for the period 1951–89 is the following (see Lefort and Solimano 1993):

$$\underset{(2.14)}{GY = 0.011} + \underset{(4.27)}{0.474\,GKNR} + 0.526\,GL - \underset{(-2.99)}{0.046\,DREC}$$

$$\underset{(-0.265)}{-0.003\,DREF}$$

Rsq(adj) = 0.651
DW = 2.04

This regression shows a negative but insignificant coefficient for the reform dummy variable (DREF) that is activated after 1985 in the GDP growth equation. This result is partly surprising, though it may reflect a small post-reform sample that fails to capture the full impact of the reform on GDP growth.

Several interesting findings stand out from the growth decomposition displayed in table 7.5. First, as noted in previous sections, the implementation of reforms in Mexico was not followed by a strong growth performance, though GDP growth has started to accelerate moderately since 1988. This upswing contrasts with the stagnation observed in the first phase of the reforms, during the period 1982–87. Second, in the pre-reform period, average annual TFP growth is around 1.2 percent, out of 6.5 percentage points of GDP growth.[20] Clearly its contribution to average growth was rather modest in comparison with the contri-

TABLE 7.5 Decomposition Analysis of Sources of Growth, Supply and Demand Factors, Mexico 1951–91 (Average Annual Change, %)

							Demand Factors[a]		
	GDP Growth	Rate of Growth of Labor	Total Labor Contrib.	Rate of Growth of Capital[b]	Total Capital Contrib.	TFP Growth	Rate of Growth Consump.	Rate of Growth Invest.	Rate of Growth of Exports
1951–91	5.26	2.92	1.54	6.12	2.90	0.82	4.99	7.08	5.43
1951–81 Pre-reform period (Developmentalist model)	6.58	3.78	1.99	7.12	3.37	1.21	5.84	9.98	5.44
1951–77 Inward-oriented growth	6.27	3.07	1.61	6.87	3.26	1.40	5.57	8.80	4.94
1978–81 Oil boom	8.63	8.57	4.51	8.76	4.15	−0.03	7.63	17.97	8.78
1982–91 Adjustment and reform period	1.16	0.25	0.13	3.02	1.43	−0.40	2.37	−1.93	5.40
1982–85 Debt crisis and first adjust. period	0.34	−0.79	−0.42	4.16	1.97	−1.21	0.53	−8.06	12.73
1986–87 Oil shock and trade opening	−1.04	−0.52	−0.27	−0.30	−0.14	−0.62	0.04	−2.66	11.40
1988–91 Stabilization and intensification of structural reforms	3.08	1.69	0.89	3.55	1.68	0.52	5.38	4.57	−4.93

Source: Lefort and Solimano 1993.

[a]The rates of growth of the demand components for the whole sample and the prereform period correspond to 1961–92 and 1961–73.

[b]Nonresidential capital adjusted by the rate of change of capital utilization.

bution of capital accumulation. Third, in the period after 1988 there is an increase in TFP growth (to 0.5 percent per year), still a low figure. Fourth, on the demand side growth was driven mainly by investment and only partly by export expansion.

Final Remarks

This chapter points in the direction of a wide variety of short-term growth responses to the adoption of stabilization and liberalization policies. Growth responded quickly to the reforms in Chile in the second half of the 1970s, and in Argentina and Peru in the early 1990s. In contrast, sluggish growth followed comprehensive stabilization and restructuring policies in Mexico and Bolivia in the 1980s, the decade of the debt crisis and the drying up of foreign financing to Latin American countries.

In a long-term perspective, existing econometric evidence on growth patterns for seven Latin American economies from the 1940s to the 1980s shows that GDP growth was mainly explained by factor accumulation, with a relatively small contribution of total factor productivity growth to GDP expansion. In addition, TFP growth exhibited a declining trend starting in the 1960s. This suggests the exhaustion (and dynamic inefficiency) of the growth pattern followed by Latin America under import substitution and state dirigisme, well before the onset of the debt crisis and the overall collapse of growth in the 1980s.

However, the restoration of growth after market reform is also complicated. The empirical evidence at the individual country level shows a long and bumpy way to sustained growth after market reform in Chile. Beyond the initial cycle of expansion (mid-to-late 1970s) and burst (1982–83), the reforms initiated in the 1970s started to pay off in terms of steady supply-driven growth just in the mid-to-late 1980s and throughout the 1990s. Econometric evidence for Chile indicates a statistically significant acceleration in TFP growth after 1974 (when the reforms started) after controlling for short-term macro fluctuations and factor accumulation. In addition, Mexico and Bolivia are still in the slow-to-moderate growth phase, ample reform notwithstanding. For Mexico a small increase in aggregate TFP growth is detected after 1988.

Summing up, growth in the golden age of state dirigisme in Latin America, say the 1940s and 1950s, was relatively high but was followed by dynamic inefficiency (low contribution of productivity growth since the 1960s); in contrast, growth in a mature and consolidated liberalized market economy is more driven by productivity growth and thus is potentially more efficient. The costly period is clearly in the transition phase when stagnation and/or instability precedes the road to prosperity.

NOTES

The author acknowledges comments by V. Corbo, D. Felix, F. Larraín, R. Frenkel, F. Hahn, M. Syrquin, L. Taylor, and participants in workshops in the University of Siena, Italy, and University Complutense's Summer School in Spain.

1. For a fuller discussion of different factors encouraging reform in Latin America and other regions, see Solimano, Sunkel, and Blejer 1994, chapters 1 and 12.
2. See Fischer 1993, Pindyck and Solimano 1993, and Bruno 1993.
3. See Patinkin 1993.
4. See Calvo and Vegh 1994, Kiguel and Liviatan 1992, Solimano 1990, and Corbo and Solimano 1991.
5. This is the mirror effect of the contractionary devaluation case pointed out by Diaz-Alejandro (1964), due to a redistributive effect between wage earners and profit recipients.
6. See Edwards 1993.
7. See Rodrik 1992.
8. See Solimano 1992.
9. See Dornbusch and Reynoso 1989 and Akyuz 1993.
10. See Servén, Solimano, and Soto 1994 for an analysis of the growth effects of privatization in developing countries.
11. The rate of GDP growth of 5.5 percent in that period corresponds to an average of nineteen economies; see Cardoso and Fishlow 1993.
12. See De Gregorio 1992, Corbo and Rojas 1993, and Lefort and Solimano 1993 for empirical analysis of growth in Latin America.
13. See Corbo and Solimano 1991.
14. See Aspe 1993 and Lustig 1992 for an analysis of Mexico.
15. See Morales 1991 for an analysis of the Bolivian case.
16. It is interesting that the "stagnationist" result holds both for the orthodox stabilization plan of Bolivia and the heterodox one of Mexico.
17. There are some important differences between the two periods, however. In the 1990s, most capital inflows are portfolio capital and foreign direct investment. In contrast, in the late 1970s and early 1980s, capital inflows took mainly the form of external borrowing from commercial banks. See Calvo, Leiderman, and Reinhart 1993.
18. In the early 1970s a socialist and/or "populist" response to the trend of stagnation (or modest growth) evident in the 1960s was tried in Chile under Allende, in Peru under Velasco-Alvarado, and in Mexico under Echeverria. These programs stressed the need for an expansion of the state sector through nationalization, coupled with more aggressive aggregate demand policies, as ways to accelerate economic growth and redistribute income. See Dornbusch and Edwards 1991, and other references contained there, for analysis of this "left-wing policy response" to the exhaustion of the import-substitution model in the region.

19. In fact, the dummy amounts to a shift in the constant of the regression, say an increase in the rate of growth of Hicks-neutral total factor productivity growth.

20. See Young 1994 for evidence of TFP growth rates for a large cross section of developing and OECD economies.

REFERENCES

Akyuz, Y. 1993. Financial Liberalization: The Key Issues. In *Finance and the Real Economy,* edited by Y. Akyuz and G. Held. UNU/WIDER.

Aspe, P. 1993. *Economic Transformation: The Mexican Way.* Cambridge, MA: MIT Press.

Bruno, M. 1993. Inflation and Growth in an Integrated Approach. NBER Working Paper 4422.

Calvo, G., and C. Vegh. 1994. Inflation Stabilization and Nominal Anchors. *Contemporary Economic Policy* 12 (2): 35–45.

Calvo G., L. Leiderman, and C. Reinhart. 1993. Capital Flows and Real Exchange Rate Appreciation in Latin America: The Role of External Factors. *IMF Staff Papers* 40 (1).

Cardoso, E. 1993. Macroeconomic Environment and Capital Formation in Latin America. In *Striving for Growth after Adjustment: The Role of Capital Formation,* edited by L. Servén and A. Solimano. Washington, D.C.: World Bank.

Cardoso, E., and A. Fishlow. 1992. Latin American Economic Development: 1950–1980. *Journal of Latin American Studies* 24: 197–218.

Chenery, H., S. Robinson, and M. Syrquin. 1986. *Industrialization and Growth.* Oxford: Oxford University Press.

Corbo, V., and A. Solimano. 1991. Chile's Experience with Stabilization Revisited. In *Lessons of Economic Stabilization and Its Aftermath,* edited by M. Bruno, S. Fischer, E. Helpmann, N. Liviatan. Cambridge, MA: MIT Press.

Corbo, V., and P. Rojas. 1993. Investment, Macroeconomic Stability, and Growth: The Latin American Experience. *Análisis Económico* 8 (1): 19–35.

Díaz-Alejandro, C. 1964. A Note on the Impact of Devaluation and the Distributive Effect. *Journal of Political Economy* 71: 577–80.

De Gregorio, J. 1992. Economic Growth in Latin America. *Journal of Development Economics* 39: 59–84.

Dornbusch, R., and A. Reynoso. 1989. Financial Factors in Economic Development. *American Economic Review, Papers and Proceedings* 79 (2): 204–209.

Easterly, W. 1993. How Much Do Distortions Affect Growth? *Journal of Monetary Economics* 23.

ECLAC (various issues). *Preliminary Economic Report on Latin America and the Caribbean.*

Edwards, S. 1993. Trade Policy, Exchange Rates, and Growth. Paper presented at the conference "Stabilization, Adjustment, and Growth." IDB, December 17–18.

Elias, V. 1992. *Sources of Growth: A Study of Seven Latin American Economies.* San Francisco: International Center for Economic Growth.

Fischer, S. 1993. Macroeconomic Factors in Growth. *Journal of Monetary Economics* 32 (3): 485–512.

Hofman, A. 1991. The Role of Capital in Latin America: A Comparative Perspective of Six Countries for 1950–1989. ECLA-UN Working Paper 4. Santiago, Chile.

International Monetary Fund (various issues).*International Financial Statistics Data Base.*

Kiguel, M., and N. Liviatan. 1992. When Do Heterodox Stabilization Programs Work? Lessons from Experience. *The World Bank Research Observer* 7 (1): 35–57.

Lefort, F., and A. Solimano. 1993. Economic Growth after Market-Based Reform in Latin America: The Cases of Chile and Mexico. Mimeo. World Bank.

King, R., and R. Levine. 1993. Finance, Entrepreneurship, and Growth: Theory and Evidence. *Journal of Monetary Economics* 32 (3): 513–42.

Lustig, N. 1992. *Mexico: The Remaking of an Economy.* Washington, D.C.: Brookings Institution.

Morales, J. A. 1991. The Transition from Stabilization to Sustained Growth in Bolivia. In *Lessons of Economic Stabilization and Its Aftermath,* edited by M. Bruno et al. Cambridge, MA: MIT Press.

Patinkin, D. 1993. Israel's Stabilization Program of 1985, or Some Basic Truths of Monetary Theory. *Journal of Economic Perspectives* 7 (2): 103–28.

Pindyck, R., and A. Solimano. 1993. Economic Instability and Aggregate Investment. NBER Working Paper 4380; also in *Macroeconomic Annual 1993,* edited by O. Blanchard and S. Fischer. Cambridge, MA: MIT Press and NBER.

Rodrik, D. 1992. Closing the Productivity Gap: Does Trade Liberalization Really Help?" In *Trade Policy, Industrialization, and Development,* edited by G. K. Helleiner. Oxford: Clarendon Press.

Servén, L., and A. Solimano, eds. 1993. *Striving for Growth after Adjustment: The Role of Capital Formation.* Washington, D.C.: World Bank.

Servén, L., A. Solimano, and R. Soto. 1994. The Macroeconomics of Public Enterprise Reform and Privatization: Theory and Evidence from Developing Countries. Mimeo. World Bank.

Solimano, A. 1990. Inflation and the Costs of Stabilization: Historical and Recent Experiences and Policy Lessons *The World Bank Research Observer* 5 (2): 167–85.

Solimano, A. 1993. How Private Investment Reacts to Changing Macroeconomic Conditions: The Case of Chile in the Eighties. In *Reviving Private Investment in Developing Countries,* edited by A. Chihibber et al. Amsterdam: North-Holland.

Solimano, A. 1992. Understanding the Investment Cycle in Adjustment Programs: Evidence from Reforming Economies. World Bank Policy Research Working Paper 921.

Solimano, A. 1994. State Dirigisme, Market Reform, and Economic Growth: A Look at the Evidence for Latin America. Mimeo. World Bank.

Solimano, A., O. Sunkel, and M. Blejer, eds. 1994. *Rebuilding Capitalism: Alternative Roads after Socialism and Dirigisme.* Ann Arbor: University of Michigan Press.

Young, A. 1994. Lessons from the East Asian NICs: A Contrarian View. *European Economic Review* 38 (3–4): 964–73.

CHAPTER 8

Growth and Convergence in the OECD: The Postwar Experience

Javier Andrés, José E. Boscá, and Rafael Doménech

Sustained economic growth, stable investment rates, substantial effort in human capital accumulation, and steady convergence in percapita income among its country members has made the postwar growth experience of the OECD somehow unique among the world's regions. OECD economies also share a good deal of social and economic institutions, such as a well-developed market structure and rather stable political systems. Finally, being a highly integrated area, the OECD also presents many fewer technological disparities than other regions.

In this chapter we study the evolution of the OECD from the perspective of the recent empirical growth literature. We highlight the main differences between the OECD and other world regions, and discuss to what extent the widely used exogenous growth model suffices to explain the most salient features of the recent economic history of the industrialized world. This question is closely related to the fundamental debate in the growth literature in the last years, namely, which is the real engine of growth? As noted by an important number of leading growth theorists (Solow [1994]; Grossman and Helpman [1994]; Romer [1994]), the importance of the variety of endogenous growth models developed in recent years is that these models have moved the discussion to a renewed interest about the ultimate determinants of the growth process over the long run. Questions regarding topics such as the role of investment in the transitional dynamics of economies reverting to their steady state that were central to the neoclassical debate are not subjects of great controversy anymore. The perspective nowadays is to determine the real forces behind the rate of growth, not denying the relevance of capital accumulation, but assigning it a role as a propagation mechanism of innovations in the economy.

Romer (1994) argues that "When I look back on my work on growth, my greatest satisfaction comes from having rejected the first round of external effects models that I tried." The reason for doing so is his belief that the notion of capital fundamentalism, in which the rate of capital accumulation is the primary determinant of economic growth, is not a realistic way to describe the real process behind economic growth. According to Romer, economists have long taken for granted some evidence that should be present in any attempt to build up a realistic model. Much of this evidence—such as the fact that technological advance comes from things that people do, and that many individuals and firms have market power and earn monopoly rents on discoveries—is difficult to reconcile with the insights of the models of growth based on a constant returns to scale technology.

In this chapter we show that much of the economic success of the OECD economies can be explained by the intense effort of these economies to increase their productive capacity as well as by the increased efficiency in the use of their resources, which in turn has been facilitated by the availability of a highly educated and trained work force. This growth has also brought about a non-negligible process of convergence in wealth levels that has no parallel in other economic regions. There have also been many less pleasant features, however, some of which are still awaiting an adequate theoretical framework. We uncover some of these and try to put forward some plausible explanations. The slowing down of the convergence process, mainly caused by the poor macroeconomic performance of the less advanced countries during the period 1975–85, is one of these. Similarly, we find difficult to reconcile the evidence found for the OECD as a whole, with the existence of substantial differences among country members, which casts some doubts on the use of the representative economy assumption in our model. Finally, we find that capital intensity has not been sufficient for growth, nor it can be taken as the only policy recipe for success. In fact, a closer inspection of the time correlations among investment and growth reveals that this correlation is not as robust as is usually assumed, suggesting that other engines of growth ought to be taken into account.

The chapter is organized as follows. In the second section, which follows, we review the evidence on growth and convergence rates, discussing the causes behind the OECD differential behavior; we also analyze the correlation among growth rates and their main determinants across countries. In the third section we study the correlation among medium-term macroeconomic indicators and growth, in search of an explanation of the poor performance of most countries during the years of the recession. The fourth section deals with the interaction between growth and the distribution of income. In the fifth section we take a

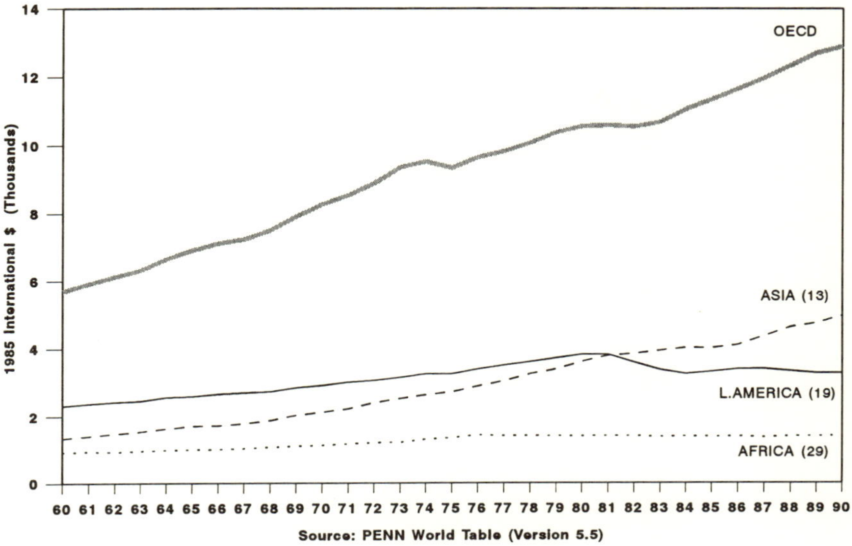

Figure 8.1a GDP per capita across world regions

more disaggregated look at the process of development within the OECD, and the sixth section concludes with some additional remarks.

Growth and Convergence in the OECD

Panel (a) in figure 8.1 compares the evolution of GDP per capita across world regions.[1] The OECD and Asia are the only regions with steady growth during the 1960–90 period;[2] Latin America grew quite fast until the mid-1970s, whereas the income per capita in Africa is not substantially higher now than it was thirty years ago. The amount of resources devoted to investments in physical and human capital is usually a key determinant in the process of growth. Indeed, the share of GDP devoted to increasing the capital stock is higher in the OECD than in other regions (panel b) and has remained fairly stable all along the sample period. The sharp increase in investment rates in Asia might also explain its economic success. As far as human capital is concerned, table 8.1 uncovers a similar pattern, although Latin America fares rather well in all seven indicators. The OECD reaches the highest values both in years of schooling (primary, secondary, and higher education) of the labor force and in enrollment rates at all levels. Africa is,

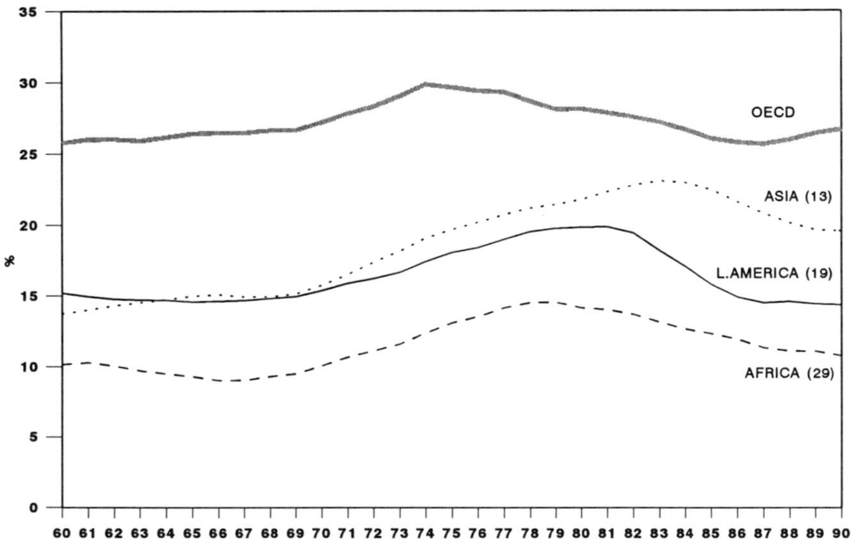

Figure 8.1b Ratio of investment to GDP (five-year moving averages)

on the other hand, at the bottom with far fewer resources devoted to accumulating human capital.

In table 8.2 we present the basic information on levels and growth rates of per capita income.[3] The average rate of growth of income per capita was 2.97 for the OECD, and slightly higher for the European Union (3.09) and the G7 (3.05); the six poorest countries[4] in 1990, on the other hand, grew at a faster rate (3.26). This growth process has been based in reasonable high investment/GDP rates (19.5), as well as in low population growth rates (0.8) and in a substantial investment in human capital (with 72.38 and 19.57 averages in secondary and university enrollment rates). Differences in saving rates explain part but not the whole of the differences in growth rates. We find fast growth associated with high savings rates in countries like Japan (5.39 growth rate and 25.21 savings rate), Finland (3.45 and 27.18) and Norway (3.23 and 29.66) as well as slow growth in countries with low savings, for example, Great Britain (2.16 and 12.2) and New Zealand (1.31 and 14.24). Variations in enrollment rates are even larger and their correlation with growth rates is less clear; some countries with very high enrollment rates (such as Denmark and the United States) have grown less than others with much less human capital investment (Turkey, Portugal, or Italy).

A first look at the information in table 8.2 suggests that the distance

TABLE 8.1 Human Capital in the OECD and Other World Regions

Region	Number of Countries	Years of Schooling				Enrollment Rates (%)		
		Total	Primary	Secondary	Tertiary	Primary	Secondary	Tertiary
OECD	24	7.20	5.14	1.79	0.35	98.5	70.3	19.6
Africa	29	1.41	1.19	0.22	0.04	55.9	10.7	1.2
Latin America	19	3.63	2.81	0.72	0.13	90.4	34.7	8.8
Asia	13	3.01	2.12	0.79	0.15	76.4	35.4	6.4

TABLE 8.2 Basic Indicators of Economic Growth in OECD Countries, 1960–1990 Averages

Country	Rates of growth (%) GDP/N	GDP/L	N	GDP/N 1960 (USA = 100)	GDP/N 1990 (USA = 100)	GDP/L 1960 (USA = 100)	GDP/L 1990 (USA = 100)	Real I/GDP	Nominal I/GDP
Australia	2.22	1.72	1.62	67.25	73.07	63.02	75.41	22.78	24.64
Austria	3.21	3.03	0.30	52.03	75.63	46.51	81.83	21.65	25.58
Belgium	3.08	3.00	0.29	53.27	74.59	53.48	93.48	16.47	20.23
Canada	2.84	1.69	1.33	66.59	86.86	73.44	87.49	18.72	22.27
Switzerland	1.89	1.76	0.80	97.20	95.85	71.87	87.45	21.57	25.78
Germany	2.65	2.81	0.44	67.73	83.61	53.82	88.94	18.75	22.49
Denmark	2.56	2.00	0.39	63.17	75.73	53.53	69.75	18.79	21.37
Spain	3.75	4.29	0.81	31.76	53.66	30.69	77.58	17.50	23.44
Finland	3.45	3.31	0.40	48.57	75.53	37.98	72.41	27.18	26.18
France	2.94	3.27	0.73	58.81	79.13	50.84	96.37	18.55	22.65
U.K.	2.16	2.11	0.31	67.85	72.56	55.02	74.14	12.02	18.21
Greece	3.96	4.38	0.66	18.97	33.83	17.47	44.63	15.49	21.50
Ireland	3.49	3.99	0.71	31.22	49.14	31.39	73.12	16.93	21.94
Iceland	3.44	2.57	1.24	50.05	76.22	48.42	73.78	23.40	25.07
Italy	3.44	3.78	0.46	47.23	73.20	42.62	93.14	18.39	23.28
Japan	5.39	5.17	0.94	29.91	80.63	23.54	76.24	25.21	31.31
Luxembourg	2.62	2.03	0.64	75.18	91.16	66.95	87.22	21.10	25.16
Netherlands	2.40	2.31	0.88	63.50	72.77	57.49	81.88	18.35	22.82
Norway	3.23	2.85	0.56	50.10	73.27	43.69	73.22	29.66	28.31
New Zealand	1.31	1.17	1.18	75.13	61.86	67.15	67.92	14.24	22.63
Portugal	4.08	4.13	0.57	20.77	38.24	16.47	39.55	18.23	25.18
Sweden	2.40	2.07	0.45	67.26	77.16	52.66	70.08	17.46	21.04
Turkey	2.96	3.69	2.40	17.43	23.36	15.13	32.02	18.22	18.73
United States	1.94	1.09	1.09	100.00	100.00	100.00	100.00	17.25	18.71
OECD	2.97	2.84	0.80	55.04	70.17	48.88	75.73	19.50	23.27
EU	3.09	3.18	0.57	49.95	66.47	44.15	76.65	17.55	22.36
G7	3.05	2.85	0.76	62.59	82.28	57.04	88.04	18.42	22.70
OECD(6)	3.26	3.61	1.05	32.55	43.35	29.72	55.80	16.77	22.24

Sources: OECD (various publications), Human Capital from UNESCO (various yearbooks and own estimates), and own calculations. GDP=Gross Domestic Product; L=Employment; N=Population; I=Investment.

OECD(6) includes only the six poorest countries in 1990.

of most countries with respect to the United States in income has fallen in relative terms, although with very different country experiences.[5] Barro and Sala-i-Martín (1991, 1992) have proposed two ways of presenting the information about the long-run path of relative incomes: σ and β convergence. The measure of σ–convergence is the time change of the standard deviation of income per capita across countries, and does not incorporate any a priori about what the relevant model of the economy

Enrollment rates		1960–1975 and 1985–1990 Averages: Rates of growth (%)			1975–1985 Averages: Rates of growth (%)		GDP/L (USA = 100)		
2nd.	3rd.	GDP/N	GDP/L	Real I/GDP	GDP/N	GDP/L	1975	1985	Real I/GDP
67.50	85.83	2.47	1.74	23.37	1.71	1.68	75.78	75.21	21.60
66.83	78.17	3.63	3.85	22.06	2.37	1.39	68.09	72.15	21.08
83.67	94.83	3.70	3.34	17.22	1.85	2.32	69.87	70.36	14.93
75.17	91.83	3.07	1.78	18.62	2.39	1.50	82.01	86.91	19.05
67.17	80.92	2.16	2.24	22.59	1.35	0.81	98.43	94.34	19.67
68.16	82.17	2.81	3.22	19.57	2.32	1.99	76.39	80.52	16.84
92.83	96.17	2.59	2.17	20.02	2.49	1.66	71.52	76.62	16.43
63.50	87.25	5.25	4.81	18.34	0.75	3.25	52.37	47.36	16.18
89.00	91.33	3.90	3.95	28.29	2.56	2.02	65.32	70.48	24.65
72.17	92.50	3.48	3.74	19.15	1.86	2.33	75.53	76.17	17.60
75.67	87.17	2.30	2.09	12.48	1.87	2.16	67.74	68.35	11.26
66.83	86.33	4.99	5.72	16.19	1.90	1.70	34.11	34.51	14.14
73.50	90.00	4.01	4.22	16.19	2.46	3.54	39.09	41.74	19.02
78.33	88.50	3.40	2.80	23.91	3.52	2.11	63.73	75.24	22.22
59.83	77.67	3.77	4.41	19.29	2.78	2.53	62.60	68.99	16.31
87.00	93.58	6.42	6.14	25.55	3.34	3.25	61.46	71.64	25.33
92.03	98.85	2.83	1.98	22.53	2.18	2.14	78.54	81.67	18.20
80.17	92.17	2.99	2.96	19.53	1.23	1.00	74.99	71.00	15.92
80.50	89.50	2.98	3.01	29.59	3.73	2.54	62.07	75.06	30.02
79.50	93.17	1.44	1.46	14.58	1.03	0.61	73.49	68.17	13.68
44.67	78.33	5.15	4.76	18.86	1.93	2.85	33.32	33.78	16.90
73.67	84.00	2.90	2.60	18.32	1.39	1.01	80.42	77.45	15.68
29.00	63.00	3.69	4.67	18.02	1.48	1.71	21.86	21.17	18.83
93.48	96.83	2.01	1.34	17.51	1.79	0.60	100.00	100.00	16.73
73.34	87.50	3.41	3.29	20.07	2.10	1.95	66.20	68.29	18.43
72.75	88.62	3.66	3.62	18.28	1.97	2.29	61.34	62.59	16.14
75.92	88.82	3.41	3.25	18.88	2.34	2.05	75.10	78.94	17.59
59.50	83.01	4.09	4.27	17.03	1.59	2.28	42.37	41.12	16.46

is. It is only a crude measure of convergence, because the variance of income across countries is contaminated by the variance of the shocks hitting the economy at any particular point in time.[6] Hence even if the economies were truly getting closer in the long run, this statistic has a lower bound given by the variance of these shocks.

The evolution of the standard deviation of (the log of) per capita income across OECD countries is depicted in figure 8.2. After a period

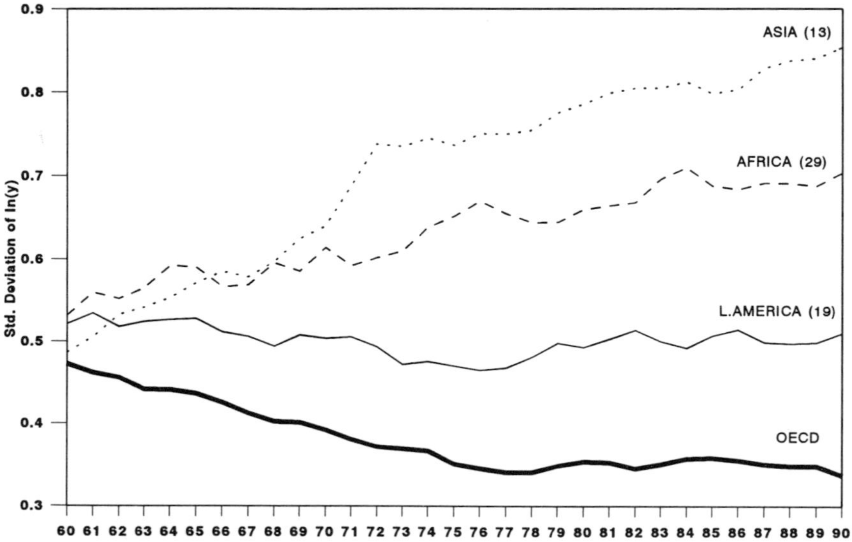

Figure 8.2 Sigma convergence across world regions

of substantial and steady reduction from 1960 to 1974, income dispersion has remained stable all through 1990. For the period as a whole, the standard deviation of per capita income has fallen by 33 percent. As figure 8.2 shows, this fall in the dispersion of incomes is not a worldwide pattern (see also Parente and Prescott 1993). Starting from comparable levels in 1960, the dispersion displays an upward trend in Asia[7] and Africa and has remained roughly constant in Latin America. The fall in dispersion within the OECD uncovers a clear pattern of convergence that has been brought about by the increased integration of goods and financial markets and the expansion of world trade, as well as by an intensive process of technological catchup. However, the unequal impact of macroeconomic shocks in the 1970s and 1980s might be behind the interruption in the convergence process in per capita incomes in the OECD from 1974 onward.

The reasons behind the tendency of many OECD economies to approach the levels of income per capita of its most advanced country members can be found in two distinctive features of the growth rates that are not present in other regions. Growth rates tend to be rather persistent, and they are negatively correlated with the initial income level. This means that yesterday's poorer countries tend to grow faster than the average today, and also that today's fast growers tend to grow fast also in the future. These two features are consistent with the predictions of a model with constant returns to scale (Solow 1956).[8] We shall use this model as the organizing framework throughout most of the rest of the chapter, to decide which variables and relationships to look at and to set up simple partitioned regression analyses. Although subject to many criticisms, this framework does not appear prima facie at odds with some of the features of the long-run evolution of the OECD economies. However, the Solow framework is just a starting point; the results in this chapter uncover many aspects that have a difficult explanation within this narrow theoretical framework, suggesting the necessity of a broader view.

Consider a regression model like equation (8.1), in which y is output per capita, x^* is its steady-state growth rate (which in this model corresponds to the rate of labor-augmenting technological progress), $\hat{y}$ is output per capita in efficiency units, and y^* its steady-state value; finally, T is the period of time considered and u is the error term.

$$(1/T) \log (y_{it}/y_{i,t-T}) = x_i^* + (1/T)(1-e^{-\beta T}) \log (\hat{y}_i^*/y_i^*) + u_{it} \,. \quad (8.1)$$

According to the expression in (8.1), economies that are above or below their steady-state income level tend to approach it monotonically at a rate β. This model encompasses the two aforementioned features: autocorrelation in growth rates and negative correlation with initial income. The second feature is the well-known β-convergence property, which is a measure of the speed at which each country's income moves toward its steady state once it has been pushed away from it by a particular shock.

As Easterly et al.(1993) have pointed out, there is very little persistence in growth rates at a worldwide level, with the exception of the OECD, in which growth rates follow a first-order autocorrelation process with declining persistence. Low persistence is difficult to explain in endogenous growth models, in which structural country characteristics determine the growth rates and hence generate inertia. Similarly, persistence should be high in exogenous growth models until countries approach their steady state and start to bounce around it, following temporary idiosyncratic shocks. In fact, the persistence in growth rates turns out to be quite substantial for the OECD, although it declines steadily from 1960 to 1990.[9]

The declining pattern of autocorrelation in growth rates might be compatible with an endogenous or an exogenous growth model, depending on whether growth rates are positively or negatively correlated with initial income levels. This is what the concept of β convergence is useful

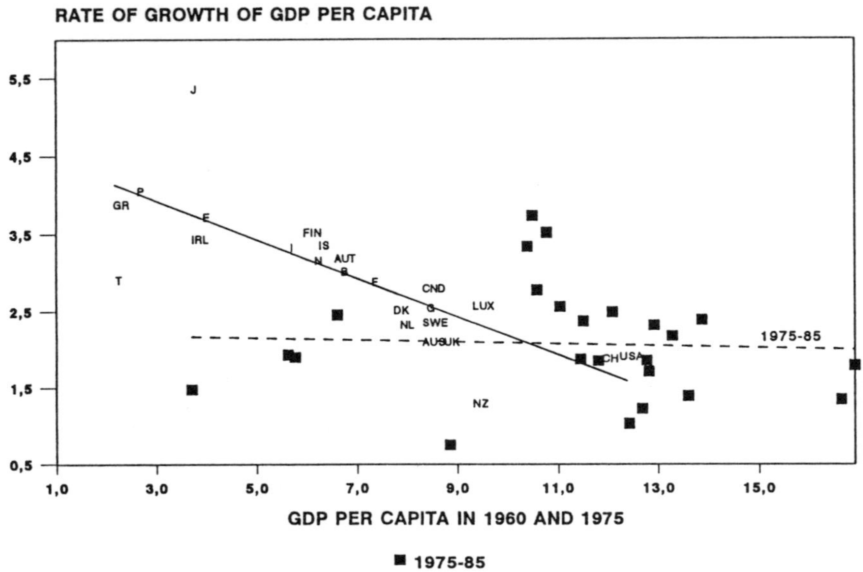

Figure 8.3a Unconditional β convergence

for, although this measure has some limitations too. First, it is a single-country implication of the model whose interpretation in a multicountry setting is not straightforward. Second, as Quah (1993b) has made clear, a significant β parameter estimated from multicountry cross-section models might be consistent with a nondegenerate distribution of incomes in the long run. Despite these shortcomings, this analysis can still deliver some useful information about the nature of the growth process in a region such as the OECD, in which the restrictive assumptions of the canonical growth model are more likely to be satisfied than anywhere else.

The absolute convergence version of the model assumes that $y_{i,t}^*$ is either constant or, at least, uncorrelated with $y_{i,t-1}$, and hence that it can be included in the error term and still obtain a consistent estimate of β in (8.1). The solid line of panel (a) in figure 8.3 displays a negative correlation among growth and initial levels of per capita income in 1960. However one of the advantages of the β-convergence model is that it allows us to relate growth rates with its main determinants. Much of the variation in growth rates might be explained by differences in accumulation rates across countries. As it is depicted in panel (b) the negative correlation among growth rates and initial income is even stronger after control-

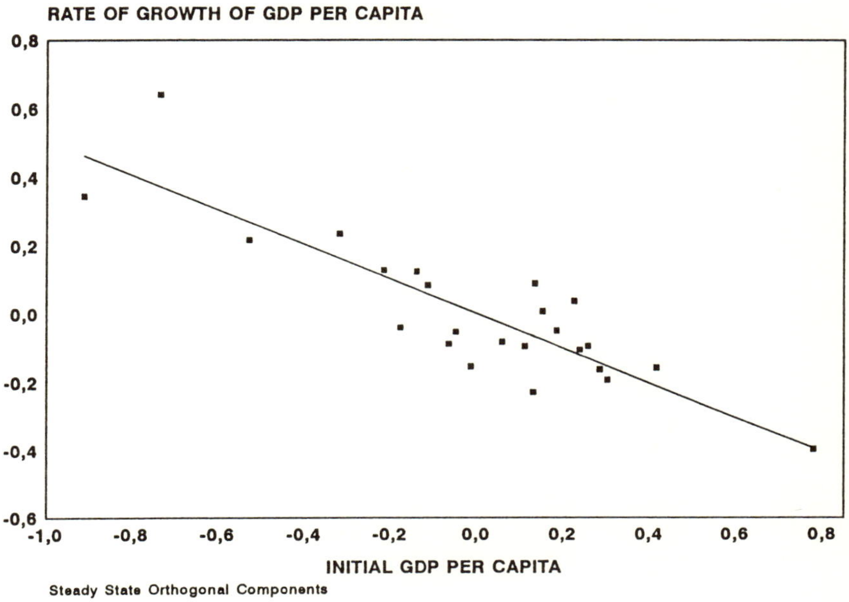

Figure 8.3b Unconditional β convergence, 1960–90

ling for the variables behind the (unobservable) steady state, that is, the savings rate, human capital accumulation, and population growth. This correlation is unambiguously negative and significant, indicating that low-income countries in 1960 enjoyed, on average, higher growth rates.[10]

The partial correlation among growth, savings and human capital accumulation is represented in figures 8.4 and 8.5. The correlation among growth and investment is positive and significant, and it remains so after controlling for initial income, population growth, and schooling. This result is stable along the sample period, although it is heavily influenced by the experience of some particular countries.[11] The same significant positive correlation is found between growth and schooling after controlling for the initial income, savings and population growth, although in this case the correlation becomes nonsignificant from 1980 onward.[12]

The evidence of a positive association among growth and investment (both in physical and in human capital), alongside the significant pattern of β and σ convergence among OECD economies, has been taken as consistent with the constant returns technology. However, be-

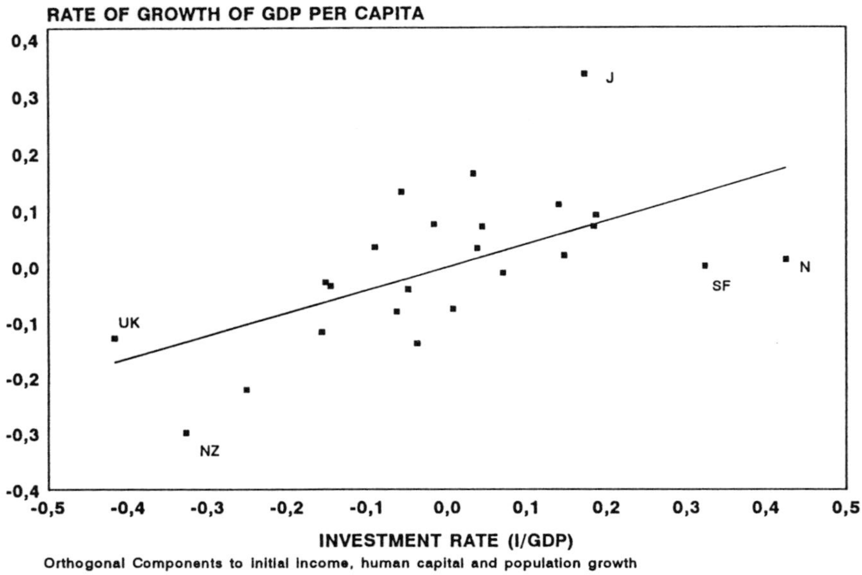

Figure 8.4 Growth and investment rates

cause the policy implications of this model differ substantially from those of the endogenous growth model, this issue should be analyzed more carefully. Some recent studies suggest that this correlation might be weak if individual country effects are taken into account (Cohen 1993) and that the direction of causality might be running from growth to capital accumulation (Blömstrom, Lipsey, and Zejan 1993). In the rest of this section we look at the causality among per capita income and accumulation rates in more detail.[13]

Tests of causality running from investment to per capita GDP are presented in table 8.3. Equations in columns 1 and 2 (5 and 6) have been estimated without controlling for country-specific time-invariant effects, whereas those in columns 3 and 4 (7 and 8) have been estimated in first differences. The models in 2 and 4 (6 and 8) include the rate of growth of population and the human capital accumulation rate as additional regressors.[14] The results differ across different specifications. When differences in constant terms are not allowed for, positive causality from human capital investment to GDP per capita and growth rates is the norm. This is especially so when other regressors are included. However, estimating the model in first differences has devastating effects for the null of causality. Causality turns out to be nonsignificant in all eight models in

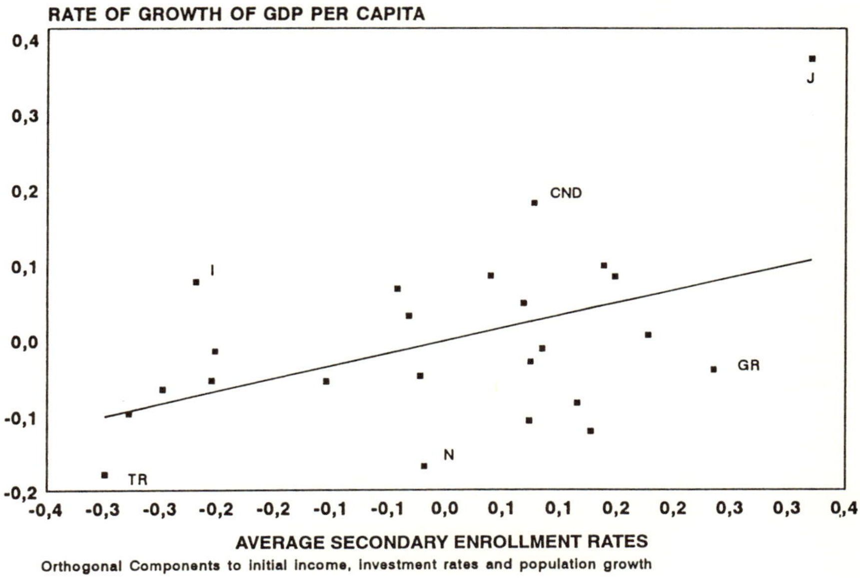

Figure 8.5 Growth and human capital

columns 3, 4, 7, and 8. Furthermore, in six of these models, the sign of the long-run impact of investment on the right-hand side variable (either GDP per capita or its growth rate) is negative.

These results are quite surprising, because some of the regressions in this table resemble very much the conventional β-convergence model as it is written in (8.1). Allowing for the possibility of parameter heterogeneity, at least in the constant term, seems to be the main reason behind this finding. We shall explore this possibility further in the fourth section; the results at this stage cast some doubts on the neoclassical interpretation of the link among investment and income per capita. Neither in levels nor in growth rates does the GDP in the OECD seem to be caused by the rate of investment. Our results, though, are consistent with those of Blömstrom, Lipsey, and Zejan (1993), who also found no evidence of causality from investment to growth after controlling for country-specific effects. In a related work Carroll and Weil (1993) find that savings fail to cause growth (or they do with an unexpected negative coefficient) for the OECD sample.

A similar analysis can be carried out for the relationship between growth and human capital accumulation. We do so using different proxies for the rate of GDP devoted to accumulating human capital.

TABLE 8.3 Causality between Investment, GDP Per Capita, and Growth

	From Investment to GDP per Capita				From Investment to Growth			
	1	2	3	4	5	6	7	8
E causality (1 lag)	yes	yes	no	no	no	yes	no	no
Sign of causality	(+)	(+)	(+)	(−)	(+)	(+)	(+)	(−)
E causality (2 lag)	yes	yes	no	no	no	yes	no	no
Sign of causality	(+)	(+)	(−)	(−)	(+)	(+)	(−)	(−)
Estimation Method	OLS	OLS	GMM	GMM	OLS	OLS	GMM	GMM
Additional regressors?	no	yes	no	yes	no	yes	no	yes

Mankiw, Romer, and Weil (1992) proposed the use of enrollment rates in secondary education. This variable has its limitations, in particular because this rate is near 100 percent for most OECD countries by the end of our sample period. Hence we have also used enrollment rates in higher education as an alternative proxy. This measure should be taken with caution too, because not all higher studies have the same impact on future production possibilities (Mulligan and Sala-i-Martín 1994). Finally we have also used three indices constructed by Barro and Lee (1993) that correspond to total, secondary, and higher years of schooling of those over age twenty-five. The data of these variables is available at five-year intervals from 1960 to 1985. We have used a pooled sample consisting of five-year averages for all variables with the exception of human capital and initial income per capita, which refer to the initial year in each interval.

Table 8.4 summarizes the analysis of causality from human capital accumulation to growth. We present two models for each of the five different human capital indices; the first one is estimated in levels, whereas the second is estimated in first differences to remove the effect of country-specific time-invariant effects. We control for time changes in the constant term as well as for other accumulation rates on the right-hand side.[15] The model is estimated using three lag structures as indicated in the table, to allow for short or long lags in the response of output to human capital accumulation. The results are somehow mixed; in the models in columns 1, 3, 5, 7, and 9 causality is always positive, being only significant in five of the fifteen cases. However, once country-specific effects are taken into account (cols. 2, 4, 6, 8, and 10), the results worsen substantially. Causality can be rejected in all fifteen possible cases, in most of which the sign of causality is even negative.[16]

These results confirm the absence of positive (statistical) causality from investment and other accumulation rates to income per capita and

TABLE 8.4 Causality between Human Capital and Growth

	3rd level		2nd level		Total Years		Years 2nd		Years 3rd	
	1	2	3	4	5	6	7	8	9	10
Causality from 1nS to 1ny										
E causality (1 lag)	yes	no	no	no	no	no	yes	no	yes	no
Sign of causality	(+)	(+)	(+)	(+)	(+)	(−)	(+)	(+)	(+)	(+)
E causality (2 lag)	yes	no	no	no	no	no	no	no	no	no
Sign of causality	(+)	(+)	(+)	(−)	(+)	(−)	(+)	(+)	(+)	(−)
E causality (3 lag)	yes	no	no	no	no	no	no	no	no	no
Sign of causality	(+)	(+)	(+)	(−)	(+)	(−)	(+)	(−)	(+)	(−)
Estimation Method	OLS	GMM	OLS	GMM	OLS	GMM	OLS	GMM	OLS	GMM

Source: Data in columns 1–4 are from UNESCO. Data in columns 5–10 are from Barro and Lee 1993.

growth. They contrast sharply with the interpretation of the standard correlation among growth and current accumulation rates that has led to the so-called capital fundamentalism (King and Levine 1994) in the analysis of growth and development. Some caution is required, however, before drawing conclusions from these results. This lack of causality should not lead us to conclude that physical and human capital are irrelevant in the growth process, as it is often claimed. Increases in the stock of physical and human capital are important features of any process of sustained growth. This evidence, though, works against the adjustment mechanism of the exogenous growth model, built into the convergence equations. If accumulation rates do not help to forecast the future income path, it means that the the long-run relationship among these variables does not hold, at least not in the way it does in the constant returns exogenous growth model. Rather than focusing in the mechanical link among accumulation and growth, the importance of investment in physical and human capital relies in its role as a means of incorporating most innovations that are the true engines of growth in the generation of endogenous growth models.

Medium-Term Economic Policies and Growth

The picture emerging in the previous section suggests that the growth process in the OECD is complex enough to be explained only by the forces behind the "catching up" hypothesis and the differences in accumulation rates in physical and human capital. The empirical growth literature has explored extensively the contribution of other economic, social, and political indicators. In this and the next section we focus in two different sets of variables that may shape the growth performance of a country. First we discuss the empirical evidence in the OECD about the connection of some economic indicators, such as inflation or export growth, with the convergence process, comparing the robustness of such relationships with the results of larger country samples such as that of Levine and Renelt (1992). Then, in the next section we analyze the interaction among income distribution and growth in the way proposed by Persson and Tabellini (1994).

As we have seen in figure 8.1, the performance of OECD countries after World War II is one of the best examples of economic convergence. This feature has been corroborated using the concept of β convergence as in figure 8.3 (panel a), where we plot the initial per capita income in 1960 against the average rate of growth from 1960 to 1990. However, in other studies we have found that even in this period, convergence in the OECD is not stable both across countries and across shorter time peri-

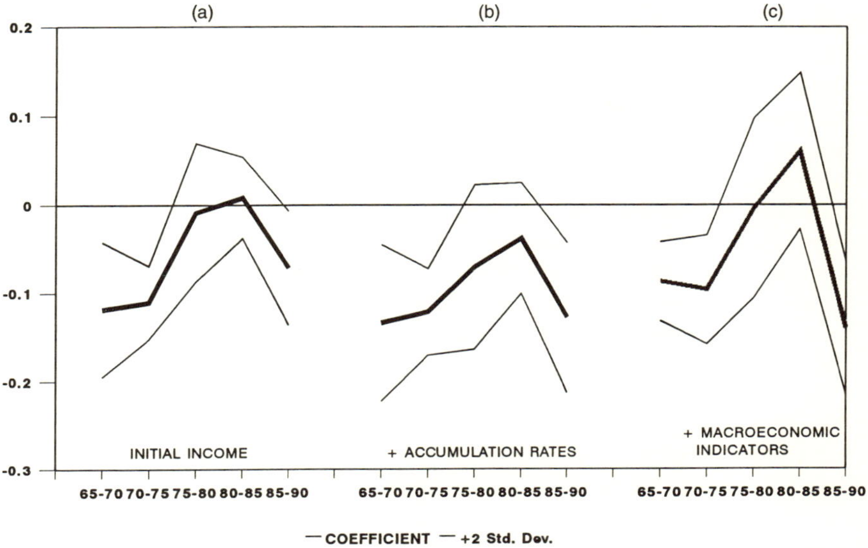

Figure 8.6 Stability of initial income coefficient

ods.[17] The dashed line in figure 8.3 is the fitted regression line of the average rate of growth in 1975–85 on income per capita in 1975, and it confirms the slowing down of the convergence process also observed in figure 8.1.

In panel (a) of figure 8.6 we show the evolution of the initial income coefficient and its confidence interval resulting from the estimation of a linear version of equation (8.1) in different periods using five-year averages. This coefficient is negative and statistically significant in three out of five periods, but it is not significant in 1975–80 and is even positive in 1980–85. Notice that, given equation (8.1), a positive coefficient on initial income implies a negative convergence coefficient (β). The first possible explanation of such behavior is that the economic turbulence experienced between 1975 and 1985 affected investment in different ways in various OECD countries, so the problem we find is the consequence of an inappropriate use of the unconditional convergence equation. Panel (b) shows the initial income coefficient when we add the accumulation rates of physical and human capital. However, the results again confirm the instability of the convergence process.

The most obvious alternative explanation for the changes in the rate of convergence is that we have omitted some variables that might account for the changes in the economic environment in each country during those years, biasing the β estimates. Table 8.5 presents the evidence in the OECD of changes in the mean and standard deviations of inflation, export and money growth, and public expenditure across different time periods. In the period from 1975 to 1985, all of these indicators display a worse performance than for the 1960–90 period as a whole. Inflation was higher while there were lower export growth rates and higher public consumption as a percentage of GDP, and money growth rates also increased. The standard deviations of these variables across countries also increased during these years, indicating that the two oil crises had unequal consequences in OECD countries. With no exceptions, there was a noticeable increase in the standard deviations and in the coefficients of variation. It seems promising on these grounds to account for the effects of the changes in these variables on the growth performance of these countries, so as to explain the structural break in the convergence process.

Some empirical evidence has pointed out the fragility of the relationship between a wide list of economic indicators and growth. Levine and Renelt (1992) found that in using a sample of 119 countries, only few variables are robustly correlated with cross-country growth rates from 1960 to 1989. In the definition of robustness they use an extreme bound analysis (EBA): if a variable remains significant and of the same sign when varying a subset of regressors in the equation, this variable is said to be robust. EBA uses equations of the form:

$$\Delta \ln y = \beta_i I + \beta_m M + \beta_z Z + u,$$

TABLE 8.5 Macroeconomic Variables, OECD

	1960–75 and 85–90	1975–80	1980–85
Means			
Inflation (%)	7.55	13.36	12.34
Exports growth (%)	7.33	4.86	4.90
Money growth (%)	12.71	14.04	13.00
Public expenditure (% of GDP)	21.92	22.69	23.18
Standard errors			
Inflation	4.19	10.23	11.94
Exports growth	2.05	2.33	3.82
Money growth	5.54	9.55	12.41
Public expenditure (% of GDP)	3.88	4.70	4.88

where *I* is a set of variables always included in the regression (the investment share of GDP, initial GDP per capita, secondary school enrollment rate, and population growth), *M* is the variable being analyzed, and *Z* is the subset of variables sequentially included in the regression. When the composition of *Z* changes, one is likely to observe changes in the estimated coefficient of the variable *M*. The EBA computes the maximum and minimum value of βm for all possible linear combinations of up to three *Z* variables.

More recently, Sala-i-Martin (1994) has argued that it would always be possible to find a specification of the above equation, in which a variable is nonsignificant. In this case, what really matters is how frequent these specifications are. Following this suggestion, Andrés, Doménech, and Molinas (1994) implement an alternative procedure. After running all possible combinations between some of the economic indicators usually considered, a variable can be classified as significant or nonsignificant, depending on the number of cases in which we can reject the null hypothesis of nonsignificance. In our analysis, *I* includes only initial GDP per capita.

Although the methodology is not strictly the same, in table 8.6 we compare the results obtained by Levine and Renelt and by Andrés, Doménech, and Molinas for a set of ten regressors. With respect to the first group of variables that Levine and Renelt include in *I*, the differ-

TABLE 8.6 Growth and Macroeconomic Variables

Variables	Levine and Renelt (1992)	Andrés, Doménech, and Molinas (1994)
Initial income	robust (−)	significant (−)
Investment share	robust (+)	significant (+)
Human capital	robust (+)	nonsignificant (+)
Population growth	fragile (−)	significant (−)[a,d]
Exports growth	fragile (+)	significant (+)
Inflation	fragile (−)	significant (−)[b]
Money growth		significant (+)[c]
Domestic credit growth	fragile (+)	
Variance of money growth		nonsignificant (−)[b]
Variance of domestic credit growth	fragile (−)	
Government consumption share	fragile (−)	nonsignificant (−)[d]
Budget surplus (% of GDP)	fragile (+)	nonsignificant (−)[c]

[a]Significant in 96% of the cases when money growth is included and in 47% when not.
[b]Significant and negative in 68% of the cases.
[c]Significant in 95% of the cases.
[d]Significant in 90% of the cases.

ence appears in the human capital variable and in population growth. The proxy of human capital used in Andrés, Doménech, and Molinas is the number of schooling years of the labor force, which is a stock variable. The significance of population growth in convergence equations in the OECD is partially driven by Turkey: the exclusion of this country decreases the rejection rate of the null hypothesis.

In the OECD, export growth is always significant in all linear combinations of the variables appearing in table 8.6 and, as opposed to Levine and Renelt's results, its significance is not affected by the inclusion of the investment rate. In OECD countries, when included simultaneously, inflation and money growth are significant in most specifications with similar but opposite coefficients. In Levine and Renelt's study, government consumption is a fragile economic indicator and is not significant at the extreme bounds, whereas in the OECD the coefficients of this variable are negative and statistically significant only in 10 percent of the cases. Finally, the budget surplus, although a fragile variable, has opposite sign in both studies, suggesting that the usual interpretation of deficits as a symptom of macroeconomic disarray, with negative effects on growth, does not apply for OECD countries. Summing up, we can conclude that in the OECD some economic indicators are robust enough to be considered in the description of the convergence process of these countries.

However, the inclusion of these variables does not restore the stability of the β coefficient, as we can observe in panel (c) of figure 8.6. In particular, after the inclusion of inflation, money and exports growth, and the variance of money growth as additional regressors in equation (8.1), the initial income coefficient remains statistically nonsignificant in the two periods between 1975 and 1985.

There must be other factors, over and above the ones we have considered, that explain the different growth patterns in recessions periods. In a previous work (Andrés, Boscá, and Doménech 1995), we put forward some alternative explanations. Less advanced countries in the OECD show cyclical fluctuations with larger frequencies than the most advanced ones. Thus it seems that macroeconomic shocks might have had more impact on the most fragile productive structures within the OECD, bringing the period of fast catching up to an end. Therefore, asymmetry emerges in this context because it is possible that the same variable (e.g., inflation) had different consequences in rich and poor countries.

Income Distribution and Growth

In the preceding section we have investigated the relationship between growth and some economic policy-related indicators. However, economic policies are also affected by economic and political institutions and by the distributional conflicts between economic agents. For example, it is frequently argued that inflation is very often a consequence of agents trying to maximize their shares in the total income of the nation. Also, it has long been stated that income distribution and the political regime can affect not only investment rate but its marginal productivity. The usual argument goes as follows. When wealth is concentrated in a small group of agents who control noncompetitive sectors, which places pressure on political institutions, investment could be oriented to firms and activities with slow potential growth. In this case, the potential marginal product of capital invested in activities of interest to the whole society is higher than in those under the control of a minority; thus savings might be low (although still higher than national investment), producing external flows of capital to high-growth countries.

Arguments of this kind led some authors, such as Persson and Tabellini (1992), to conclude that economic policies are the result of social and political institutions; that is, variables such as inflation, export growth, or government spending, for example, are not exogenous but endogenous variables, to be explained by other variables such as income and wealth distribution or political and social rights. From our perspective, it is difficult to simplify this position in terms of contrastable predictions such as those used in convergence equations. As a matter of fact, growth, economic policies, and political institutions interact with one another in such a way that is difficult to isolate causality relationships among them. Income distribution is a good example of this. In democracies with high inequality in the distribution of income, a large share of voters favor more redistributive polices that heavily tax high incomes and promote more transfers and social expenditures. Higher taxes imply slower growth through a slower capital accumulation; however, more public spending can imply faster growth if redistributive policies are implemented through more public education. Therefore, in the folowing periods less inequality in income distribution can be a consequence either of higher or slower growth. In any case it must be clear that income distribution can affect growth and vice versa. For our purposes it is more useful to avoid contemporaneous correlations and to analyze the effects of income distribution on future growth.

Before exploring the empirical relationship between growth and income distribution in the OECD, it is worthwhile to summarize some of the testable hypotheses found in the theoretical literature. In Meltzer and Richard (1981), democratic societies with inequalities among voters promote redistribution through higher taxes that harm growth. The same argument is used in Persson and Tabellini (1994): income taxes will be higher in more unequal democracies, but this will not be the case in nondemocratic countries where there is no such relationship between income distribution and growth. In Alesina and Rodrik (1992), more concentrated wealth distributions lead to lower growth in democracies because voters will be willing to tax physical and human capital, while in nondemocratic countries the relationship between growth and wealth distribution is ambiguous. Persson and Tabellini (1992) follow a similar route. These authors claim that more concentrated factor ownership is likely to create lobbies and pressure groups operating both in democratic and authoritarian countries that prevent investment from going to the most productive sectors in the economy. However, it is difficult to maintain that this argument does not operate also when income is unequally distributed; provided that income and wealth distribution are positively correlated, as we will see later on.

Another way to analyze the impact of income distribution on growth is through its implications for human capital accumulation. Perotti (1993) argues that very unequal societies prevent a large proportion of the population from having enough income to invest in education. In Saint-Paul and Verdier 1993, the main channel of redistribution is public education, such that, in democracies, more inequality could increase growth because the pressures for redistribution imply more human capital accumulation; however, in nondemocratic countries, inequality might slow growth because it implies less support for public spending in education. Galor and Zeira (1993) explore the implications of credit rationing on accumulation rates, showing that when credits markets are imperfect, wealth distribution affects economic activity. In such economies, individuals who inherit large bequests can invest in human capital, receiving wages as skilled workers and also leaving large inheritances.

In the context of an analysis of debt rescheduling, Berg and Sachs (1988) state that income inequality affects political and economic management in different negative ways (making coups d'état more likely, producing social unrest, hindering the adoption of correct economic policies, etc.), producing distortions that may also negatively affect growth. In Murphy, Shleifer, and Vishny 1989, economies in which income and wealth are more equally distributed can experience sustained growth after the introduction of innovations or following an export boom. This is due to the fact that in these economies a large proportion of the population can benefit from these positive shocks, which produce externalities that are the sources of additional improvements in the national wealth, taking advantage of larger markets where the usual multiplier effects apply.

To summarize, there are different ways in which income distribution can affect growth, but this influence is in general expected to be negative. Briefly, we can display the following empirical implications of the models we have reviewed:

1. More inequality may be correlated with higher future taxes in democracies.
2. More inequality may be correlated with lower future investment rates.
3. More inequality may produce less investment in private or total education as a consequence of poverty traps.
4. More inequality may promote more public spending in education as a means of redistribution.
5. More wealth and income concentration may decrease the marginal efficiency of investment.
6. Inequality may produce political and economic distortions.
7. Inequality may reduce the impact of positive supply and demand shocks.

Our next step is to examine some of the the evidence, in particular that related directly to growth experiences, with special emphasis on the differences and similarities between OECD and non-OECD countries. As we have already mentioned, we tried to use data on income distribution at the beginning of the period analyzed. To avoid using a small sample of countries, we have employed the data reported by Ahluwalia (1976), which presents the income shares of quintiles around 1970 from a compilation undertaken by the World Bank's Development Research Center. From this sample we omit the data for six socialist countries. For most OECD countries and those not included in Ahluwalia's data set, we used the older World Bank estimates from the *World Development Report*. Using this information we have computed the Gini coefficients for these countries.[18] Table 8.7 gives a preliminary picture of the income distribution across different world regions. As we can see, OECD countries had income more equally distributed, while inequality is very marked in the eighteen Latin American countries considered. Only in the income received by the first quintile are there not very appreciable differences between the OECD and Asian countries. We also have examined information about land ownership concentration, although the sample of countries is smaller.[19] Figure 8.7 shows the positive correlation between income and land ownership distributions. As we see, the variance within OECD countries is higher in the latter variable than in income distribution. In this case, land concentration is higher in OECD

TABLE 8.7 Income and Land Ownership Distribution across World Regions

		Income Shares of Quintiles				Gini Coefficients	
	Bottom 20%	Second Quintile	Third Quintile	Fourth Quintile	Top 20%	Income	Land Ownership
OECD	5.85	11.70	16.91	23.09	42.00	0.344	0.603
	(22)	(21)	(21)	(21)	(21)	(22)	(18)
Africa	5.27	8.94	13.15	19.49	53.16	0.433	0.501
	(18)	(18)	(18)	(18)	(18)	(18)	(9)
Latin America	3.68	7.22	11.82	19.39	57.89	0.483	0.813
	(18)	(18)	(18)	(18)	(18)	(18)	(15)
Asia	5.52	9.40	13.79	20.53	50.73	0.406	0.565
	(13)	(13)	(13)	(13)	(13)	(13)	(8)

Sources: For most countries income distribution data refer to years circa 1970. When possible, data for OECD countries come from World Bank's *World Development Report*. For other countries, data come from Ahluwalia (1976). Information on land ownership distribution comes from Taylor and Hudson (1972) and Taylor and Jodice (1983), reproduced in Persson and Tabellini (1992).

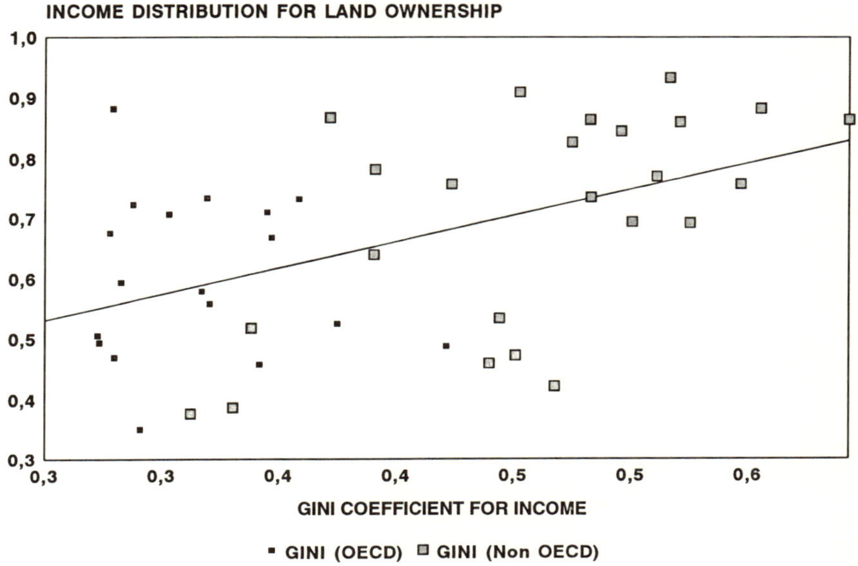

Figure 8.7 Income and land ownership distributions

than in Asian and African countries, although again Latin American countries show the greater disparities.

In figure 8.8 we plot the Gini coefficient of income against the average growth rate from 1960 to 1990. At first glance there is no clear correlation between income distribution and growth in the OECD or in non-OECD economies. However, this figure does not take into account the role of other variables that we know can have an important influence on growth, such as the initial income per capita or accumulation rates.

In table 8.8 we analyze the influence of income and land ownership distribution on growth, once we have discounted the effects of the variables just mentioned. In columns (1) and (2) we estimate the base growth equation including initial income (RGDP), the log of investment shares (I/Y), population growth rates (n), and a proxy of human capital accumulation as regressors (ENROL). To ensure comparability among the two samples, data on national accounts and population come from version 5.5 of *Penn World Tables* (Summers and Heston 1991). In the case of non-OECD countries, human capital is measured by primary school enrollment rate averages, while in the OECD equation we use tertiary enrollment rates averages, from Barro and Lee 1993. With the exception of population growth in non-OECD countries, all variables

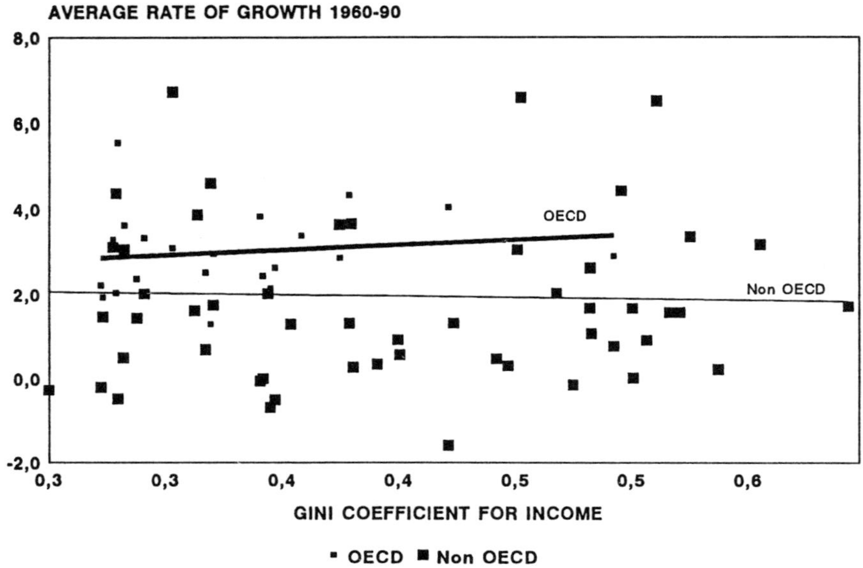

Figure 8.8 Income distribution and growth

are statistically significant. When we add income and wealth distribution variables to the regression, the best estimates are obtained using the Gini coefficient on income (GINI) for the OECD and the land ownership distribution (GINILA) for non-OECD countries, although in both samples higher inequality in income and land ownership imply lower growth rates.[20] Columns (3) and (4) show that there is a substantial increase in the goodness of fit in both samples, although more important in non-OECD countries in relative terms. We have also estimated these equations including political rights variables as a way of controlling for the different effect that inequalities may have in democracies and nondemocracies. However, these variables were not significant and they did not affect the results obtained for the Gini coefficients. Another interesting result is the asymmetry between both samples when we include the government consumption share in the growth regression. This variable is not statistically significant in either sample when income or wealth distributions are not included; however, it becomes significant for OECD countries when GINI is in the regression, as in column (5).

Finally, we have estimated two additional regressions with the investment rates as a dependent variable. In that case, there are again important differences between both samples. Thus human capital is a

TABLE 8.8 Growth and Distribution

	Growth				Investment		
	1 Non-OECD	2 OECD	3 Non-OECD	4 OECD	5 OECD	6 Non-OECD	7 OECD
Constant	7.27	−0.24	10.35	8.05	8.15	−7.30	−26.4
	(1.01)	(0.07)	(1.52)	(1.91)	(2.07)	(1.89)	(0.67)
1nRGDP	−1.65	−1.88	−0.95	−2.24	−2.21		7.36
	(5.62)	(7.92)	(2.66)	(8.32)	(9.07)		(1.84)
Enrollment	2.67	4.21	3.20	4.80	4.94	18.25	
	(2.28)	(3.41)	(2.62)	(5.10)	(5.10)	(5.38)	
1n (n + 0.05)	−0.23	−3.36	2.06	−2.82	−3.71		
	(0.08)	(3.78)	(0.83)	(3.35)	(5.60)		
1n (I/GDP)	1.43	2.70	1.58	2.06	1.63		
	(2.65)	(3.11)	(3.04)	(3.35)	(2.85)		
GINI				−5.03	−4.78	17.69	−54.00
				(2.37)	(2.40)	(1.82)	(2.73)
GINILA			−4.60				
			(2.81)				
AGRIL							0.40
							(3.72)
1n (G/GDP)					−0.65		
					(2.93)		
r^2 Adj.	0.388	0.806	0.466	0.863	0.871	0.483	0.381
Number of observations	46	23	46	22	22	46	18

key variable in non-OECD countries and, surprisingly, GINI has a positive influence on investment rates, although this result could be partially driven by the presence of some outliers. In OECD countries, however, income inequalities have a negative bearing on investment after controlling for initial income and the percentage of the labor force in the agricultural sector (data taken from the *World Development Report*). The positive influence of the latter variable reflects the potential allocation of resources from the primary sector to higher growth sectors.

To summarize, a more egalitarian income distribution seemed to have positive effects on growth in OECD countries. There are, however, different aspects of the relationships among income distribution, spending in public and private education, and transfers from government that need further analysis.[21] In particular, it is possible that the two oil crises had negative effects on income distribution and therefore could be an additional obstacle to the convergence process.

On Country Specificities of the Growth Process in the OECD

In previous sections we have presented a broad picture of some of the main characteristics of the growth performance of the OECD as a whole. Although some of the features of the long-run evolution of the OECD are quite consistent with the standard augmented neoclassical growth model, we have found some evidence concerning the causality implications among variables that is difficult to reconcile with that model. In this section we extend our search for sources of the inability of this model to explain the long-run evolution of a region as homogeneous as the OECD.

The Solow model is a single-country model that has been widely used in the last decade to explain the growth process of groups of countries. Before using a single-country model in a multicountry setting, however, some requirements should be met. For instance, the assumption of parameter homogeneity in estimating multicountry regressions should be tested, rather than imposed, as is common practice in most empirical studies. There are a variety of reasons, both empirical and theoretical, for concentrating some effort on bringing country specificities to the forefront of the analysis. Econometrically this means sometimes using only dummy variables to control for country idyiosyncratic effects, whose implications are not very important theoretically. More troublesome is the fact that these country specificities can go beyond a simple time invariant country effect, and denote even different model structures for different countries or groups of countries. In such cases this would mean that the estimated equation is simply misspecified. To be more precise, a good fit in a cross-country convergence regression, or a well-established first-order autoregressive pattern in growth rates, is not sufficient empirical evidence to unambiguously support the canonical neoclassical growth model. From a theoretical point of view, there are good reasons to believe so.

First, one has to ask if endogenous growth-type models are a reasonable benchmark for describing the pattern of growth and limited convergence exhibited by the OECD data. As noted, one key distinction between exogenous and endogenous models is that in the former accumulation rates affect the relative position of countries in the long run, but not the growth rate, while in the latter these variables and other social, political, and macroeconomic indicators can have a bearing on long-run growth rates. In fact, a significant partial correlation between growth rates and investment in physical and human capital is compatible with either an exogenous or an endogenous growth framework. We showed in the second section that in addition to the significant partial correlation, the exogenous model requires causality running from accumulation rates to growth rates, which the data do not exhibit.

From an empirical point of view, given that endogenous growth models constitute a realistic alternative to the neoclassical framework, there is a difficult problem to solve. Most empirical work in growth theory, though motivated by endogenous growth models has tested earlier growth models rather than endogenous propositions themselves. One important distinctive fact about many endogenous-type models is that the equations that govern the dynamics of growth in different countries need not be the same, so that multicountry analysis can be inappropriate. The reason is that serious degree-of-freedom constraints would prevent testing of differences among all the countries in all estimated coefficients of the model. As Pack (1994) states, in practice this means testing the insights of the new growth theory against the economic evolution of individual countries using time-series data.

Given the descriptive aim of this chapter, we are not going to try to develop here any kind of formal test to discriminate between exogenous and endogenous models. We simply want to show, using the variables implied by the augmented neoclassical model, that the growth and convergence implications of such a model can be seriously at odds with the empirical evidence, if we proceed to a more detailed disaggregated country-by-country analysis. In doing so, let us present a quick review of some findings in the empirical convergence literature. Table 8.9 contains a summary of some selected recent results from convergence regressions

TABLE 8.9 Some Selected Results on Convergence

Authors' Method	Estimation	Sample	Convergence Speed	Test of Constant Returns to Scale	Observations
Mankiw, Romer, and Weil (1992)	OLS cross-section	75 non-oil countries 1960–85	0.0186	accepted	
Mankiw, Romer, and Weil (1992)	OLS cross-section	22 OECD countries 1960–85	0.0206	accepted	
Durlauf and Johnson (1992)	OLS cross-section	14,34,27,and 21 countries, 1960–85	0.0626 0.0036 0.0152 −0.0020		Regression tree breaks in the sample: 4 convergence clubs.
Cohen (1993)	OLS cross-section	89 non-oil Countries, 1960–88	0.0116		
Cohen (1993)	SURE (2 equations)	66 non-oil countries, 1970–88			System is explosive: nonconvergence. Takes into account explicitly the law of motion of physical and human capital.
Knight, Loayza, and Villanueva (1992)	PANEL $N = 98$, $T = 5$	98 industrial and developing countries, 1960–85	0.0391	rejected	Controls for time and country-specific effects. Chamberlain estimation method.
Knight, Loayza, and Villanueva (1992)	PANEL $N = 81$, $T = 5$	81 non-oil countries, 1960–85	0.0499	rejected	Controls for time and country-specific effects. Includes openness to trade and public infrastructure indicators.
Andrés and Boscá (1994)	NL3LS $N = 24$, $T = 5$ POOLING	8 and 16 OECD countries, 1960–90	0.0270 0.0570		Time dummies included. Countries split into 2 convergence clubs. High convergence speed in leading club.

stemming from the augmented neoclassical growth model. These works differ either in the estimation technique employed or in the sample used, and the broad picture we can draw is that the well-known 2 percent convergence speed may be questioned. Results from Mankiw, Romer, and Weil (1992) are taken as reference for comparison, and the criterion for selecting the other results is mainly that these studies share a concern for exploiting the time dimension of the data, which allows for control of differences in structural or unobservable country characteristics.

Durlauf and Johnson (1992) claimed that the process of convergence can be limited. They find evidence that there may be country groups in which convergence takes place at a high rate (6.2 percent) coexisting with other groups in which convergence does not occur. These results have to do with threshold effects depending on the level of development of the countries. Employing completely different techniques and samples, other authors point out the shortcomings of the augmented Solow model. Cohen (1993) discusses the robustness of the human capital variable, stressing the inexistence of convergence when the dynamics of accumulation are taken into account. Knight, Loayza, and Villanueva (1992) find high convergence rates (5 percent) when countries' specificities are controlled for, showing in addition formal tests against the constant returns to scale technology.

Finally, it is worth emphasizing the results obtained by Andrés and Boscá (1994), because they present findings that are consistent with the existence of at least two different technologies inside the OECD, which is known to be the most homogeneous region, where the assumptions of the augmented Solow model are more likely to hold. Using standard econometric techniques, the authors provide a formal and explicit test of the equality of technolodical parameters across different estimated convergence equations, for different country groups. In addition, they present a more efficient alternative to the regression tree procedure of Durlauf and Johnson (1992) to identify the existing technological clubs inside the OECD. This methodology relies on the existence of country-specific effects that are interpreted as evidence from differences in the initial technological level among countries. Applying this procedure, Andrés and Boscá (1994) find that the maintained assumption of a common technology among the OECD countries (from 1960 to 1990) does not hold. They identify at least two different groups inside the OECD with markedly different technological parameters. The augmented Solow model explains reasonably well the evolution of the less advanced technology countries[22] and yields a low convergence rate (2.7 percent). Convergence inside the more advanced technology group[23] of countries is much faster (5.7 percent), although the implausible parameter values obtained cast some doubts on the validity of the Solow model in accounting for the long-run evolution of this group.[24] The main result of this study is not against convergence, which occurs at different rates inside every group, but against neoclassical convergence dynamics.

The important idea we want to emphasize is that by abandoning the imposition of parameter homogeneity and allowing for differences in the constant term and in the slope parameters, we find many results that cast reasonable doubts at least about the 2 percent convergence speed, and even about the model itself. The results indicate that we find significant structural differences among countries if we allow for them. Pack's (1994) claim about using time-series data in the empirical growth literature should be extended to the augmented neoclassical growth model. There are powerful reasons to believe this, mainly because we are employing a representative country model in a multicountry analysis. The usual reason for not doing so is that the time dimension of the growth problem leaves too few data points to test the model for every country alone. In other words, thirty annual observations yield limited information about the steady state, given that they are contaminated by short-run cyclical fluctuations. Nevertheless, we can remove these cyclical fluctuations in a number of ways that leave us with enough annual observations to estimate the model for every country. In Andrés, Boscá, and Doménech 1994b, we justify the utilization of these smoothing methods to construct the so-called data fields (namely, data sets with approximately equal time and individual dimensions). Using, for instance, the Hodrick-Prescott filtering method, we are left with thirty annual observations for the twenty-four OECD countries. This allows us to run a separate convergence regression for every country, the results of which are presented in a simplified way in table 8.10.

The results from estimating the model with time-series date for every country are at first glance astonishing. The initial income coefficient, which contains the implicit convergence rate, is negative and significant in fourteen of the twenty-four countries. If the model is supposed to be a good description of the growth process in every country, this would imply that in Australia, Ireland, Portugal, and Japan, where the initial income coefficient is estimated to be positive and significant, the pattern has been from divergence to their own steady states. More striking is to take a look at the implicit convergence rates that arise from these estimates. They range from −51 percent in Japan to 197 percent in Turkey, with the average convergence rate for all the countries at 24 percent. Another interesting result from these estimates is that the human capital coefficient is only significant and positive in nine countries, being negative or nonsignificant in the remaining countries (similar re-

TABLE 8.10 Mean Group Estimator: Sign and Significance of the Coefficients (Data: Hodrick-Prescott Filtered)

	Constant	Initial Income	Investment Rate	Population Growth	2nd Enrollment Rate	Trend	Lambda
Australia	N.S.(−)	S.(+)	S.(+)	S.(+)	N.S.(−)	N.S.(−)	−0.06
Austria	S.(−)	S.(−)	S.(+)	S.(−)	S.(+)	S.(+)	0.29
Belgium	N.S.(−)	S.(−)	S.(+)	N.S.(+)	S.(+)	S.(+)	0.02
Canada	S.(+)	N.S.(−)	S.(−)	S.(+)	S.(−)	S.(+)	0.17
Switzerland	S.(−)	S.(−)	S.(+)	S.(−)	S.(+)	S.(+)	0.30
Germany	S.(−)	S.(−)	S.(+)	S.(−)	S.(+)	S.(+)	0.03
Denmark	N.S.(−)	N.S.(−)	N.S.(+)	N.S.(−)	N.S.(−)	N.S.(+)	0.50
Spain	S.(+)	S.(−)	S.(+)	S.(+)	S.(+)	S.(+)	1.12
Finland	S.(−)	S.(−)	S.(+)	S.(−)	S.(+)	S.(+)	0.10
France	S.(−)	S.(−)	S.(+)	S.(−)	N.S.(+)	S.(+)	0.44
U.K.	S.(+)	S.(−)	S.(+)	N.S.(+)	N.S.(+)	S.(+)	0.59
Greece	S.(−)	S.(−)	S.(+)	N.S.(−)	N.S.(−)	S.(+)	0.15
Ireland	S.(−)	S.(+)	S.(+)	S.(−)	S.(+)	S.(−)	0.22
Iceland	S.(+)	N.S.(−)	S.(+)	N.S.(+)	S.(−)	S.(+)	0.07
Italy	S.(+)	S.(−)	S.(−)	S.(+)	N.S.(+)	S.(+)	0.15
Japan	S.(−)	S.(+)	S.(+)	S.(−)	N.S.(+)	S.(−)	−0.51
Luxembourg	N.S.(+)	S.(−)	N.S.(+)	N.S.(+)	N.S.(+)	S.(+)	0.09
Netherlands	S.(−)	S.(−)	S.(+)	S.(−)	N.S.(−)	S.(+)	0.05
Norway	S.(−)	S.(−)	S.(+)	S.(−)	N.S.(−)	S.(+)	0.44
New Zealand	N.S.(−)	N.S.(+)	N.S.(+)	N.S.(−)	S.(−)	N.S.(−)	−0.05
Portugal	S.(−)	S.(+)	S.(+)	S.(−)	S.(+)	N.S.(−)	−0.02
Sweden	N.S.(+)	N.S.(+)	N.S.(−)	N.S.(+)	S.(+)	N.S.(−)	−0.13
Turkey	N.S.(+)	N.S.(−)	N.S.(+)	N.S.(+)	N.S.(+)	N.S.(+)	1.97
USA	S.(−)	S.(−)	S.(+)	S.(−)	S.(+)	S.(+)	0.21
Averages	−0.13	−0.14	0.09	−0.05	0.00	0.33	0.24
t-statistic	(0.19)	(0.60)	(0.85)	(0.18)	(0.23)	0.54)	

sults can be found for the population growth coefficient). The most robust result in these estimations is the significant positive partial correlation between growth and investment in physical capital.

Pesaran and Smith (1993) have dicussed how to obtain consistent estimates of the mean coefficients in a multicountry framework, showing that the mean coefficients can be consistently estimated using precisely the information contained in table 8.9. The so-called mean group estimator (MGE) coefficients are obtained simply by taking averages of the coefficients estimated in separate regressions for every country.[25] The average coefficients for the OECD are presented in the table, with the respective *t*-statistics. The results are sufficiently expressive; none of the coefficients of the convergence regression is statistically significant at conventional levels. How do we interpret these results? First, we have to notice that the MGE takes into account differences in all the coefficients and not only in the constant term, as do other panel estimation techniques. Looking at the variety of country experiences and at the adequacy of the Solow model country by country, it does seem reasonable that the mean coefficients are not significant. When the model is estimated imposing parameter homogeneity, as is the case for example in Mankiw, Romer, and Weil's (1992) estimations shown in table 8.9, all structural differences among countries are left to be explained by differences in accumulation rates. In this case the average steady state can have very little to do with the real long-run prospects of individual countries.[26] Simply put, the message is that allowing for parameter heterogeneity (taking full account of country specificities) enables one to better specify the steady state of each country.

In table 8.11 we want to qualify some of the results presented in the preceding paragraph. What happens with the MGE coefficients if we impose constant returns to scale (CRS) in the estimation of the convergence regression for every country? The first result is that the constant returns to scale restriction is only valid in seven countries (Canada, Denmark, Iceland, Luxembourg, Portugal, Turkey, and the United States) as is shown in the last column of the table. But the surprising fact is that the imposition of the CRS technology allows us to rescue the conventional results of the convergence regression literature. All the coefficients have the right sign and are precisely estimated with the exception of the human capital coefficient, which remains nonsignificant. There is, however, an important difference with respect to conventional convergence results: the average speed of convergence is 17 percent instead of the universal 2 percent. If this rate of convergence were the true one, this would imply that countries take 4.5 years to return to their steady state after having been moved away from it. Although country differences in the conver-

TABLE 8.11 Mean Group Estimator Imposing Constant Returns to Scale (Data: Hodrick-Prescott Filtered)

	Constant	Initial Income	Investment Rate	Population Growth	2nd Enrollment Rate	Trend	Lambda	p-value
Australia	N.S.(−)	S.(−)	N.S.(+)	N.S.(−)	S.(+)	N.S.(+)	0.15	0.00
Austria	S.(−)	S.(−)	S.(+)	S.(−)	S.(+)	S.(+)	0.92	0.00
Belgium	S.(−)	S.(−)	S.(+)	S.(−)	S.(+)	S.(−)	0.01	0.00
Canada	S.(+)	S.(+)	S.(−)	S.(+)	S.(−)	S.(+)	−0.02	0.30
Switzerland	S.(−)	S.(−)	S.(+)	S.(−)	S.(+)	S.(+)	1.23	0.00
Germany	S.(+)	S.(+)	S.(−)	S.(+)	N.S.(−)	S.(−)	−0.33	0.00
Denmark	N.S.(−)	S.(−)	S.(+)	S.(−)	N.S.(−)	S.(+)	0.35	0.92
Spain	S.(−)	S.(−)	S.(+)	S.−)	S.(+)	S.(+)	0.11	0.00
Finland	S.(−)	S.(−)	S.(+)	S.(−)	S.(+)	S.+)	0.03	0.00
France	S.(−)	S.(−)	S.(+)	S.(−)	S.(−)	S.(+)	0.23	0.00
U.K.	N.S.(+)	N.S.(+)	N.S.(+)	N.S.(+)	S.(−)	N.S.(−)	−0.01	0.00
Greece	S.(−)	S.(−)	S.(+)	S.(−)	N.S.(+)	S.(+)	0.10	0.00
Ireland	S.(+)	N.S.(+)	S.(−)	S.(+)	S.(+)	N.S.(−)	0.20	0.00
Iceland	S.(+)	S.(−)	S.(+)	S.(−)	S.(−)	S.(+)	0.15	0.07
Italy	S.(−)	S.(+)	S.(+)	S.(−)	N.S.(−)	N.S.(−)	−0.12	0.00
Japan	S.(−)	S.(−)	S.(+)	S.(−)	N.S.(−)	S.(+)	0.12	0.00
Luxembourg	N.S.(−)	S.(−)	S.(+)	S.(−)	N.S.(−)	S.(+)	0.07	0.51
Netherlands	S.(−)	S.(−)	S.(+)	S.(−)	N.S.(+)	S.(+)	0.07	0.00
Norway	S.(+)	S.(−)	S.(+)	S.(−)	N.S.(−)	S.(+)	0.17	0.00
New Zealand	S.(−)	S.(−)	S.(+)	S.(−)	N.S.(−)	S.(−)	0.14	0.00
Portugal	S.(−)	S.(+)	S.(+)	S.(−)	S.(+)	S.(−)	−0.02	0.87
Sweden	S.(−)	S.(−)	S.(+)	S.(−)	S.(+)	S.(+)	0.05	0.02
Turkey	S.(−)	S.(−)	S.(+)	S.(−)	S.(+)	S.(+)	n.a.	0.30
USA	S.(−)	S.(−)	S.(+)	S.(−)	S.(+)	S.(+)	0.13	0.21
Averages	−0.49	−0.16	0.13	−0.13	0.00	0.38	0.17	
t-statistic	(2.66)	(3.54)	(3.74)	(3.86)	(0.34)	(3.08)		

gence rate are wide, intuitively it seems more reasonable that on average countries take between four and ten years to return to their own steady state,[27] instead of the thirty-five years implied by the 2 percent convergence rate. We are not going to discuss whether the imposition of constant returns to scale is reliable; in fact, the p-value of formal F-tests presented in the table tells us that for the majority of countries in the sample (seventeen of the twenty-four countries), this assumption is rejected. The message is nevertheless that imposing some structure to the data, we can rescue conventional convergence results.

To sum up the results presented in this section, we have seen that as we move from more to less restricted models—that is, imposing first parameter homogeneity, allowing then for time-invariant specific effects and, finally, allowing for differences both in the constant and in the slopes—the landscape changes dramatically and with a clear pattern. First, some variables like human capital become less or nonsignificant, and the convergence rate becomes bigger; and second, all variables can become nonsignificant. These results naturally deserve more detailed study to establish their robustness, which is beyond the scope of this chapter.

Summary and Final Remarks

Since 1960 there has been a substantial reduction in the dispersion of per capita income within the OECD. This process can be explained by two features that distinguish the OECD from other economic regions: a negative correlation among growth rates and initial income, and a substantial persistence in growth rates. These features, along with a significant correlation among growth accumulation rates, favor an interpretation of the recent OECD economic history in accordance with the predictions of the constant returns model of growth. This in turn has popularized the automatic link between accumulation and growth, whereby economic success is believed to arise mainly out of a steady investment effort. A closer inspection of the time correlation among accumulation rates and growth suggests that this might well be far too naive. Because investment and human capital formation do not cause growth, in a statistical sense, their role in the growth process must be seen as facilitating the incorporation of innovations that constitute the true engines of growth, according to most models of endogenous growth.

The process of convergence within the OECD has not been stable all along the sample period. In fact, convergence proceeded quite rapidly from 1960 through 1975 and has virtually stopped since then. Since catch-up has been quicker in periods of fast growth, this suggests that poorer countries are the principal beneficiaries of worldwide expansions, whereas they lose ground in recessions. The unequal impact of the macroeconomic shocks of the 1970s and 1980s along with a less fortunate policy response to them in some countries is an obvious candidate to explain this structural break. Actually, in contrast to some previous studies in this field, we find that the long-term success of OECD economies is inextricably linked to their short-run performance. Inflation variability is harmful for growth, whereas exports and openness enhance it. The impact of other variables on growth rates is also quite robust. This takes us halfway to accounting for the interruption of the process of catching up, but the structural break remains even after allowing for these policy variables, and more research is needed to solve this puzzle. Similarly, the contribution to growth of a stable social and political environment in OECD economies cannot be denied. Although the pattern of total correlation among growth and income inequality is not very clear, matters are different once we control for other variables in growth equations. In particular, the indicators of inequality in the distribution of income and wealth appear negative and significant in augmented growth regressions.

Accumulation rates and disparities in initial incomes, jointly with income inequality and short-run macroeconomic indicators, account for a substantial proportion of the total variation in growth rates within the OECD. However, structural differences, technological or otherwise, also matter. We have shown that by including country-specific time-invariant effects, the fit of growth regressions improves significantly, and as it does also when time-variant specific effects are allowed in. When standard growth and convergence regressions are estimated for each country, some of the well-known OECD-wide results no longer hold. Although convergence, in the sense of mean reversion of the income per capita series, is a feature of many individual countries, both the pattern of correlation with accumulation rates and the size of the parameters does not correspond with what would be expected according to the constant returns to scale model. This result suggests that we must be cautious in drawing policy implications on the basis of representative economy models and that country-specific characteristics, national institutions, and initial conditions might influence the long-run performance of OECD economies more heavily than has been usually thought.

NOTES

This chapter is part of the project "Growth, Convergence, and Macroeconomic Performance" carried out at the Ministry of Finance of Spain and the University of

Valencia. We would like to thank César Molinas for useful suggestions. The support of DGICYT PB92-1036 is gratefully acknowledged.

1. This section relies partially on section 2 of Andrés, Boscá, and Doménech 1995.

2. Data in this figure are from the *Penn World Tables* 5.5 (Summers and Heston 1991). To avoid breakpoints in the series, we have considered only those countries in the data set with available information through the period 1960–90. This reduces the number of observations to twenty-four OECD, twenty-nine African, nineteen Latin American, and thirteen Asian countries in all years.

3. Data in this table come mainly from OECD statistics using OECD PPP's rather than from *Penn World Tables* 5.5. See Dabán, Doménech, and Molinas 1994 for further details.

4. OECD (6) hereafter: Turkey, Portugal, Greece, Ireland, Spain, and New Zealand.

5. Consider, for instance, the cases of Germany, Canada, Australia, and the United Kingdom, with similar per capita incomes in 1960. Whereas Canada and Germany got very close to the U.S. level by 1990 (about 85 percent), the other two countries were still well below it (less than 75 percent).

6. In addition, the standard deviation is a single parameter that does not capture some interesting aspects of the distribution dynamics (Quah 1993a).

7. In this case, due to the extraordinary success of the newly industrialized countries of the Far East.

8. Besides this explanation, Ben-David (1993) has pointed out that convergence in the OECD has been promoted by trade liberalization, which came with the removal of quantitative restrictions between member countries.

9. The estimated coefficient of the autoregressive process ranges from 0.7 in 1965–70 to -0.1 in 1985–90. Furthermore, the virtual absence of inertia during 1980–90 coincides with the increase in macroeconomic turbulence during these years.

10. Similar results have been obtained by Mankiw, Romer, and Weil (1992), Dolado, Goria, and Ichino (1994), and Andrés, Doménech, and Molinas (1995), among others.

11. In particular, the case of Japan, with its extraordinary high rates of savings and growth during the sample period, has strong influence on this result.

12. Secondary schooling rates have very little variance by the end of the sample period. Later we consider alternative proxies for human capital accumulation in the OECD.

13. For a more rigorous analysis of this issue, see Andrés, Boscá, and Doménech 1994a.

14. The initial level of GDP per capita is also included in columns 6 and 8.

15. In all cases, these additional regressors appear significant and with the correct sign. When these variables are not controlled for, positive causality is overwhelmingly rejected.

16. A similar analysis is carried out in Andrés, Boscá, and Doménech 1994a,

with the rate of growth of GDP per capita as the right-hand variable. The results there largely confirm the lack of causality discussed here.

17. See Andrés, Doménech, and Molinas 1995 and Andrés, Boscá, and Doménech 1995.

18. We have used the linear approximation by giving the following expression: Gini = $1-2\,(0.9q_1 + 0.7q_2 + 0.5q_3 + 0.3q_4 + 0.1q_5)$. Data for Greece come from Cromwell 1977, where is available the Gini coefficient and the share of income going to the poorest 20 percent of the population in 1962.

19. Information on land ownership distribution comes from Taylor and Hudson 1972 and Taylor and Jodice 1983, reproduced in Persson and Tabellini 1992.

20. For countries for which the GINILA variable is not available but GINI is, we used their fitted value coming from the following regression:

$$\begin{aligned} \text{GINILA} = \underset{(3.15)}{-0.641} + \underset{(8.05)}{1.347}\ \text{GINI} + \underset{(4.25)}{0.094}\ \ln\text{RGDP}_{60}. \end{aligned}$$

21. González-Páramo (1994) has analyzed the role of public policies as determinant of income redistribution in OECD countries. He found that government transfers as a share of GDP is a statistically significant variable to explain income inequalities. However, these results worsen when he adds public spending in health and education.

22. These countries being: Turkey, Greece, Portugal, Ireland, Spain, New Zealand, Finland, and Norway.

23. Some mild evidence is also presented that the advanced technology group could be split into two subgroups: an intermediate technology group (Iceland, Italy, Austria, Belgium, Netherlands, Denmark, United Kingdom, and Australia) and a leading technology group (the United States, Canada, Switzerland, Germany, Luxembourg, France, Sweden, and Japan).

24. For instance, the investment coefficient is not significant for the advanced countries.

25. For a discussion of the conditions under which the mean group estimator is consistent, see Pesaran and Smith 1993. In Andrés, Boscá, and Doménech 1994b, we show that these conditions are satisfied in our sample.

26. It might well be the case, as documented in Andrés and Lamo 1994, that most country observations never cross the average steady state.

27. If we exclude Austria and Switzerland (with abnormally high convergence rates) from the calculation of the mean convergence rate, we obtain a 7 percent average convergence rate, which means taking ten years to return to the steady state after a shock to the growth rate.

REFERENCES

Alesina, A., and D. Rodrik. 1992. Distribution, Political Conflict, and Economic Growth: A Simple Theory and Some Empirical Evidence. In *Political*

Economy, Growth, and Cycles, edited by A. Cukierman, Z. Hercowitz, and L. Leiderman. Cambridge, MA: MIT Press.

Ahluwalia, M.S. 1976. Inequality, Poverty, and Development. *Journal of Development Economics* 3: 307–42.

Andrés, J., and J. Boscá. 1994. Technological Differences and Convergence in the OECD. Mimeo. Dirección General de Planificación. Ministerio de Economía y Hacienda. Madrid.

Andrés, J., J. Boscá, and R. Doménech. 1994a. Testing the Neoclassical Growth Model: A Causality Approach. D-9405. Dirección General de Planificación. Ministerio de Economía y Hacienda. Madrid.

Andrés, J., J.E. Boscá, and R. Doménech. 1994b. Data Fields and Convergence Regressions: Results for the OECD. D-9406. Dirección General de Planificación Económica. Ministerio de Economía y Hacienda.

Andrés, J., J. Boscá, and R. Doménech. 1995. Main Patterns of Economic Growth in OECD Countries. *Investigaciones Económicas* 19 (1): 35–63.

Andrés, J., R. Doménech, and C. Molinas. 1994. Growth and Macroeconomic Performance. Mimeo. Dirección General de Planificación. Ministerio de Economía y Hacienda. Spain.

Andrés, J., R. Doménech, and C. Molinas. 1995. Growth and Convergence in OECD Countries: A Closer Look. In *Catch-up and Convergence in Postwar Europe: Quantitative Aspects*, edited by B. van Ark and N. Crafts. Cambridge: Cambridge University Press.

Andrés, J., and A. R. Lamo. 1994. Dynamics of the Income Distribution across the OECD Economies. Mimeo. Centre for Economic Performance. London School of Economics.

Barro, R., and J.W. Lee. 1993. International Comparisons of Educational Attainment. *Journal of Monetary Economics* 32: 363–94.

Barro, R., and X. Sala-i-Martín. 1991. Convergence across States and Regions. *Brookings Papers on Economic Activity* 1: 107–182.

Barro, R., and X. Sala-i-Martín. 1992. Convergence. *Journal of Political Economy* 100: 223–51.

Ben-David, D. 1993. Equalizing Exchange: Trade Liberalization and Income Convergence. *Quarterly Journal of Economics* 108(3): 653–79.

Berg, A., and J. Sachs. 1988. The Debt Crisis. Structural Explanations of Country Performance. *Journal of Development Economics* 29: 271–306.

Blomstrom, M., R. Lipsey, and M. Zejan. 1993. Is Fixed Investment the Key to Economic Growth? NBER Working Paper 4436.

Carroll, C., and D. Weil. 1993. Saving and Growth: A Reinterpretation. NBER Working Paper 4470.

Cohen, D. 1993. Two Notes on Economic Growth and the Solow Model. Discussion Paper 780. Centre for Economic Policy Research.

Cromwell, J. 1977. The Size Distribution of Income: An International Comparison. *Review of Income and Wealth* 23(3): 291–311.

Dabán, T., R. Doménech, and C. Molinas. 1994. International and Intertemporal Comparisons of Real Product in OECD Countries: A Growth

Sensitivity Analysis. Mimeo. Dirección General de Planificación. Ministerio de Economía y Hacienda. Madrid.

Dolado, J., A. Goria, and A. Ichino. 1994. Immigration and Growth in the Host Country: Evidence from Pooled Country Data. *Journal of Population Economics* 7 (2): 193–215.

Dolado, J. J., and H. Lütkepohl. 1994. Making Wald Test Work for Cointegrated VAR Systems. Mimeo. CEMFI.

Durlauf, S., and P. Johnson. 1992. Local versus Global Convergence across National Economies. NBER Working Paper 3996.

Easterly, W., M. Kremer, L. Pritchett, and L. Summers. 1993. Good Policy or Good Luck? Country Growth Performance and Temporary Shocks. *Journal of Monetary Economics* 32: 458–93.

Galor, O., and J. Zeira. 1993. Income Distribution and Macroeconomics. *Review of Economic Studies* 60: 35–62.

González-Páramo, J.M. 1994. Gasto Social y Crecimiento Económico en el Estado de Bienestar. Mimeo. Universidad Complutense. Madrid.

Grossman G., and E. Helpman. 1994. Endogenous Innovation in the Theory of Long- Run Growth. *Journal of Economic Perspectives* 8(1): 23–44.

King, R., and R. Levine. 1994. Capital Fundamentalism, Economic Development, and Economic Growth. *Carnegie-Rochester Conference Series on Public Policy* 40: 259–92.

Knight, M., M. Loayza, and D. Villanueva. 1992. Testing the Neoclassical Theory of Economic Growth: A Panel Data Approach. IMF Working Paper, WP/92/106.

Levine, R., and D. Renelt. 1992. A Sensitivity Analysis of Cross-Country Growth Regressions. *American Economic Review* 82: 942–63.

Lucas, R. 1988. On the Mechanics of Economic Development. *Journal of Monetary Economics* 22(1): 3–42.

Mankiw, G., D. Romer, and D, Weil. 1992. A Contribution to the Empirics of Economic Growth. *Quarterly Journal of Economics* 107: 503–530.

Meltzer, A., and S. Richard. 1981. A Rational Theory of the Size of Government. *Journal of Political Economy* 52: 914–27.

Mulligan, C.B., and Sala-i-Martín. 1994. Measures of the Aggregate Value of Human Capital. Mimeo. Yale University.

Murphy, K., A. Shleifer, and R. Vishny. 1989. Income Distribution, Market Size, and Industrialization. *Quarterly Journal of Economics* 104(3): 537–64.

Pack, H. 1994. Endogenous Growth Theory: Intellectual Appeal and Empirical Shortcomings. *Journal of Economic Perspectives* 8(1): 55–72.

Parente S., and E. Prescott. 1993. Changes in the Wealth of Nations. *Quarterly Review* (Federal Reserve Bank of Minneapolis) 17: 3–13.

Perotti, R. 1993. Political Equilibrium, Income Distribution, and Growth. *Review of Economic Studies* 60: 755–76.

Persson, T., and G. Tabellini. 1992. Growth, Distribution, and Politics. In *Political Economy, Growth, and Cycles*, edited by A. Cukierman, Z. Hercowitz, and L. Leiderman. Cambridge, MA: MIT Press.

Persson, T., and G. Tabellini. 1994. Is Inequality Harmful for Growth? *American Economic Review* 84(3): 600–21.

Pesaran, M. H., and R. Smith. 1993. Estimating Long-Run Relationships from Dynamic Heterogenous Panels. Mimeo. Trinity College and Birkbeck College.

Quah, D. 1993a. Empirical Cross-Section Dynamics in Convergence Hypothesis. *European Economic Review* 37: 426–34.

Quah, D. 1993b. Galton's Fallacy and Tests of the Convergence Hypothesis. *Scandinavian Journal of Economics* 95(4): 427–43.

Romer, P. M. 1994. The Origins of Endogenous Growth. *Journal of Economic Perspectives* 8(1): 2–22.

Sala-i-Martin, X. 1994. Cross-sectional Regressions and the Empirics of Economic Growth. *European Economic Review* 38: 739–47.

Saint-Paul, G., and T. Verdier. 1993. Education, Democracy, and Growth. *Journal of Development Economics* 42: 399–407.

Solow, R. 1956. A Contribution to the Theory of Economic Growth. *Quarterly Journal of Economics* 70: 65–94.

Solow, R. 1994. Perspectives on Growth Theory. *Journal of Economic Perspectives* 8(1): 45–54.

Summers, R., and A. Heston. 1991. The Penn World Table (Mark 5): An Expanded Set of International Comparisons, 1950–88. *Quarterly Journal of Economics* 106(2): 327–68.

Taylor, C., and M. Hudson. 1972. *World Handbook of Political and Social Indicators*. 2d. ed. New Haven: Yale University Press.

Taylor, C., and D. Jodice. 1983. *World Handbook of Political and Social Indicators*. 3d. ed. New Haven: Yale University Press.

United Nations. *UNESCO Statistical Yearbook*. Various issues.

World Bank. *World Development Report*. Oxford: Oxford University Press. Various issues.

CHAPTER 9

Financial Development and Economic Growth

José De Gregorio and Pablo E. Guidotti

Ever since the pioneering contributions of Goldsmith (1969), McKinnon (1973), and Shaw (1973), the relationship between financial development and economic growth has remained an important issue of debate.[1] Numerous studies have dealt with different aspects of this relationship at both the theoretical and empirical levels. At a basic level, several studies have attempted to establish whether financial deepening leads to improved growth performance, and have endeavored to analyze the strength of this relationship. Other studies have focused on identifying the channels of transmission from financial intermediation to growth.

The original contributions to this literature all coincide in suggesting that there is a strong positive correlation between the extent of financial development and economic growth. However, they emphasize different channels of transmission. While the main focus in Goldsmith (1969) is on the relationship between financial development and the efficiency of investment, McKinnon (1973) and Shaw (1973) influenced to a large extent by the success stories of Southeast Asia, emphasize the role played by financial liberalization in increasing savings and, hence, investment.

Research on the relationship between financial development and growth has received a new source of inspiration from the rapidly expanding "endogenous growth" literature. By focusing on cases in which the marginal product of capital always remains positive, this literature provides a natural framework in which financial markets affect long-run, and not just transitional, growth. Models in this spirit by Bencivenga and Smith (1991) and Greenwood and Jovanovic (1990), for instance, emphasize how the creation and growth of financial institutions lead to a positive relationship between financial intermediation and economic growth. Most of these studies tend to emphasize the role of financial intermediation in improving the efficiency of investment, rather than its volume. That is, financial intermediaries play a central role in allocating capital to its best possible use. The following section provides a brief overview of these theoretical developments.

Although empirical studies often find a positive relationship between indicators of financial development and growth, much controversy remains about how these results should be interpreted. There are two main sources of controversy. First, there is debate over the issue of how to measure empirically the extent of financial intermediation. Typically, financial intermediation has been proxied largely by the level of the real interest rate and by various monetary aggregates, all of which pose significant problems of interpretation. A brief review of these issues is provided in the third section. The second area of controversy concerns the channel of transmission from financial development to growth. Although some studies find support for the McKinnon-Shaw hypothesis, others conclude that there is no clear relationship between measures of financial development and savings or investment rates.

The purpose of this chapter is to reexamine the empirical relationship between financial development and long-run growth by using the ratio of bank credit to the private sector to GDP as the indicator of financial development. This indicator, as we argue in more detail later, has a clear advantage over measures of real interest rates or monetary aggregates such as M1, M2, or M3, in that it more accurately represents the actual volume of funds channelled to the private sector. Therefore the ratio of bank credit to the private sector to GDP is more directly linked to investment and economic growth.

Our empirical investigation is carried out in the four section using two different data sets. First, we extend Barro's (1991) cross-country growth regressions for a sample of ninety-eight countries during the period 1960–85, by including our proxy for financial development as an additional explanatory variable.[2,3] Second, using De Gregorio's (1992) panel data set for twelve Latin American countries during 1950–85, we explore the relationship between financial intermediation and growth in Latin America.

Recent empirical work has studied the relationship between financial development and economic growth. Most notably, King and Levine (1993a, 1993b) carry out a detailed empirical investigation on the relationship between several indicators of financial depth and economic growth. While they analyze a large cross-section of countries as being affected equally by financial development, we show that the impact of financial development on growth, although broadly positive, changes according to regions, time periods, and levels of income. In addition, and unlike previous work, we examine whether financial development affects growth positively by increasing the volume of investment, its efficiency, or both. This issue is important since the theory does not provide clear predictions on the sign of the relationship between financial development and investment. Moreover, some important cases discussed below imply that this relationship could be even negative, despite a net positive effect of financial development on growth.

The following are our main results. First, using Barro's (1991) data set we find a positive effect of our measure of financial development on long-run growth of real per capita GDP. This positive effect is particularly strong in middle- and low-income countries. We argue that the weak relationship observed in high-income countries is due to the fact that financial development occurs to a large extent outside the banking system, while our proxy for financial development focuses on banking sector development. We also find that the relationship is stronger in the 1960s than in the 1970s and 1980s.

Second, our findings suggest that the effect of financial intermediation on growth is due mainly to its impact on the *efficiency* of investment, rather than its *volume*. We find that only one fourth of the effect of our measure of financial development on growth is channeled through the volume of investment, the rest being explained by improved efficiency of investment. The relative importance of improved efficiency of investment is higher in low- and middle-income countries than in high-income countries.

Third, when we explore the relationship between our measure of financial intermediation and economic growth in Latin America, we find a robust and significant *negative* correlation. This effect, which may appear puzzling, is interpreted in light of the extreme experiments of financial liberalization witnessed by Latin America during the 1970s and 1980s, which subsequently collapsed. The fifth section provides an example of how, in the absence of proper regulation, more financial intermediation may be associated with *lower* efficiency of investment. This case illustrates not only the importance of a large amount of financial intermediation, but that the quality of this intermediation, influenced to a large extent by economic policy, is also crucial.

The chapter is organized as follows. The following section provides a brief overview of the analytical literature. The third section discusses how to measure the degree of financial development. The fourth section presents the empirical evidence, and the fifth section provides an example of why financial development may be negatively related to growth. The sixth section concludes.

Financial Intermediation and Economic Growth: An Analytical Overview

To organize the ensuing discussion, it is useful to consider the following production function which, for simplicity, is assumed to depend only on the capital stock:

$$y_t = f(k_t), \tag{9.1}$$

where y_t and k_t denote output and the stock of capital at time t, respectively. By totally differentiating equation (9.1) and denoting the rate of growth of output by $\hat{y}$, the savings rate (dk/y) by s, and the marginal productivity of capital by ϕ, we have:

$$\hat{y}_t = \frac{dk_t}{y_t} f'(k_t) = s_t \phi_t. \tag{9.2}$$

By equation (9.2), the rate of output growth is the product of the savings rate and the marginal productivity of capital.

In the traditional literature on growth, emphasis has been placed on the dynamic process that would lead the economy to a steady-state equilibrium in which (per capita) output growth would eventually cease. The assumption of decreasing marginal productivity of capital plays a crucial role in ensuring convergence to such a steady-state equilibrium. In the context of equation (9.2), decreasing marginal productivity of capital implies that ϕ_t (and, hence, output growth) goes to zero as k_t grows over time.[4] The new literature on endogenous growth, in contrast, considers a mechanism in which the marginal productivity of capital does not converge to zero as capital grows.[5] Therefore emphasis is placed on situations where it is possible for (per capita) real output to grow endogenously, even in the absence of exogenous productivity growth.

Financial development has a dual effect on economic growth. On the one hand, the development of domestic financial markets may enhance the efficiency of capital accumulation (hence increasing ϕ_t). On the other hand, financial intermediation can contribute to raising the savings rate and thus the investment rate (hence increasing s_t).[6] The former effect is first emphasized by Goldsmith (1969), who also finds some positive correlation between financial development and the level of real per capita GNP. He attributes this correlation to the positive effect that financial development has in encouraging more efficient use of the capital stock:

> Irrespective of whether or not the existence and development of a financial superstructure increases the aggregate volume of saving and investment and thus accelerates the rate of economic growth beyond what would have otherwise been, there is no doubt that it results in a different allocation of capital expenditures among and within sectors, types of tangible assets, and regions. (p. 398)

In addition, Goldsmith argues that the process of growth has feedback effects on financial markets by creating incentives for further financial development.

McKinnon (1973) and Shaw (1973) extend the earlier argument by noting that financial deepening implies not only higher productivity of capital but also a higher savings rate and therefore a higher volume of investment. Unlike Goldsmith, where growth and financial intermediation are both thought of as endogenous, the focus of McKinnon and Shaw is on the effects of public policy regarding financial markets on savings and investment. In particular, McKinnon and Shaw argue that policies that lead to financial repression—for example, controls that result in negative real interest rates—reduce the incentives to save. Lower savings, in turn, result in lower investment and growth. Thus they conclude that higher interest rates resulting from financial liberalization induce households to increase savings. As will be discussed in more detail later on, the empirical validity of the McKinnon-Shaw hypothesis has been challenged by various authors. Díaz-Alejandro (1985), for instance, argues that the Latin American experience shows that financial deepening is unlikely to increase savings; therefore, the main contribution of financial deepening to growth should be thought of as increasing the marginal productivity of capital, rather than the volume of savings and investment.

Recent theoretical work has incorporated the role of financial factors in models of endogenous growth in an attempt to analyze formally the interactions between financial markets and long-run economic growth. Greenwood and Jovanovic (1990) present a model in which both financial intermediation and growth are endogenous.[7] In their framework, the role of financial institutions is to collect and analyze information to channel investible funds to the investment activities that yield the highest return. Since the activity performed by financial intermediaries involves costs, Greenwood and Jovanovic (1990) show that there is a positive two-way causal relationship between economic growth and financial development. On the one hand, the process of growth stimulates higher participation in financial markets, thereby facilitating the creation and expansion of financial institutions. On the other hand financial institutions, by collecting and analyzing information from many potential investors, allow investment projects to be undertaken more efficiently and, hence, stimulate investment and growth.

Bencivenga and Smith (1991) present a model in which individuals face uncertainty about their future liquidity needs. They can choose to invest in a liquid asset (which is safe but has low productivity) and/or an illiquid asset (which is riskier but has high productivity). In this framework, the presence of financial intermediation increases economic growth by channelling savings into the activity with high productivity, while allowing individuals to reduce the risk associated with their liquidity needs. Although individuals face uncertain liquidity needs, banks, by the law of large numbers, face a predictable demand for liquidity and can therefore allocate investment funds more efficiently. In the absence of financial intermediaries, individuals may be forced to liquidate their investment (i.e., their savings held in illiquid assets) when liquidity needs arise. Thus the presence of banks also provides the benefit of eliminating unnecessary liquidations. Interestingly, Bencivenga and Smith (1991) show in their model that growth increases even when aggregate savings are reduced as a result of financial development, the reason being the dominant effect that financial development has on the efficiency of investment.

Along similar lines, Levine (1992) analyzes the effects of alternative financial structures on economic growth. In his model, financial institutions raise the fraction of total savings devoted to investment and avoid premature liquidations of capital. Banks, stock markets, mutual funds, and investment banks enhance growth by promoting the efficient allocation of investment through various channels.

Saint-Paul (1992) develops a model where financial markets affect technological choice. In this model, agents can choose between two technologies: One technology is highly flexible and allows productive diversification, but has low productivity; the other is rigid, more specialized, and more productive. The economy is exposed to shocks to consumer preferences, which may result in a lack of demand for some products. Therefore, in the absence of financial markets risk-averse individuals (consumer-producers) may prefer technological flexibility rather than high productivity. Financial markets, in contrast, allow individuals to hold a diversified portfolio to insure themselves against negative demand shocks and, at the same time, to choose the more productive technology.

In a somewhat different approach, Roubini and Sala-i-Martin (1992) analyze the relationship between financial intermediation and growth by emphasizing the role of government policy. In particular, they develop a model in which financial repression becomes a tool that governments may use to broaden the base of the inflation tax. Thus financial repression yields higher seigniorage to finance government expenditures. In an optimal taxation framework where the tax instruments at the government's disposal are the inflation tax and an income tax that is subject to tax evasion, Roubini and Sala-i-Martin (1992) show that high income tax evasion induces policymakers to repress the financial system and set a high inflation rate in an attempt to generate higher revenues from the inflation tax. Because financial repression reduces the productivity of capital and lowers savings, it hampers growth.

From a different perspective, De Gregorio (1993) and Jappelli and Pagano (1994) analyze the effects of financial market developments on the savings rate. They concentrate attention on the effect of borrowing constraints—that is, the inability of individuals to borrow freely against future income—on economic growth. This work shifts the focus from the effects of financial markets on the production side of the economy to their effects on household behavior. A result common to both studies is that the full or partial inability of individuals to borrow against future income induces them to increase savings. The reason is that when individuals are unable to borrow, they must build up financial wealth by increasing savings in order to finance current consumption. Thus these studies suggest that, in general, financial deepening on the side of consumer credit is unlikely to increase savings. This result is consistent with casual observation in Latin America, where episodes of financial liberalization have not increased savings rates.

The implication from De Gregorio 1993 and Jappelli and Pagano 1994 that the relaxation of borrowing constraints is unlikely to stimulate savings does not necessarily imply that such a form of financial deepening will result in lower growth. De Gregorio (1993), in fact, suggests that the relationship between borrowing constraints and growth will ultimately depend on the importance of the effect of borrowing constraints on the marginal productivity of capital relative to their effect on the volume of savings. In particular, this study shows that a relaxation of borrowing constraints increases the incentives for human capital accumulation. This effect is likely to increase the marginal product of capital and hence may lead to higher growth despite the reduction in savings.

Measurement of Financial Intermediation

This section provides an overview of the main issues that arise in connection with the choice of proxies for the level of financial intermediation.

Interest Rates, Financial Intermediation, and Growth

The McKinnon-Shaw hypothesis suggests that the level of financial intermediation should be closely related to the prevailing level of the real interest rate, because the level of the real interest rate, when held below their normal competitive levels, indicates the extent of financial repression. According to this view (see, for instance, Fry 1988), a positive real interest rate stimulates financial savings and financial intermediation, thereby increasing the supply of credit to the private sector. This in turn stimulates investment and growth. While the main channel of transmission emphasized by the McKinnon-Shaw hypothesis is the effect of real interest rates on the volume of savings, it is also recognized that positive real interest rates make the allocation of investible funds more efficient, thus providing an additional positive effect on economic growth. We argue, in contrast, that real interest rates are a poor indicator of financial intermediation and, more generally, of financial development.

The view that growth is positively related to the level of real interest rates finds empirical support in a number of studies.[8] Most of these studies do not attempt to establish which is the precise channel of transmission from real interest rates to growth. Dornbusch (1990), in contrast, addresses this issue and shows that, although there appears to be a positive relationship between growth and real interest rates, this relationship cannot be attributed to the main channel of transmission emphasized by the McKinnon-Shaw hypothesis. In particular, Dornbusch (1990) finds that financial savings are not related to the level of real interest rates, and that the positive effect of real interest rates on growth does not come through its effect on the volume of investment. In contrast, Fry (1988) finds a much stronger positive effect of real interest rates on financial savings than on the national income definition of savings. Khan and Villanueva (1991) suggest that positive real interest rates are a good proxy for the efficiency of capital accumulation. In view of these findings, one could conclude that a plausible interpretation for the significance of the real interest rate in explaining growth performance reflects the fact that the real interest rate is acting as proxy for the productivity of investment, rather than for financial repression. Therefore the discussion again turns to the question of the specific channel through which financial intermediation affects growth: the level and/or the efficiency of investment.

A more fundamental criticism of the McKinnon-Shaw hypothesis and of the resulting policy implication that high interest rates are beneficial for economic growth is provided by the recent literature focusing on policy credibility. This literature emphasizes that high real interest rates may reflect factors that do not bear any relation to the marginal productivity of capital on account, for instance, of public expectations of inflation and/or outright repudiation of government obligations and, more generally, lack of credibility of economic policies.[9]

As emphasized by Calvo and Coricelli (1992) in the case of Eastern European economies, real interest rates may also reflect such factors as the presence of a fragile financial structure, a poor regulatory environment, and the lack of a proper legal framework to safeguard property rights. All of these factors cause high risk premia to be embodied in interest rates. Moreover, as discussed in the literature on stabilization and financial markets in the late 1970s and early 1980s, high real interest rates may have negative supply-side effects on working capital.[10] This line of research argues that, because of this effect, financial liberalization can have negative consequences for output when firms are heavily dependent on working capital. The conclusion that emerges from all of these arguments is that high real interest rates may indeed have a negative impact on investment and economic growth through, for instance, credit rationing, increased production costs, or the creation of an internal debt problem as a result of the accumulation of significant amounts of arrears across domestic financial and production units.

A recent study by Greene and Villanueva (1991), which explores the determinants of private investment in a large sample of developing countries for the period 1975–87, finds a robust and quantitatively significant negative relationship between real interest rates and private investment. In a study focused on the relationship between interest rates and growth, Gelb (1989) finds no relationship between aggregate investment and real interest rates.

As noted by Calvo and Guidotti (1991), the conflicting evidence presented above regarding the relationship between real interest rates and economic growth suggests an inverted U-curve type of relationship. Very low (and negative) real interest rates tend to cause financial disintermediation and hence tend to reduce growth, as implied by the McKinnon-Shaw hypothesis. Artificially low interest rates may create an excess demand for funds, so that investors have to be rationed, and consequently banks may face problems or may lack the incentive to allocate available credit to the most efficient projects. On the other hand, very high real interest rates that do not reflect improved efficiency of investment, but rather a lack of credibility of economic policy or various forms of country risk, are likely to result in a lower level of investment as well as a concentration in excessively risky projects. At intermediate levels real interest rates do not appear to be closely associated with growth, reflecting no clear-cut relationship between real interest rates and savings and investment. Fry (1993) finds support for this inverted U-curve by adding a quadratic term on interest rate in a growth regression. Evidence adduced by Roubini and Sala-i-Martin (1992) also provides some support for this view. They find a significantly positive relationship between real interest rates and growth when episodes of very negative interest rates (below −5 percent per year) are examined, and no significant relationship when episodes of moderately negative real interest rates are considered.

In sum, these considerations suggest that real interest rates are likely to be rather poor indicators of the degree of financial intermediation, although they may be good indicators of the efficiency of investment. Therefore the impact of real interest rates on growth cannot be easily interpreted as measuring the effect of financial development on growth.

Monetary Aggregates and Financial Intermediation

Monetary aggregates provide an alternative set of variables to measure the extent of financial development. A number of empirical studies have used a wide variety of monetary aggregates to analyze the correlation between financial intermediation and economic growth.[11] As in the case of real interest rates, however, the use of monetary aggregates as a proxy for the degree of financial intermediation presents problems. In particular, as noted by King and Levine (1993a), different definitions of monetary aggregates may act as proxies for different roles of financial intermediation. And in some cases, monetary aggregates may be very poor indicators of the extent of financial development.

Consider first the more liquid forms of monetary aggregates, such as M1 or a broader measure such as M2. These are the aggregates likely to pose the most significant problems. In principle, it may be argued that the original McKinnon-Shaw hypothesis implies that a monetized economy reflects a highly developed capital market; hence a high degree of monetization should be positively related to growth performance. The basic problem with this argument lies in the fact that financial markets have two main functions (Fama 1980): to channel funds from agents willing to save to those requiring funds (credit allocation or portfolio management), and to provide liquidity (or transactions) services. More important, the ability of the financial sector to allocate credit efficiently and to provide a medium of exchange are not necessarily related. While the aspect of financial intermediation that is thought to be related to investment and growth is that which refers to the ability of financial markets to allocate credit, a liquid aggregate such as M1—and in some cases M2—is mainly related to the ability of the financial system to provide liquidity, or a medium of exchange.

Therefore one can envision situations in which a high level of monetization—say, measured by the ratio of M1 to GDP—is the result of financial underdevelopment, while a low level of monetization is the result of a high degree of sophistication of financial markets, which allows individuals to economize on their money holdings. An example of the former case is provided by the so-called monetary overhang in Eastern Europe and the former Soviet Union. Before the implementation of market-oriented reforms, those economies had been—and most still remain—highly monetized compared to Western economies, mainly reflecting the lack of alternative assets that would serve as stores of value. Interestingly, this type of relationship is consistent with the analysis of Bencivenga and Smith (1991), which shows why financial repression may induce an increase in the stock of liquid assets relative to GDP.

An example of the latter case—that is, one in which low monetization is associated with a very sophisticated financial market—is provided by a number of economies where sustained high inflation has resulted in a steady demonetization. This phenomenon, however, has been largely stimulated by an increasing sophistication of financial markets, which allows individuals to economize on the real cash balances needed for transactions purposes.

To overcome some of the previously mentioned problems, a less liquid monetary aggregate has sometimes been used to proxy for the degree of financial intermediation. For example, Gelb (1989) uses the ratio of a broad definition of money, M3, to GDP as a proxy for financial depth, and the change in M3 divided by GDP as a measure of financialization. Similarly, the indicator in which King and Levine (1993a) focus most attention is in liquid liabilities of the financial system (M3 and when not available, M2). Although these measures may be more related to the degree of credit market development than narrower definitions of money, they may still be influenced by factors other than financial depth. In particular, because M3 still includes liquid assets (M1), Neal (1988) has relied on indicators of quasi-liquid assets by subtracting M1 from M2.

In our ensuing analysis we use the ratio of domestic credit to the private sector to GDP as a proxy for the degree of financial intermediation. It corresponds to credit granted to the private sector by the central bank and commercial banks (line 32d from the International Monetary Fund's *International Financial Statistics*), as a fraction of GDP: we henceforth refer to this variable as CREDIT. The main advantage of CREDIT over other monetary aggregates is that because it excludes credit to the public sector, it represents more accurately the role of financial intermediaries in channelling funds to private market participants. Thus this is the definition of financial intermediation that should be more closely related to the level and efficiency of investment, and hence to economic growth.[12]

However, the use of CREDIT is subject to caveats as well. In particular, although CREDIT appears to be the most appropriate indicator of the degree of financial intermediation that occurs through the banking system, it may be a weaker indicator of financial development broadly defined, to the extent that a significant portion of financial development occurs outside the banking system. This phenomenon appears to be most relevant in industrial countries, which have experienced significant nonbank financial innovation (see Goldstein et al. 1992). Nevertheless, it is likely that the two forms of financial development—that is, bank and nonbank—are positively correlated.[13] Thus the presence of financial innovation outside the banking system will show up in the form of a smaller coefficient for CREDIT (more on this in the next section). In developing countries, in contrast, most of financial development has occurred within the banking system. Therefore in these countries CREDIT is likely to be a better proxy for financial development broadly defined.

Finally, as in the case of monetary aggregates, including CREDIT on the right-hand side of output growth equations may induce endogeneity problems. This is the case if, as suggested by Goldsmith (1969), one expects the degree of financial intermediation to be endogenous. In that case the error term in the growth equations should be positively correlated with CREDIT, introducing a positive bias in the coefficient for CREDIT. In the next section we use CREDIT measured at the beginning of the period of estimation to overcome the endogeneity problem. Because it is unlikely that this practice solves the endogeneity problem, the empirical results of the next section should be interpreted cautiously, as suggestive of broad correlations rather than indicating a causal relationship.

Empirical Evidence

In this section we present the results for the cross-section of countries used by Barro (1991), which comprises about 100 countries during the period 1960–85, and then for the panel data of twelve Latin American countries, using six-year average data for the period 1950–85, examined by De Gregorio (1992).

Large Cross Section of Countries

The first set of results extends the cross-section regressions of Barro (1991). The results of adding our proxy for the degree of financial intermediation (CREDIT) to those regressions are presented in tables 9.1 and 9.2. The basic specification follows Barro 1991. It includes as explanatory variables measures of human capital accumulation based on primary and secondary school enrollment ratios in 1960, GDP per capita in 1960, the average level of government spending over GDP, and Barro's proxies for political instability. Unlike Barro (1991), we did not include dummies for each continent as explanatory and PPP investment deflators deviations with respect to the mean. Because their presence did not affect the results, they were dropped to simplify the exposition. The estimations were carried out using OLS, and the standard errors were computed using White's robust procedure.[14]

Regressions (1) and (2) correspond to the full sample of countries for the period 1960–85. They show that per capita real output growth is positively correlated with CREDIT. The remaining parameter estimates are in line with those found by Barro (1991). As discussed in the previous section, it is important to disentangle the effects of financial intermediation on the volume of savings and investment from those on the efficiency of investment. To examine this issue, equation (9.2) excludes the volume of investment from equation (9.1). If the main channel through which financial intermediation affects growth is the volume of investment, then the coefficient of CREDIT should increase substantially when investment is excluded as an explanatory variable, because CREDIT would also be capturing its indirect effects on growth through fostering investment. In contrast, as indicated by regression (2), the coefficient of CREDIT increases by a third. This suggests that approximately one-fourth of the effect of CREDIT on growth is transmitted through the volume of investment, while the remaining three-fourths reflect the effect of CREDIT on the efficiency of investment. Thus these findings support the hypothesis that the effects of financial intermediation on growth, as indicated by most of the literature, are primarily transmitted through an increase in the marginal productivity of capital. These results can be confirmed by estimating investment equations with the same explanatory variables as in the growth regression. The coefficient on CREDIT is equal to 0.1. Using the coefficient of investment of regression (1) implies that 10 percentage points increase in CREDIT increases growth by 0.18 percentage points via efficiency and 0.07 via investment.[15] Similar computations can be done using table IX from King and Levine 1993a, which shows that the total

TABLE 9.1 Financial Intermediation and Growth (Data from Barro 1991. Full Sample and High-Income Countries)

Regression No.	(1)	(2)	(3)[a]	(4)[a]	(5)	(6)	(7)
Credit	0.018	0.024	0.015	0.019	0.010	0.009	0.005
	(2.30)	(3.58)	(1.74)	(2.55)	(1.71)	(1.40)	(−0.67)
Constant	0.018	0.025	0.020	0.026	0.018	0.027	0.007
	(2.51)	(3.89)	(2.39)	(1.71)	(2.03)	(2.33)	(−0.35)
Investment rate	0.066		0.059		0.096	0.051	0.088
	(1.90)		(1.71)		(2.82)	(1.24)	(1.72)
Primary school	0.013	0.018	0.018	0.026	0.002	−0.011	−0.015
enrollment (initial year)	(2.14)	(2.94)	(3.03)	(3.78)	(0.36)	(−1.15)	(−0.40)
Secondary school	0.024	0.032	0.021	0.031	0.044	0.033	−0.001
enrollment (initial year)	(2.08)	(3.31)	(1.93)	(3.29)	(3.48)	(4.37)	(−0.11)
GDP per capita	−0.007	−0.008	−0.008	−0.008	−0.007	−0.005	−0.007
(initial year)	(−6.28)	(−6.61)	(−6.35)	(−6.70)	(−5.64)	(−3.74)	(−1.87)
Government	−0.113	−0.112	−0.133	−0.147	−0.161	−0.049	−0.015
spending	(−3.80)	(−3.80)	(−3.32)	(−4.40)	(−4.22)	(−1.55)	(−0.40)
Revolutions and	−0.017	−0.019	−0.016	−0.016	−0.023	−0.045	−0.066
coups per year	(−2.75)	(−2.80)	(−2.37)	(−2.42)	(−2.80)	(−4.23)	(−2.91)
Index of	−0.002	−0.004	−0.002	−0.003	−0.003	0.008	0.015
assassinations	(−1.03)	(−1.60)	(−1.01)	(−1.57)	(−1.04)	(1.74)	(1.74)
Sample	full sample	full sample	full sample	full sample	high income	high income	
	1960–85	1960–85	1960–85	1960–85	1970–85	1960–85	1970–85
R^2	0.57	0.54	0.60	0.57	0.50	0.73	0.66
No. of observations	95	95	72	72	95	31	31

Notes: Dependent variable: Average GDP per capita growth for the period 1960–85. t-statistics in parentheses. Standard errors were computed using White's robust procedure. CREDIT corresponds to the ratio between domestic credit to the private sector (line 32d IFS) and GDP average for the period, except in regressions (3) and (4) (see note a). For a description of the rest of the variables, see Barro 1991.

[a]CREDIT is measured at the beginning of the period: average 1960–62.

TABLE 9.2 Financial Intermediation and Growth (Data from Barro 1991. Middle- and Low-Income Countries)

Regression No.	(8)	(9)	(10	(11)	(12)
CREDIT	0.044	0.054	0.048	0.135	0.081
	(2.16)	(2.77)	(2.39)	(3.62)	(1.01)
Constant	0.015	0.022	0.017	0.042	0.033
	(1.08)	(1.40)	(1.02)	(3.86)	(1.74)
Investment rate	0.103		0.117	0.099	0.148
	(2.38)		(1.02)	(1.89)	(2.22)
Primary school	0.026	0.031	0.019	−0.003	−0.015
enrollment (initial year)	(2.33)	(2.33)	(1.75)	(−0.31)	(−0.87)
Secondary school	−0.033	−0.013	0.014	0.139	0.121
enrollment (inital year)	(−1.79)	(−0.56)	(0.66)	(4.70)	(3.80)
GDP per capita	−0.015	−0.012	−0.016	−0.087	−0.050
(initial year)	(−2.77)	(−2.10)	(−4.18)	(−4.40)	(−1.55)
Government	−0.127	−0.138	−0.203	−0.139	−0.187
spending	(−3.35)	(−3.55)	(−3.97)	(−3.21)	(−2.42)
Revolutions and	−0.011	−0.012	−0.017	−0.013	−0.022
coups per year	(−1.55)	(−1.45)	(−1.95)	(−1.26)	(−1.39)
Index of	−0.000	−0.004	−0.014	−0.022	−0.009
assassinations	(−0.15)	(−1.38)	(−0.39)	(−3.12)	(−0.59)
Sample	middle-income	middle-income	middle-income	low-income	low-income
	1960–85	1960–85	1970–85	1960–85	1970–85
R^2	0.78	0.73	0.72	0.62	0.47
No. of observations	32	32	32	32	32

Notes: Dependent variable: Average GDP per capita growth for the period 1960–85. t-statistics in parentheses. Standard errors were computed using White's robust procedure. CREDIT corresponds to the ration between domestic credit to the private sector (line 32d IFS) and GDP. For a description of the rest of the variables, see Barro 1991.

effect of increasing liquid liabilities by 10 percentage points on growth is 0.34 percentage points, from which 0.25 are due to higher efficiency.

An important issue in cross-country growth regressions has been the endogeneity of the regressors. In our case, it could be argued that CREDIT is an endogenous because financial development facilitates growth, but, as reviewed in previous sections, economic growth also induces financial deepening.

A procedure to overcome this potential problem is to use the variable measured at the beginning of the period (e.g., King and Levine 1993a). In our case this would mean to use CREDIT measured around 1960. Although this approach does not capture the dynamic interactions between financial development and growth, it answers the question of whether countries that started with more developed financial markets were able to grow faster in subsequent years. Regressions (3) and (4) use average CREDIT during 1960–62 instead of the average for 1960–85. They show that the alternative periods considered to measure CREDIT do not change the results. The reason is that CREDIT is highly persistent over time, and hence, CREDIT at the beginning of the period is a very good predictor of CREDIT in the next years.[16] This result highlights an even more important point that the endogeneity problem may not be that critical after all. Indeed, theory suggests that economic growth induces growth in the financial system, but this has no implications regarding the size of the financial system with respect to GDP, which is what CREDIT measures. The endogeneity problem would be serious if the growth of CREDIT were used as an independent variable.

As discussed in the second section, CREDIT may be a weak indicator of financial development in situations where substantial financial innovation occurs outside the banking system. Under these conditions, higher growth is not necessarily accompanied by a higher volume of credit to the private sector. To explore this issue we examined the relationship between CREDIT and growth across subperiods and across subsamples of countries. In particular, the above considerations suggest the following conjectures: *(a)* the effect of CREDIT on growth should be weaker in the 1970s and 1980s, as these periods are associated with higher financial innovation outside the banking system, and *(b)* the effect of CREDIT on growth should be weaker in industrial countries, where financial innovation outside the banking system has been the largest. Results support the validity of these conjectures. Regression (5) restricts the sample to the period 1970–85. It shows that for the entire group of countries the correlation between CREDIT and growth is smaller than for the 1960–85 sample. The coefficient on CREDIT falls to approximately half of that obtained for the full sample. The same result obtains using De Long and Summers's (1991) data set, where the coefficient of CREDIT in the 1975–85 period is about a quarter of the level that obtains in the 1960–75 period.

To explore further the robustness of previous results and to see the patterns that emerge across different stages of development, we run the regressions for different sub-samples of countries classified according to their levels of income in 1960. The original sample of 98 countries in Barro 1991 was divided into high-income countries (32 countries), middle-income countries (33 countries), and low-income countries (33 countries). The countries included in each group are listed in Table A.1 in Appendix A. The sample of low-income countries is composed mainly of African countries.[17] The findings for high-income countries are presented in table 9.1, while the results for middle-income and low-income countries are presented in table 9.2.

Compared to the rest of the sample, the effect of financial development on growth in high-income countries is relatively small. In particular, the effect in the period 1970–85 is not significantly different from zero, as shown by regression (7). As discussed earlier, the contrast between the periods 1960–85 and 1970–85 may reflect the significant financial innovation outside the banking system that occurred in industrialized countries during the 1970s and 1980s. Alternatively, this result may suggest that increased efficiency from further financial development in high-income countries may have reached the stage of diminishing returns.

As table 9.2 shows, the impact of CREDIT on growth increases significantly as one moves progressively from high-income to low-income countries. However, while this finding is consistent with our previous conjecture, it should be noted that it could also reflect a larger bias in the coefficient in the sample of low- and middle-income countries. As discussed in the previous section, if CREDIT is endogenous then the bias is likely to be positive. Further research will be required to assess more precisely the presence of such a bias. Table 9.2 also reveals that the effect of CREDIT on growth declines in the period 1970–85 for both groups of countries. Unlike the case of high-income countries, it is less clear that in low-income countries this fact can be explained in terms of increased development of non-bank financial intermediation.

When the volume of investment is included in the sample of middle-income countries (regression [8]), the increase in the size of the coefficient on CREDIT is rather small. A similar result is obtained for the sample of low-income countries, where the coefficient increases from 0.135 to 0.146 when investment is excluded. The largest value is obtained for the sample of high-income countries, where the coefficient increases from 0.009 to 0.015. Overall these findings suggest that, except for high-income countries, the effect of financial development on the volume of investment is relatively small, and hence most of the beneficial effect on growth comes from the increased efficiency of investment.

Although our focus is on financial intermediation, it is worth noting some other interesting results that emerge from table 9.2. First, the effect of initial levels of primary and secondary school enrollment ratios differs significantly across groups of countries. Second, government consumption and Barro's (1991) indices of political instability are in general negatively related with growth in all groups of countries, although magnitudes and significance levels differ across them. Third, all groups of countries show some degree of conditional convergence.

Latin American Countries

We now analyze the Latin American experience in greater detail. For this purpose we extend the results of De Gregorio (1992). The basic specification includes investment rates, literacy rates as a proxy for human capital, foreign investment, inflation, GDP per capita in 1960, and government spending. The estimations are carried out using panel data with random effects, and the standard errors are computed using White's robust procedure. The main results are presented in table 9.3.

The inclusion of CREDIT as an explanatory variable does not alter the coefficients of other explanatory variables—with the exception of government spending which becomes insignificant. Interestingly, the coefficient of CREDIT is significantly negative. This result is obtained under many specifications and appears to be robust when estimated in the full sample. In addition, as regressions (13) and (14) show, a negative effect is found regardless of whether investment is included as a right-hand-side variable. This result is in sharp contrast with those obtained in the previous subsection; because of its robustness it merits further examination.

Before analyzing in more detail the result regarding the coefficient of CREDIT, it is interesting to note that after CREDIT is included in the regression the effect of inflation on growth is still negative, and with a value statistically unchanged compared to that which obtains when CREDIT is excluded. It has been argued that the negative correlation between inflation and growth may simply reflect the fact that inflation is a proxy of financial repression. The results presented in table 9.3 show that inflation exerts a negative effect on growth even after we control for the degree of financial development.

Regressions (15) to (17) present results for some selected subsamples. Regressions (15) and (16) show that the effects of CREDIT are not significant during the first half of the sample, the 1950s and 1960s. In

TABLE 9.3 Finanial Intermediation and Growth in Latin America (Data from De Gregorio 1992)

Regression No.	(13)	(14)	(15)	(16)	(17)
CREDIT	−0.092	−0.104	−0.041	−0.027	−0.087
	(−3.20)	(−3.83)	(−0.72)	(−0.52)	(−2.20)
Constant	−0.051	−0.056	0.010	0.003	−0.063
	(−1.85)	(−2.29)	(0.51)	(0.19)	(−3.09)
Investment rate		0.176		0.062	0.050
		(3.33)		(1.79)	(0.93)
Literacy rate	0.116	0.069	0.045	0.030	0.105
($x10^{-2}$)	(3.56)	(2.08)	(1.75)	(1.09)	(1.94)
Foreign investment	0.345	0.345	0.637	0.604	0.284
	(2.30)	(3.02)	(4.60)	(4.69)	(1.94)
Inflation (log)	−0.763	−0.855	0.084	−0.017	−0.930
($x10^{-2}$)	(−3.20)	(−4.27)	(0.44)	(−0.10)	(−4.35)
GDP per capita	−1.024	−0.681	−0.915	−0.787	−0.860
(1960) ($x10^{-5}$)	(−4.27)	(−2.83)	(−4.10)	(−3.79)	(−4.15)
Government	−0.074	−0.031	−0.001	−0.003	−0.063
spending	(−0.99)	(−0.50)	(−0.19)	(−0.07)	(−1.00)
Sample	1950–85	1950–85	1950–74	1950–74	Excludes Argentina, Brazil, and Chile
R^2	0.45	0.55	0.53	0.59	0.66
No. of observations	62	62	38	38	46

Notes: Dependent variable: Average GDP per capita growth in six-year periods during 1950–85. *t*-statistics in parentheses. Standard errors were computed using White's robust procedure, and the estimations were done using panel data with random effects. CREDIT corresponds to the ratio between domestic credit to the private sector (line 32d IFS) and GDP. For a description of the rest of the variables, see De Gregorio 1992.

other words, the negative effect of CREDIT on growth is attributable mainly to the last subperiods of the sample; that is, there is a strong negative correlation between financial intermediation and growth during the 1970s and 1980s in Latin America. Finally, regression (17) shows that the negative correlation between CREDIT and growth is still present when Argentina, Brazil, and Chile (countries that might be thought, a priori, to be driving the results) are excluded from the sample.

The previously mentioned findings constitute the first evidence we are aware of that there are cases where a robust negative relationship exists between financial intermediation and growth.[18] At first glance, this evidence may appear puzzling. In our view, however, these findings are less controversial once one considers that the negative relationship between financial intermediation and growth is obtained for Latin American countries during the 1970s and 1980s, a set of countries and a time period when financial markets were exposed to extreme conditions. In particular, we think our findings may reflect the effects of experiments of extreme liberalization of financial markets followed by their subsequent collapse. The following paragraphs attempt to explain the reason for the apparent contradiction between the results obtained for Latin America and those presented earlier.[19]

After years of financial repression in Latin America, the 1970s witnessed substantial efforts to liberalize domestic capital markets in several of these countries. Many of these experiments collapsed in the early 1980s (see Díaz-Alejandro 1985). The liberalization of financial markets was often undertaken in the context of poor regulatory environments, resulting in very fragile financial systems. The negative effects of lack of regulation were compounded by widespread expectations that the financial system would be bailed out in the event of failure. In many cases, this led to massive overlending. Therefore a high degree of financial intermediation in the sample of Latin American countries was often a sign of a fragile and over-exposed financial system, rather than one that was efficiently allocating credit.

An important feature of the Latin American experience is the massive government intervention after the collapse of financial systems. This intervention most likely validated expectations and hence appears to be an essential factor in explaining the behavior of the banking systems in periods preceding their collapse. Regardless of the existence of formal deposit insurance, governments bore most of the costs of financial crises by bailing out banks and protecting depositors. The fact that government bailouts occurred independently of the presence of formal deposit insurance legislation strongly suggests that their policy of not bailing out failing banks was simply time inconsistent; all agents realized that the government had an incentive to intervene after a collapse occurred and that, consequently, it could not stick to its announced policy of nonintervention. As the Latin American experience illustrates,[20] banks may act on the assumption that the government will provide some degree of relief in the event of a crisis.

There are several possible reasons behind a government's incentive to intervene in the event of a financial crisis. A traditional explanation is that governments do not want the public to think that the financial system can collapse; consequently, they let it be known that relief will be provided at the first sign of a portending crisis. After this has happened, people tend to expect the government to repeat this action at later dates. Another explanation is that because of political pressure (or preferences), governments do not want depositors—particularly holders of small deposits—to suffer significant losses. Therefore, regardless of governments' assurances that there will not be a bailout of financial institutions, and even in the absence of formal deposit insurance, private agents may expect that some form of relief will be forthcoming to banks and/or depositors in the event of a crisis. In turn, the expectation of a bailout induces inefficient behavior on the part of banks. Banks will tend to be less careful in evaluating credit applications and, as a result, they may end up overlending. This inefficiency is likely to translate into a reduction of long-run growth. The next section provides an example to illustrate this point.[21]

These considerations suggest that the negative relationship between financial intermediation and long-run growth observed in the sample of Latin American countries comes from a negative effect on the efficiency of investment, rather than from effects on the volume of investment. In fact, these considerations point toward the possibility that more financial intermediation may be associated with overlending rather than with rationing. Thus more financial intermediation could be associated with higher but less efficient investment.

The conjecture that the negative relationship between financial intermediation and growth is due to a loss of efficiency is borne out by the empirical findings in table 9.3. As was the case with the regressions run on Barro's 1991 data set, regressions (13) and (14) show that the coefficient of CREDIT increases slightly (from −0.10 to −0.09) once investment is included as an explanatory variable. Hence the volume effect appears to be positive, although small. The Latin American experience and our empirical findings can be rationalized in the following example.

Overlending and Financial Crises: An Example

This section provides an example to illustrate the possibility that in the absence of proper regulation, expectations about government intervention in the case of a financial crisis may lead to overlending by banks, coupled with a loss of efficiency in the allocation of funds.

To keep the analysis simple we consider the behavior of a single bank in an unregulated financial market when it knows (or believes) that in the event of a crisis it will be partially bailed out by the government. Furthermore, we assume that there is an infinitely elastic supply of funds so that we can abstract from the effects of financial markets on the volume of savings.

In each period, a representative bank can finance a continuum of projects. Each project, indexed by x, requires a unitary loan and yields a return equal to αx. Parameter α is common to all projects and is stochastic. It takes the value α^h with probability h and α^ℓ with probability $1 - h$. Since $\alpha^h > \alpha^\ell$, superscript h represents a high-productivity state of nature and ℓ a low-productivity one. The return x is assumed to be uniformly distributed over the range $[\underline{x}, \bar{x}]$; for normalization it is assumed that $\bar{x} - \underline{x}$ is equal to unity.

The loan contract stipulates an interest rate equal to $r - 1$; hence, amortization plus interest equals r in the case that αx is greater than r. In the event that αx is less than r, all of the return on the project (i.e., αx) is paid to the bank. It is assumed that all projects are profitable in the state of high productivity; hence, $\underline{x}\alpha^h > r$. Thus the bank is able to obtain full repayment on its loan in high-productivity states. In contrast, it is assumed that in low-productivity states only projects with return $x > x^*$ receive a positive net return. That is, x^* is such that $\alpha^\ell x^* = r$. This implies that in low-productivity states the bank gets partial repayment on loans invested in the subinterval of projects yielding a return below x^*.

Banks, in turn, pay interest to depositors at the rate $\rho - 1$, regardless the realization of α. Since the bank may make losses in low-productivity states, it may need government relief to be able to meet the interest payment to depositors in full. It is assumed, therefore, that the government bails out banks by paying a fraction b of the payments owed to depositors in the event that productivity is low. This implies that a bank that lends to all projects with return higher than δ pays $(1 - b)\rho(x - \delta)$ to depositors from its own resources when $\alpha = \alpha^\ell$. The fraction b is the minimum bailout that keeps the bank solvent. Hence one may think of b as an indicator of the fragility of the financial system; for a given size of loss a higher b means the bank has a lower capacity to absorb that loss from its own resources (e.g., capital plus reserves).

The main purpose of banks is to review the various projects to determine their quality. The technology for evaluating projects is such that, by paying a cost $c(\delta)$, the bank can determine whether a project has a return x greater or less than a given value δ. Presumably, distinguishing whether a project is very good or very bad is cheap. What is costly is to evaluate projects of average quality. Thus a reasonable shape for the cost function $c(\delta)$ is as shown in figure 9.1. The cost function $c(\delta)$ can be thought of as the amount of resources spent by a bank in screening projects. We assume that x^* is below x^m, where x^m is the value of x that maximizes $c(\delta)$. Finally, to have a well-behaved cost function, we assume that for all x below x^* the cost function is convex.

Because banks make profits lending to all projects when $\alpha = \alpha^h$, but incur losses for a range of projects with $x < x^*$ if $\alpha = \alpha^\ell$, the optimal strategy for a representative bank is to choose a value of δ, lend to all projects with $x > \delta$, and deny loans to the rest.

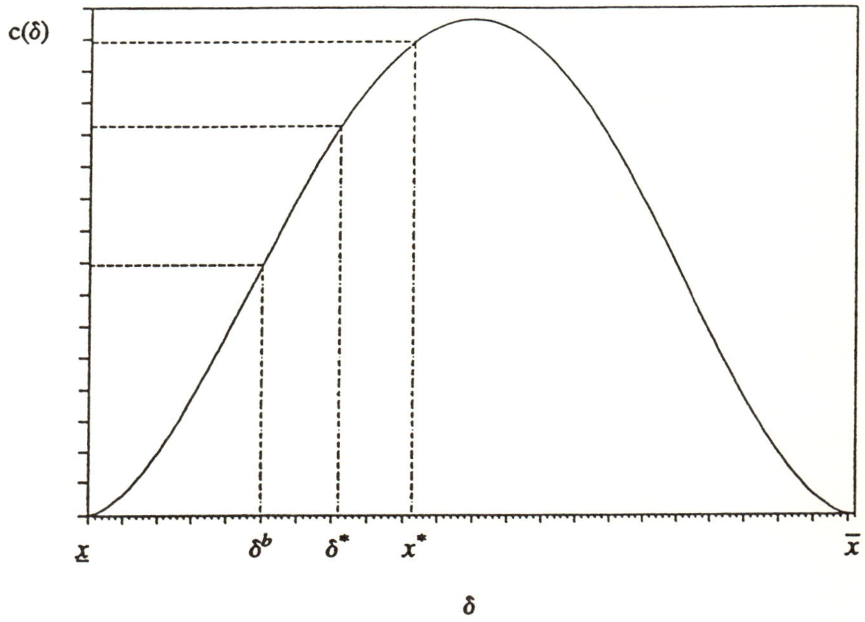

Figure 9.1 Screening costs

We can now characterize the optimal choice of δ. Expected bank profits are given by:

$$\begin{aligned} \mathrm{E}\pi &= h(r-\rho)(\bar{x}-\delta) + (1-h)[r(\bar{x}-x^{*}) + \int_{\delta}^{x^{*}} \alpha^{\ell} x dF(x) \\ &\quad - (1-b)\rho(\bar{x}-\delta)] - \mathrm{c}(\delta) \qquad (9.3) \\ &= h(r-\rho)(\bar{x}-\delta) + (1-h)[(\bar{x}-x^{*}) + \frac{\alpha^{\ell}}{2}(x^{*2}-\delta^{2}) \\ &\quad - (1-b)\rho(\bar{x}-\delta)] - \mathrm{c}(\delta). \end{aligned}$$

The optimal choice of δ, denoted by δ^{*}, is given by the following condition:

$$c'(\delta^{*}) = \rho[h + (1-h)(1-b)] - hr - \alpha^{\ell}\delta^{*}(1-h). \qquad (9.4)$$

Equation (9.4) states that, at the optimum, the bank equates the expected marginal benefit with the marginal cost—that is, interest plus screening costs—associated with an additional unit of lending, $\bar{x} - \delta$. Because c(δ) is convex over the relevant range, equation (9.4) implies that there is a positive relationship between the amount of bank lending, $\bar{x} - \delta$, and the size of the bailout expected from the government, b. Moreover, equation (9.4) implies that higher financial fragility—as measured by a higher b—is not only associated with more lending, but also with less screening on the part of banks.

In sum, this example shows how, because of government incentives to provide relief to the financial system during crisis, the level of financial intermediation—measured by bank lending to the private sector—may be positively associated with lower productivity of investment and with greater fragility of the financial system. In turn, this type of consideration may explain why, in situations where the financial system is liberalized and allowed to operate under a poor regulatory environment, higher financial intermediation may have negative effects on growth performance, as suggested by recent Latin American experience.

Conclusions

This chapter has examined the empirical relationship between financial development and economic growth. The review of the literature and our empirical findings suggest that, by and large, financial development leads to improved growth performance. This effect, however, varies across countries and over time. Furthermore, as the Latin American experience of the 1970s and 1980s demonstrates, there may be instances where unregulated financial liberalization and expectations of government bailouts can lead to a negative relationship between the degree of financial intermediation and growth. Thus the removal of financial repression requires an appropriate regulatory framework to avoid costly financial crisis. Our findings also strongly suggest that the main channel of transmission from financial development to growth is the effect on the efficiency of investment, rather than its level.

APPENDIX A: CLASSIFICATION OF COUNTRIES

TABLE A.1 Classification of Countries by Income per Capita in 1960

High Income	Middle Income	Low Income
United States	Hong Kong	Ivory Coast
Switzerland	Peru	Zambia
Luxembourg	Cyprus	Korea (South)

TABLE A.1 Continued

High Income	Middle Income	Low Income
Canada	Costa Rica	Thailand
New Zealand	Nicaragua	Sudan
Denmark	Singapore	Madagascar
Venezuela	Greece	Zimbabwe
Germany	Jamaica	Haiti
Australia	Portugal	Pakistan
Sweden	Guyana	Nigeria
Norway	Colombia	Morocco
United Kingdom	Brazil	Ghana
Trinidad and Tobago	Algeria	India
Netherlands	Malta	Cameroon
Iceland	Guatemala	Egypt
France	Turkey	Indonesia
Belgium	Panama	Botswana
Finland	Ecuador	Central African Republic
Austria	Jordan	Nepal
Uruguay	Malaysia	Kenya
Italy	El Salvador	Liberia
Argentina	Mauritius	Bangladesh
Chile	Papua New Guinea	Swaziland
Israel	Paraguay	Togo
South Africa	Sri Lanka	Burundi
Ireland	Dominican Republic	Uganda
Spain	Bolivia	Zaire
Japan	Philippines	Burma
Mexico	Taiwan	Ethiopia
Iran	Tunisia	Sierra Leone
Fiji	Gabon	Rwanda
Barbados	Senegal	Malawi
	Honduras	Tanzania

NOTES

We have greatly benefited from comments by Michael Bruno, Panicos Demetriades, Kenneth Kletzer, Malcolm Knight, Felipe Larraín, Ross Levine, Matthew Saal, Delano Villaneuva, and two anonymous referees. Any remaining errors are our responsibility.

1. The terms "financial development" and "financial intermediation" are used interchangeably for the purpose of this chapter. Financial development, however, should be thought of as a broader concept that also includes financial innovations that occur outside the banking system. Because of the lack of data regarding nonbank financial innovation in developing countries, the degree of

financial development is effectively measured by the level of financial intermediation by the banking system.

2. Like other recent studies (for instance, Jappelli and Pagano 1994 and Roubini and Sala-i-Martin 1992), this chapter follows the strategy of adding new variables to Barro's (1991) basic cross-country regressions to analyze their impact on growth. Jappelli and Pagano (1994) also use the data set of De Long and Summers (1991).

3. To check the robustness of our results, we also used De Long and Summers's (1991) data set. The results are very similar to those obtained using Barro's (1991) data set, which suggests that our findings are robust across data sets.

4. Of course, with depreciation of the capital stock and a positive rate of time preference, the steady-state equilibrium is reached for a bounded level of k_t (see, for instance, Solow 1956 and Blanchard and Fischer 1989).

5. See, for example, Romer 1986, Lucas 1988, and Grossman and Helpman 1991.

6. To simplify the discussion we assume the economy to be closed, so investment equals savings. It could be assumed that the economy is open and there is in addition an upward-sloping supply of funds (Fry 1993) or some other form of imperfect capital mobility such as the lack of collateral to obtain foreign financing for human capital accumulation (Barro, Mankiw, and Sala-i-Martin 1994). In all of these cases more national saving would encourage capital accumulation, and the implications for growth would be qualitatively similar to those of the closed economy.

7. See also Greenwood and Smith 1994.

8. See, for example, Fry 1988, World Bank 1989, Gelb 1989, Polak 1989, Easterly 1990, Khan and Villaneuva 1991, and Roubini and Sala-i-Martin 1992.

9. See, for instance, Calvo 1988, Calvo and Guidotti 1991, Guidotti and Kumar 1991, and Persson and Tabellini 1990.

10. See Cavallo 1977, Taylor 1983, and van Wijnbergen 1983, among others.

11. See, for example, McKinnon 1973, Gelb 1989, Neal 1989, and Fry 1988. Typical monetary aggregates are scaled by dividing them by some other macroeconomic aggregate, such as GDP. King and Levine (1993a) present a wide set of indicators and discuss their advantages and problems.

12. King and Levine (1993a, 1993b) also use this variable as an indicator of financial depth. They also use credit to the private sector as a ratio of total credit, which represents to whom banks are lending. However, this variable may take a large value not only because a large volume of total credit is intermediated to the private sector, but also because financial depth, and hence total credit, is small.

13. To the extent that financial innovation induces a substitution away from bank credit—say, by inducing firms to resort to the stock market or other forms of direct financing—one could envision a situation in which a negative relationship between bank credit and growth performance obtains as the result of a negative correlation between bank credit and nonbank intermediation. However, we do

not think that this is a relevant possibility. Later on we will present a case—that is, Latin America—in which a negative relationship between CREDIT and growth is observed. Especially because those results are obtained in a context where growth performance is very weak (and therefore no development of nonbank intermediaries is expected), they are interpreted as arising from lack of proper financial regulation, rather than from nonbank financial innovation.

14. The measure of government spending excludes education and defense expenditure in order to proxy for government consumption. None of the results change if total government expenditure is used.

15. The regression is

$$\text{Investment} = \underset{(3.82)}{0.095} + \underset{(3.50)}{0.098}\ \text{CREDIT} + \text{other vars.}$$

with *t*-statistics in parentheses, $R^2 = 0.56$, and number of observations = 95.

16. Regressions (1) and (2) are basically the same if the sample is restricted so as to have the same number of observations as those of regressions (3) and (4). The coefficient of a regression of the average of CREDIT for 1960–85 on the average for 1960–62 is equal to 0.94. In addition, in King and Levine 1993a the results are also similar when liquid assets are measured as the average for 1960–89 or at the beginning of the period (see tables 7 and 8).

17. Barro's (1991) sample includes twelve Latin American countries and thirty-seven African countries.

18. Gertler and Rose (1991) examine the correlation between CREDIT and the level of real per capita income using panel data for sixty-nine developing countries with annual observations during the period 1950–88. They find a significant positive correlation except when they run the regression in first differences, where they find a negative coefficient, that is, the rate of growth of income and the rate of growth of CREDIT are negatively correlated. Although those results are not fully comparable to ours and they dismiss this correlation as stemming from business cycle rather than long-run correlations, the similarity with our findings is noteworthy.

19. We reran all regressions in table 9.3 with commercial bank credit to the private sector (line 22d) as a ratio of GDP instead of CREDIT. This measure excludes central bank credit to the private sector because in some instances central bank credit could be more related to fiscal developments than financial intermediation. The results of table 9.3 are robust to this change in the proxy for financial intermediation.

20. In the United States the case of Continental Illinois and the S & L crisis are examples of massive bailouts.

21. In a related context, Isard, Mathieson, and Rojas-Suárez (1992) present a model in which government's protection (implicit or explicit) of depositors may reduce their incentive to evaluate the financial position of banks. This in turn reduces market discipline and increases financial fragility.

REFERENCES

Barro, Robert J. 1991. Economic Growth in a Cross Section of Countries. *Quarterly Journal of Economics* 104 (2): 407–33.

Barro, Robert J., N. Gregory Mankiw, and Xavier Sala-i-Martin. 1995. Capital Mobility in Neoclassical Models of Growth. *American Economic Review* 85: 103–115.

Blanchard, Olivier J., and Stanley Fischer. 1989. *Lectures on Macroeconomics*. Cambridge, MA: MIT Press.

Bencivenga, Valerie, and Bruce D. Smith. 1991. Financial Intermediation and Endogenous Growth. *Review of Economic Studies* 58 (2): 195–209.

Calvo, Guillermo A. 1988. Servicing the Public Debt: The Role of Expectations. *American Economic Review* 78 (4): 647–61.

Calvo, Guillermo A., and Fabrizio Coricelli. 1992. Stagflationary Effects of Stabilization Programs in Reforming Socialist Countries: Enterprise-Side vs. Household-Side Factors. *World Bank Research Review* 6 (1): 71–90.

Calvo, Guillermo A., and Pablo E. Guidotti. 1991. Interest Rates, Financial Structure, and Growth: Bolivia in a Comparative Perspective. Unpublished manuscript. Washington, D.C.: International Monetary Fund.

Cavallo, Domingo. 1977. Stagflationary Effects of Monetarist Stabilization Policies. Ph.D. diss. Harvard University.

De Gregorio, José. 1992. Economic Growth in Latin America. *Journal of Development Economics* 39 (1): 58–84.

De Gregorio, José. 1993. Borrowing Constraints, Human Capital Accumulation, and Growth. Unpublished manuscript. Washington, D.C.: International Monetary Fund.

De Long, Bradford, and Lawrence Summers. 1991. Equipment Investment and Economic Growth. *Quarterly Journal of Economics* 104 (2): 445–502.

Díaz-Alejandro, Carlos F. 1985. Good-Bye Financial Repression, Hello Financial Crash. *Journal of Development Economics* 19 (1–2): 1–24.

Dornbusch, Rudiger. 1990. Policies to Move from Stabilization to Growth. In *Proceedings of The World Bank Annual Conference on Development Economics*: 19–48.

Easterly, William. 1990. Endogenous Growth in Developing Countries with Government-Induced Distortions. Unpublished manuscript. Washington, D.C.: World Bank.

Fama, Eugene. 1980. Banking in the Theory of Finance. *Journal of Monetary Economics* 6 (1): 39–57.

Fry, Maxwell J. 1988. *Money, Interest, and Banking in Economic Development*. Baltimore: Johns Hopkins University Press.

Fry, Maxwell J. 1993. Financial Repression and Economic Growth. Working Paper IFGWP-93–07, International Finance Group. Birmingham, UK: University of Birmingham.

Gelb, Alan. 1989. Financial Policies, Growth, and Efficiency. World Bank Working Paper WPS 202.

Gertler, Mark, and Andrew Rose. 1991. Finance, Growth, and Public Policy. World Bank Working Paper WPS 814.

Goldsmith, Raymond W. 1969. *Financial Structure and Development.* New Haven: Yale University Press.

Goldstein, Morris, David Folkers-Landau, Mohamed A. El-Erian, Steven M. Fries, and Liliana Rojas Suárez. 1992. *International Capital Markets: Developments, Prospects, and Policy Issues*. World Economic and Financial Survey. Washington, D.C.: International Monetary Fund.

Greene, Joshua, and Delano Villanueva. 1991. Private Investment in Developing Countries. *IMF Staff Papers* 38 (1): 33–58.

Greenwood, Jeremy, and Boyan Jovanovic. 1990. Financial Development, Growth, and the Distribution of Income. *Journal of Political Economy* 98 (5): 1076–1108.

Greenwood, Jeremy, and Bruce D. Smith. 1994. Financial Markets in Development and the Development of Financial Markets. *Journal of Economics, Dynamics, and Control.*

Grossman, Gene, and Elhanan Helpman. 1991. *Innovation and Growth in the Global Economy*. Cambridge, MA: MIT Press.

Guidotti, Pablo E., and Manmohan Kumar. 1991. Domestic Public Debt of Externally Indebted Countries. IMF Occasional Paper 80.

Isard, Peter, Donald Mathieson, and Liliana Rojas-Suárez. 1992. A Framework for the Analysis of Financial Reforms and the Cost of Safety Nets. IMF Working Paper WP/92/31.

Jappelli, Tulio, and Marco Pagano. 1994. Savings, Growth, and Liquidity Constraints. *Quarterly Journal of Economics* 109 (1): 93–109.

Khan, Mohsin S., and Delano Villanueva. 1991. Macroeconomic Policies and Long-Term Growth: A Conceptual and Empirical Review. IMF Working Paper WP/91/28.

King, Robert G., and Ross Levine. 1993a. Finance and Growth: Schumpeter Might Be Right. *Quarterly Journal of Economics* 108 (3): 717–38.

King, Robert G., and Ross Levine. 1993b. Finance, Entrepreneurship, and Growth. *Journal of Monetary Economics* 32 (3): 513–42.

Levine, Ross. 1992. Financial Structure and Economic Development. World Bank Working Paper WPS 849.

Lucas, Robert E. 1988. On the Mechanics of Economic Development. *Journal of Monetary Economics* 22 (1): 3–42.

McKinnon, Ronald I. 1973. *Money and Capital in Economic Development.* Washington, D.C.: Brookings Institution.

Neal, Craig R. 1988. Macro-Financial Indicators for One Hundred Seventeen Developing and Industrial Countries. Background paper for the *World Development Report 1989*. Washington, D.C.: World Bank.

Persson, Torsten, and Guido Tabellini. 1990. *Macroeconomic Policy, Credibility, and Politics*. London: Harwood Academic Publishers.

Polak, Jacques. 1989. *Financial Policies and Development.* Paris: OECD Development Center Studies.

Romer, Paul. 1986. Increasing Returns to Scale and Long-run Growth. *Journal of Political Economy* 94 (5): 1002–37.
Roubini, Nouriel, and Xavier Sala-i-Martin. 1992. Financial Repression and Economic Growth. *Journal of Development Economics* 39 (1): 5–30.
Saint-Paul, Gilles. 1992. Technological Choice, Financial Markets and Economic Development. *European Economic Review* 36 (4): 763–81.
Shaw, Edward S. 1973. *Financial Deepening in Economic Development.* New York: Oxford University Press.
Solow, Robert. 1956. A Contribution to the Theory of Economic Growth. *Quarterly Journal of Economics* 70 (1): 65–94.
Summers, Robert, and Alan Heston. 1990. The World Penn Table (Mark 5): An Expanded Set of International Comparisons, 1950–1988. *Quarterly Journal of Economics* 104 (2): 327–68.
Taylor, Lance. 1983. *Structuralist Macroeconomics.* New York: Basic Books.
van Wijnbergen, Sweder. 1983. Credit Policy, Inflation and Growth in a Financially Repressed Economy. *Journal of Development Economics* 13 (1–2): 45–65.
World Bank. 1989. *World Development Report.* New York: Oxford University Press.